IGNITE
YOUR FAITH

IGNITE YOUR FAITH

365 DEVOTIONS
TO SET YOUR FAITH ON FIRE

FROM THE EDITORS OF CAMPUS LIFE'S IGNITE YOUR FAITH

Revell
a division of Baker Publishing Group
Grand Rapids, Michigan

© 2009 by Christianity Today International

Published by Revell
a division of Baker Publishing Group
P.O. Box 6287, Grand Rapids, MI 49516-6287
www.revellbooks.com

Printed in the United States of America

Library of Congress Cataloging-in-Publication Data
Ignite your faith : 365 devotions to set your faith on fire / editors of Campus Life's Ignite Your Faith.
    p. cm.
    ISBN 978-0-8007-3388-9 (pbk.)
    1. Christian teenagers—Prayers and devotions. I. Campus Life's Ignite Your Faith.
BV4850.I36 2009
242'.63—dc22
                                           2009022235

09   10   11   12   13   14   15   7   6   5   4   3   2   1

CONTENTS

5

Contents

Contents

HOW TO USE THIS BOOK

TWO WAYS TO SET YOUR FAITH ON FIRE

Option 1: Look for what interests you. This book is arranged by topics. Many of these topics are labeled with a Bible or faith theme (for example, "What's So Great about Jesus?"). Other topics deal head-on with a life issue (for example, "Lust"). Still others dig pretty deeply into a spiritual discipline (for example, "Your Prayers Matter"). With this in mind, you might want to find a topic that grabs you, spend your devotional times going through that topic, and then move on to another topic of interest.

Option 2: Do a devotion a day. It's a great spiritual discipline to read a devotion each day of the week. We've got you covered for a year. Just start at the beginning and keep going until you've read all 365 devotions. Don't freak out if you miss a day here or there. Each reading is pretty short. It will be easy to get caught up in order to keep yourself moving forward.

9

Keep this in mind: This book isn't simply something to put on your spiritual to-do list. It's been created to help you grow in your faith, strengthen your relationship with Christ, and dig deeper into the Bible. It's also meant to help you apply God's Word to everyday life. In fact, application is huge. Plan to take action by completing the many activities and spiritual exercises you'll find throughout these pages. In doing so, we believe you'll discover that Christ is shining a little more brightly through all you do.

So find a topic of interest or flip to the first devotional, and prepare to *ignite your faith*.

DAY 1 I Don't Get It

I believe the Bible is God's Word, but there's a lot of stuff I can't understand—like people who live to be six hundred years old. Is that all true?

—Anonymous

How about you?

* What are your own questions about the Bible? Write 'em here.

Pray your questions

* Ask God your questions. Turn them into a prayer.

> For the word of God is alive and powerful. It is sharper than the sharpest two-edged sword, cutting between soul and spirit, between joint and marrow. It exposes our innermost thoughts and desires.
>
> —Hebrews 4:12 NLT

DAY 2 The Bible Didn't Mean Much to Me

I plopped down on the couch and looked around at all the people who had come to my youth group's Bible study. I went almost every week to the regular Sunday night meetings and just didn't see any reason to go to another church activity. But Kelly, my youth group leader and someone I really respected, told me it was really important to take time out to study the Bible. So I decided to give it a shot.

There were lots of new people, and Kelly wanted us to get to know each other. She asked us each to talk about how we'd become Christians. When it was my turn, I shifted nervously in my chair, cleared my throat, and began.

11

"I became a Christian when I was nine." I paused, feeling a lump form in my throat and my eyes fill with tears. "It was the year my mother died of breast cancer. . . . She was a Christian, but that didn't make it any easier."

When I finally stopped talking, I got a lot of hugs—even from people I didn't know. I saw that Kelly had been crying too.

The following week, I went back to the Bible study. Kelly started the night off by reading James 1:22: "Do not merely listen to the Word. . . . Do what it says."

As I listened to Kelly, I felt kind of guilty. I'd spent a lot of time reading the Bible—but honestly, it didn't mean that much to me. While I wasn't really a bad person, I know I didn't work that hard at applying God's Word to my life.

"Live your life according to the Bible," Kelly went on. "Let it be your guide."

With that challenge, Kelly asked each of us to have daily devotions and memorize Bible verses. She said one of the best ways to do this was to have an accountability partner—someone you talked to each week to make sure you were on track with your devotions.

I wasn't sure if I wanted to make this kind of commitment, but Kelly volunteered to be my partner. I really liked her and I wanted to know God better, so I agreed.

Kelly called me once a week to see if I was keeping up with my devos. As the weeks passed, we started having some really great and even deep talks about God and life.

One night, I told Kelly I still struggled with my mom's death. She didn't say much, but mostly listened. She also assured me that God really loved me and wanted the very best for me. In a soft, gentle voice, she quoted Jeremiah 29:11: "'For I know the plans I have for you,' declares the LORD, 'plans to prosper you and not to harm you, plans to give you hope and a future.'" That conversation with Kelly really helped me. I'd always known in my head that God loved me, but now I was able to feel it in my heart too. And it wasn't only Kelly's words that helped me feel God's love. The way she reached out to me and cared about me showed me just how much God loved me.

12

Throughout the year, I became really close with Kelly and everyone else in the Bible study. And as we all got to know the Bible and God better, I was able to come to peace with losing my mom. I no longer doubted that God loved me.

—Emily

What changed?

* How'd Emily's attitude change toward the Bible? Why the change?

Who?

* Who helps you understand God's Word? Nobody? Who could you ask to help you study the Bible?

DAY 3 How the Bible Helps

My friend Jim was trying to copy off my paper during a chemistry test, but I told him to stop it. As he tried to convince me to help him out, Ephesians 4:25 came into my head:

Each of you must put off falsehood and speak truthfully to his neighbor.

My friend blamed me for the bad grade he got on the test and didn't talk to me for days. It would have been easier to let Jim cheat. At least he wouldn't have gotten mad at me. But it comes down to what the Bible teaches about honesty. And God wants me to be honest in everything I do—even if it means making a friend mad.

—Matt

Shortly after my aunt was killed in a car accident, a student from my school died from a severe asthma attack. Then a short time later, a close friend of mine was taken to the emergency room because of an asthma attack. Frightening questions went through my mind: *What if something horrible happened to me? What if I suddenly found myself close to death?* As I prayed about my fears, God reminded me of this truth from his Word:

13

Every day of my life was recorded in your book. Every moment was laid out before a single day had passed.

—Psalm 139:16 NLT

I needed that reassurance—that God knows my life from beginning to end. And even though my circumstances seemed to scream otherwise, he was in total control. With God's help, I am learning that each day is a special gift. I must make the most of it—no matter what.

—Allison

How have you been helped?

* What Scripture is really meaningful to you? When has Scripture shown you that you've been heading in the wrong direction? How has Scripture kept you from going in the wrong direction?

Every part of Scripture is God-breathed and useful one way or another—showing us truth, exposing our rebellion, correcting our mistakes, training us to live God's way. Through the Word we are put together and shaped up for the tasks God has for us.

—2 Timothy 3:16–17 Message

DAY 4 Cool Quotes from Famous Dead People

The Scriptures were not given to increase our knowledge but to change lives.

—*Dwight Moody*

When you read God's Word, you must constantly be saying to yourself, "It is talking to me and about me."

—*Søren Kierkegaard*

It is Christ himself, not the Bible, who is the true Word of God. The Bible, read in the right spirit and with the guidance of good leaders, will bring us to him.

—*C. S. Lewis*

The Bible is alive, it speaks to me; it has feet, it runs to me; it has hands, it lays hold of me.

—*Martin Luther*

14

React

* Which quote do you like the most? Why? Are any of the quotes hard to understand? If so, who could help you make sense of any quote you don't get?

Write your own quote about the Bible

DAY 5 God's Big Rescue Plan

The Bible isn't just a bunch of random, out-of-touch stories. It's one big, connected story about God's plan to be with us. And it all started in the Garden of Eden—a place where he could hang out face-to-face with his friends. Of course, Adam and Eve blew it and had to leave paradise. So God launched a five-phase rescue mission:

Phase 1—God goes camping. After God rescued the Israelites from Egypt, he told them to build a big mobile tent (the tabernacle). This was where God revealed himself in a bright, glowing cloud (Exod. 40:34). It was God's way of saying, "Hey, I'm still with you guys." But the tabernacle was also a big reminder of what was lost because of sin. There was a special room inside where God's presence dwelled. Because of sin, people couldn't go in there. They were separated from God by a thick curtain. Only the high priest could go beyond that curtain—and he could only do so once a year after being purified with lots of sacrificial blood (Leviticus 16).

Phase 2—God moves into a big house. Around 1000 BC, King David started thinking, *Maybe it's time we upgraded God's tent. We need to build him a temple.* His son Solomon actually pulled off David's plan for

15

a huge temple. When the project was finished, "the cloud filled the temple of the LORD" (1 Kings 8:10). This time, though, God's presence dwelled in a more permanent structure. Unfortunately, God's people stopped following him and began worshiping idols. So God left the building: "Then the glory of the LORD rose . . . [and] departed" (Ezek. 10:4, 18 TNIV).

Phase 3—God gets his feet dirty. Then God came to us in Jesus Christ, stepping even deeper into the junk of the world. He came not only to rescue us from sin but also to show us how to bring a bit of God's kingdom to earth (Matt. 6:10; Luke 11:2). As always, we messed up. We murdered God. But God's rescue plan was unstoppable. Matthew 27:51 says that at the very moment Jesus died "the curtain of the temple was torn in two from top to bottom." Yep, that curtain separating sinful people from a holy God ripped in half. Jesus's ultimate blood sacrifice let us all cross over into God's presence. Catch that? All those Old Testament sacrifices kept pointing to Jesus's once-and-for-all sacrifice.

Phase 4—God lights a fire. But Jesus didn't stay dead. He rose from the grave and ascended into heaven. Then something big happened: the disciples "saw what seemed to be tongues of fire that separated and came to rest on each of them. All of them were filled with the Holy Spirit" (Acts 2:3–4). After that, the disciples started speaking God's truth in a bunch of different languages "as the Spirit enabled them," and about three thousand people became followers of Jesus in one day. This was the start of the church. "Tongues of fire" sounds strange, but think back to that shiny cloud. God's presence was now *very close* to each disciple through each tiny cloud of fire. It's like God is saying, "I am with you, Matthew. I am with you, Peter. I am with you, John. . . ." Each disciple had become a temple where God dwelled! The same is true of every believer: "Your body is a temple of the Holy Spirit, who is in you" (1 Cor. 6:19).

Phase 5—Home sweet home. Revelation 21:3 says, "I heard a loud shout from the throne, saying, 'Look, God's home is now among his people! He will live with them, and they will be his people. God himself will be with them'" (NLT). So heaven will be just like the Garden of Eden—we'll walk and talk with God face-to-face, only this time it'll be permanent. Mission accomplished.

—Sam

Close your eyes . . .

* Well, close them after you've read this. With your eyes closed imagine a really awful situation. If your imagination needs a jump start, think about a really scary scene from a movie. Now, imagine *what it's like to be rescued* from that awful situation. What feelings come to mind? Now open your eyes and think about how God has rescued you.

DAY 6 Pray Scripture

Let's say you come across 1 Peter 5:7: "God cares for you, so turn all your worries over to him" (CEV). Turn that verse into a prayer: "Lord, I'm going to trust you and give you all my worries. I know you will take care of me." Do this with passages that express needs and also with those that praise or thank God.

—Rebecca

I have taken your words to heart so I would not sin against you.
—Psalm 119:11 NCV

DAY 7 The Miracle Loogie (Todd's fake interview with a for-real Bible character)

Q: So what did Jesus do for you?

A: He rubbed spit in my face. It was great.

Q: What? He just rubbed spit on you?

A: Well, no—not just spit. He put dirt in it too. It was muddy spit. You see, I'd been blind my whole life. Jesus made up his spit-mud and smeared it over my eyes. He then told me to go wash it off. When I did, I could see for the first time ever! It changed my life.

Q: Wow! Did you think the spit-mud would work?

A: I guess I just trusted him. I followed what he said and I saw the good results. I knew he was different from other people. I knew he was of God. But when he later said he was the Son of God, I didn't even ques-

17

tion. How could I not believe he was God after the way he changed me? I could do nothing else but worship him.

Q: But didn't you think that was a weird way to heal your eyes?

A: Ha! Who am I to question how God works? We aren't going to understand how he does things. I mean, I didn't know what Jesus was doing when I heard him spit in the dirt. I sure wasn't expecting *that*! But I let him work. And it was obviously the right way. It helped me see and led me to worship him.

Q: Do you think other blind people minded Jesus coating spit-mud on their faces?

A: See, that's the cool way about how God works! Besides working in weird and mysterious ways we can't understand, he works in *different* ways. He healed my blindness with spit-mud. But he healed other blind people by touching their eyes [Matt. 9:29], with only spit [Mark 8:22], or by just seeing their faith [Mark 10:52]. God works that way all the time. He's not going to answer my prayer the same way he does yours. He's not predictable. He's amazing! And when he works in your life, you just gotta tell somebody!

Q: Why? Why tell people?

A: Why wouldn't you? It's funny, when I first got my sight, all my neighbors kept asking me about it. And all I could tell them was what I knew: I was blind, Jesus healed me. And then these religious leaders kept asking me, and I just told them over and over: I was blind, Jesus healed me. I couldn't understand why no one would believe in this man. I wanted so badly for them to see how he worked in my life! See, Jesus didn't just help me to see, but he used that miracle to help me see the truth about him. And when you feel God work in your life, you can't help but embrace him. And you want everyone to have that. You want them to let him work in *their* lives. And that's why I tell people about him.

What changed?

* Besides gaining his sight, how was this Bible character changed? What actions did he take because of what Jesus did in his life? What does

the man's response say to you about the changes God brings about in your own life?

* *Read the real story:* Who is the real Bible character behind Todd's fake interview? Find out in John 9:1–38.

Better than spit

Then the blood of Jesus, God's Son, cleanses us from every sin.

—1 John 1:7 NCV

DAY 8 Tough Question

My reputation is so bad that my pastor and youth pastor have a hard time believing I actually want to change my life. And I do, but it's so hard. And it seems that every step I take, I always take two steps back. How can I change?

—Anonymous

How about you?

* How would you answer the question? Write it out.

Praying4U

* Do you have a friend who's struggling to overcome a bad reputation? Maybe it's someone who knows some changes need to be made but struggles to make those changes. Spend a minute in prayer for your friend. Then send a text simply to say you're praying for this friend.

19

DAY 9 | I Felt So Dirty

Ugh! I moaned as I studied my reflection in my bedroom mirror. *Who is this girl staring back at me?*

I had been raised in a Christian home and had done Christian things, like going to youth group and Bible study. To most people around me, including my parents, I looked like a model Christian girl. In reality, though, I'd never made a decision to follow Christ. I'd also been lying to my parents about the guys I'd been going out with. My mom and dad believed I had good morals when it came to dating. But I didn't. I'd let guys push me to do just about anything short of having sex with them. I suddenly felt so dirty and ashamed. As I stared at that mirror, I didn't even know who I was anymore.

I decided I needed to talk to my youth leader, hoping she could help me straighten out my life. She encouraged me to turn my problems and my life over to God. She also said I should be honest with my parents.

It took me about a week, but I finally worked up the courage to tell my mom what had been going on. My heart raced from fear of how she would react. As I continued to talk, I could see the hurt in her eyes. She sat there, stunned, then finally said, "I'm glad you told me. I'll talk to your father about this." I was thankful that I wouldn't have to tell Dad—that would have been even more difficult than talking to Mom. Thankfully, he too was supportive, loving, and forgiving. While I wasn't punished, my parents let me know they would be more strict about how I spent my free time.

Over the next few weeks, I thought a lot about what my youth leader had said about turning my life over to God. Eventually, I went to her and said I was ready to become a Christian. We prayed together. I confessed my sins and asked Christ to forgive me and come into my life. Afterward, it felt like a huge weight had been taken off my shoulders.

That was more than a year ago. Since then, the Bible has really come alive for me. I find it easier to pray, and I feel like God is listening when I talk to him. I also spend time with Christian friends. They encourage me to keep my priorities straight by keeping God first.

Christ has definitely given me more joy and true happiness than I thought possible.

—Cristen

What about you?

* Is there anything that's making you feel ashamed or dirty?

* Do you need to talk to someone—like your youth pastor—about your need for a new life in Christ?

* If you're already a Christian, do you need to let go of a bad habit or attitude that's dragging you down?

* Do you need to talk to someone about a sin or struggle you can't overcome on your own?

DAY 10 Shiny and New

Have you ever cleaned a very dirty penny with an old toothbrush, salt, and vinegar? If not, give it a try. Dip the toothbrush in vinegar, sprinkle some salt on it, and then start scrubbing. It's kind of amazing how clean and shiny the penny becomes. It looks brand new. And that's kind of like when you tell God you're sorry and really mean it. He cleans you up and makes your heart all clean and shiny.

Get cleaned up

But if we confess our sins, he will forgive our sins, because we can trust God to do what is right. He will cleanse us from all the wrongs we have done.

—1 John 1:9 NCV

DAY 11 Throw It Off

Throw off your old sinful nature and your former way of life, which is corrupted by lust and deception.

—Ephesians 4:22 NLT

21

Grab some loose change

* Place two or three coins in the palm of each hand. Look at those coins and imagine they represent sins or bad habits you have in your life. With the coins still in your palms, close your hands. Squeeze them into tight fists and think again about the sins or bad habits the coins represent. Think about how tightly you're holding on to things that hurt you, drag you down, or damage your relationships. Now, turn your hands over and open them quickly, letting the coins fall out. Imagine letting go of your sins or bad habits in the same way you've let go of those coins.

DAY 12 Put It On

Let the Spirit renew your thoughts and attitudes. Put on your new nature, created to be like God—truly righteous and holy.

—Ephesians 4:23–24 NLT

* What are some qualities you think God likes to see in his followers? Write them down. Need some help? Read Colossians 3:12 and Galatians 5:22–23.

DAY 13 What's New?

A new heart

I will remove their stubborn hearts from them. And I will give them hearts that obey me.

—Ezekiel 11:19 NIrV

A *new birth*

You have been born again, and this new life did not come from something that dies, but from something that cannot die. You were born again through God's living message that continues forever.

—1 Peter 1:23 NCV

A *new creation*

If anyone belongs to Christ, there is a new creation. The old things have gone; everything is made new!

—2 Corinthians 5:17 NCV

DAY 14 My Friends See the New Me

After I became a Christian at a youth conference a couple of years ago, I was worried about how my nonbeliever friends would react to my new life in Christ. Would they think I'd turned into some kind of a weird religious freak? But when I arrived at school on that Monday after the conference, I was the one really surprised. My actions and attitudes toward friends, homework, and teachers were more upbeat and positive. No, it wasn't like I was totally unrecognizable. But I was different—in a good way.

I'd always thought that being a Christian meant limited freedom and a lot less fun, but that wasn't true at all. I felt like I was really enjoying life for the very first time ever. And other people could see this change right away. They weren't turned off by the change either. In fact, many of them seemed drawn to it. They were interested in knowing why I was different—and this created many opportunities to talk about how Christ had changed my life for the better.

—Kennen

* *How has Christ changed you?* Or how would you like him to change you? List three ways:
  1.
  2.
  3.

23

DAY 15 New Beginnings

The notebook page,
squeezed into a tight, crinkled ball,
rests on the left-hand corner
of my desk, just like
last week's, last month's, last year's
regrets, mistakes, lost opportunities,
and crushed dreams.

At the center of the desk I notice
a fresh page and a new pen
filled with unused ink;
I hesitate for a moment,
staring at the wad of paper;
my heart turns heavy and sad.

I look again at the blank page;
there it is, waiting for me to capture
new opportunities to love, to serve,
and to reach out to the world around me.
I warily place the pen's tip on the page;
before I know it, the ink flows with incredible ease,
and I am writing a new chapter in my life.

—Marie

* What new chapter would you like to write in your own life? Journal
your thoughts, jotting down changes you'd like to make, attitudes
you'd like to change, dreams you'd like to fulfill.

DAY 16 Loving the Unlovable

Perhaps Jesus's toughest teaching is to "love your neighbor as yourself" (Mark 12:31). Sure, that *seems* easy enough—until you really think about what it means. You don't get to pick your neighbors. They're everyone: strange outcasts, mean bullies, annoying people, and little brothers who shampoo your hair as you sleep (maybe that's just me). *Clearly*, I used to think, *all of these people are unlovable.*

Were Jesus's expectations too high? I mean, he never had to go to high school. Well, that's a cool thing about Jesus. He wasn't just God on High shouting down orders. He experienced what we experience. When he told us to live a certain way, it was coming from a guy who'd been there. He lived on earth—and probably knew his share of bullies and weirdos. And he had little brothers.

However, Jesus understood two important truths: (1) Everyone is created in God's image. So if we're worthy of love, so is everyone else because of who made them. (2) Because of sin, we're all really unlovable. But Christ changed the rules by offering love, grace, and forgiveness (Rom. 5:8). If God can love us, surely we can love those around us.

But how do we *do* it?

Pastor Andy Stanley once pointed out something that blew my mind. At the Last Supper, Jesus was in the same room with a bunch of people about to betray him, deny him, and desert him. And he knew it. Talk about hard-to-like people. But what does Jesus do? "He got up from the meal, took off his outer clothing, and wrapped a towel around his waist. After that, he poured water into a basin and began to wash his disciples' feet, drying them with the towel that was wrapped around him" (John 13:4–5).

Whoa. He's surrounded by guys who don't deserve his love or respect. And he washes their feet. Right here, Jesus shows how to love the unlovable. It's not just tolerating them. Or not making fun of them. Or pretending you love them. Instead, we should *serve* them.

Here's why: (1) Serving gives us a way to move love from some mushy, hard-to-grasp emotion to an action. (2) Serving someone changes how we see them. If you're continually looking to help someone, it's very hard to think they're worthless. It's very hard to hate them.

25

Of course, it'd be weird to whip out a towel and lather up a bully's feet. But you can look for opportunities to help somebody out. Maybe it's holding a door open when someone is carrying his band instrument. Or spotting someone a dollar for a soda when she's short on change.

—Todd

Your serve list

* Make a list of three people in your life you might consider "unlovable" and look for ways to serve them this week.

1.
2.
3.

DAY 17 Annoyance into Love

Take the things you see in people that annoy you and turn them into a prayer.

—Timothy Jones

Fill-in-the-blanks prayer

* Lord,

When I think of ___(person)___, I naturally just feel ___(emotion)___. The way ___(person)___ always ___(verb)___ and ___(verb)___ just makes me ___(adjective)___. Help me to see ___(person)___ as you do. Help me see why they do what they do. Help me to turn my ___(emotion)___ toward those annoyances into love, kindness, and patience. Most of all, allow me to extend grace. Amen.

DAY 18 The Day I Made the Bully Cry

"Cec-cec-cecily. He-he-hey-hey, Ce-ce-cily!" Daniel cackled, making fun of my stutter.

I looked at the floor and set my backpack on my lap, hoping he'd find somebody else to torment. But he kept mimicking my stutter.

"I don't sound like that!" I yelled. I pulled out my iPod and cranked up the volume. My plan worked, until Daniel ripped the earphones from my head.

"Whatcha jammin' to? Something Latino?" he asked with a chuckle.

"Why would you say that?" I asked.

"Cuz you're Mexican," he answered.

"I'm Cuban!" I corrected him.

"Cuban . . . dirty Mexican—same thing," Daniel huffed, rolling his eyes.

My blood boiled. I sprang to my feet. "You wanna name call? I've got one for you, zit face! Your cheeks and forehead are bumpier than a BMX track!"

The bus erupted in laughter. My pulse raced as I celebrated by high-fiving one of Daniel's frequent victims.

—Cecily

Intermission

* **What do you think of Cecily's revenge? How would you feel if you were her? If you were Daniel? Did he get what he deserved?**

* **Read Matthew 5:38–48.**

. . . the rest of the story

As I turned to high-five another frequent victim, I noticed Daniel was fighting back tears. I had totally humiliated him. I suddenly felt ashamed.

Although there was a part of me that felt like Daniel deserved what he got, I knew God wouldn't see it that way. His rude behavior didn't give me the right to act just as horribly. I certainly hadn't loved my enemy. I took a deep breath, swallowed my pride, and said, "Daniel, that was a jerky thing for me to say. I'm sorry."

He muttered, "Whatever," then turned away and stared out the window. For the next five minutes he was silent—until we got to my stop. As I brushed past him to exit the bus, he murmured, "Me too."

—Cecily

DAY 19 Dealing with Mean People

Get fiery revenge!

> If your enemies are hungry, give them food to eat. If they are thirsty, give them water to drink. You will heap burning coals of shame on their heads, and the LORD will reward you.
>
> —Proverbs 25:21–22 NLT

Be nice to their donkeys

> If you find your enemy's ox or donkey loose, take it back to him. If you see the donkey of someone who hates you lying helpless under its load, don't walk off and leave it. Help it up.
>
> —Exodus 23:4–5 Message

DAY 20 Do WHAT?

> I say to you, do not resist the one who is evil. But if anyone slaps you on the right cheek, turn to him the other also.
>
> Matthew 5:39 ESV

This verse has always struck me as a pain in the cheek. Though once it was a pain in a friend's cheek.

We were standing in line in a high school P.E. class, waiting for the coach to show up. Harry, a classic bully, insulted my friend Steve and slapped him in the face. There was a stunned silence as everyone wondered what was going to happen next.

That's when I said, "Harry, quit picking on him."

Harry walked up to me, put his nose near mine, and said, "What you going to do about it?"

It's rare to be confronted physically like this. More often we're assaulted by words—when someone tells lies about us or insults us. Things can get pretty tense when that happens, and we wonder what we should do. When we're challenged or insulted or assaulted, instinct says, "Defend yourself." "Stand up for your rights." "Nobody talks to you this way!" "Show them a thing or two."

But Jesus says, "Don't go there. It's not about you and your rights. It's about overcoming evil. And the only way to finally conquer this brand of evil is by absorbing it."

Absorbing? Think about it this way: when water is poured on a rock, the rock's hardness simply repels the water, which splashes all over the place. But when water is poured on a sponge, the sponge soaks it up. It's kind of like that with evil. We can resist evil with hard words or actions, but it will only spread. Instead, we can, in a small way, stop it from spreading if we absorb it with love.

This takes a lot of humility. And patience. And help from God. But it can be done.

When Harry said, "What you going to do about it?" I knew my options were limited. If I swung at him, we'd be enemies forever. There'd be lots of bad blood and more fights to come. Maybe others would get involved. Water would splash all over the place.

I simply said, "Look, Harry, I'm not going to fight you. But I want you to stop bothering Steve."

After what seemed like an hour (it was probably only five seconds), he walked away. I quietly let out a sigh of relief.

Does Jesus mean that you should stand by and do nothing if you or a friend is being attacked? Does he mean armies shouldn't defend their citizens against terrorists? Hardly. Most Christians believe there is a place for defending victims of such aggression (Rom. 13:1–7). Extreme evil must be checked by force (that's why we have police), and will not be completely conquered until Jesus comes to establish his just kingdom.

In the meantime, Jesus says that the everyday evil of insults and slaps and slander can be overcome. How? By soaking it up in love.

—Mark

Think about it

* How have you turned the other cheek? When have your actions caused more splashing instead of absorbing? How might you have acted differently?

DAY 21 Nice for One Day

Jackson had bushy eyebrows that connected in the middle, a dopey walk, and an annoying habit of never leaving my friends and me alone. One day, while shooting hoops, my friends finally lost it.

After a barrage of insults from Dylan and Trent, I told Jackson, "I'd split if I were you." He didn't budge.

"Beat it!" Trent insisted as he grabbed Jackson by the shirt collar and flung him to the floor. Jackson sprang up and started swinging his fists in self-defense, grazing Dylan's chin with his knuckle.

"You little punk!" Dylan yelled as he hurled a left hook into Jackson's face, knocking him to the ground. Jackson slowly stood and headed for the gym door as Dylan and Trent cheered.

Although Jackson irritated me, I decided the only decent thing to do was find Jackson and see if he was OK. I found him all alone in the locker room.

"Are you OK, man?" I asked.

Jackson wouldn't respond.

"What were you thinking? I told you to leave!"

"Are you kidding me?!" Jackson said. "You're gonna pin this on me? All I wanted was to hang with you guys."

He sat down on the wooden bench, pressing his shirtsleeve to his bloody lip.

"Listen, man," I said. "I'm sorry this happened. The guys were way outta line."

"And how 'bout you?"

"What about me?" I asked. "What did I do?"

"Forget it," Jackson said, shaking his head. "I thought we could be friends. Clearly, I was wrong."

"Hey, I came looking for you, didn't I?" I said defensively.

"What? You expect me to thank you for being decent to me one day out of the past two months?" Jackson asked.

—Josh

* How do you think Josh felt? What would you do in reaction?

* Think about times you've been in Jackson's shoes. Or Dylan's. Or Josh's.

* How is dealing with a well-meaning annoying person similar to and different from dealing with an enemy?

* Think of someone you wish treated you better. Is there anyone you treat that same way?

DAY 22 Stick It in Your Head

Choose the verse below that applies the most to you right now and memorize it.

> Here is a simple rule of thumb for behavior: Ask yourself what you want people to do for you; then grab the initiative and do it for them!
> —Luke 6:31 Message

> If it is possible, as far as it depends on you, live at peace with everyone. Do not take revenge, my friends, but leave room for God's wrath, for it is written: "It is mine to avenge; I will repay," says the Lord. . . . Do not be overcome by evil, but overcome evil with good.
> —Romans 12:18–19, 21

> The LORD is the stronghold of my life—of whom shall I be afraid? . . . Though an army besiege me, my heart will not fear; though war break out against me, even then will I be confident.
> —Psalm 27:1–3

DAY 23 From Enemy to Royalty

Second Samuel 9 is one of the most beautiful and Christlike glimpses of how to treat an enemy.

Mephibosheth's granddad was Saul, Israel's king. Good deal, huh? Well, not really, because Grandpa Saul's rebellion against God led to his death and the murder of all his sons. The new king of Israel was David. In those days, a king would establish his rule by killing any of the last king's relatives. So Mephibosheth assumed things were not looking good for him and went into hiding.

Meanwhile, David *was* searching for Mephibosheth, but not to kill him. Actually, David's best buddy was Meph's father. When David found the hiding son, the king said: "Don't be frightened. . . . I'd like to do something special for you in memory of your father Jonathan. To begin with, I'm returning to you all the properties of your grandfather Saul. Furthermore, from now on you'll take all your meals at my table" (2 Sam. 9:7 Message).

Instead of ending the life of his enemy's grandson, David gave him a life by making him a part of the royal family.

—Jarrett

Retell it!
* Make this story into a movie or rewrite it into a modern-day short story.

DAY 24 Quick, Grab a Pen . . .

* Write down five facts you know about Jesus. Don't do a lot of thinking; just quickly jot down what comes to mind:
  1.
  2.
  3.
  4.
  5.

DAY 25 6 Reasons People Followed Jesus

1. Jesus loved people. Jesus had a very big heart for little kids (Matt. 19:13–15), for people who were suffering (Mark 5:25–34), for the spiritually lost (Luke 19:1–9), for those rejected by the popular crowd (Matt. 9:9–12), and for those society condemned (John 8:1–11). He also loved those who seemed to have it all together. This doesn't mean he was easy on arrogant religious leaders. He could really rip into them (Matt. 6:1–24). Jesus also had some strong warnings for rich people who let their money get in the way of loving God (Matt. 19:23–24). But those reactions came out of love. After all, it was a religious leader who heard Jesus say the words we find in John 3:16—a verse proclaiming God's sacrificial love for all.

2. Jesus was all about helping people in need. He fed the hungry (Mark 6:32–44) and healed the hurting (Matt. 8:1–17). Even as he was dying on the cross, he couldn't overlook the needs of his own mother. With his body twisted from unspeakable pain, he looked toward John and asked his good friend to take care of his mom (John 19:25–27).

3. Jesus was "God in the flesh." When Jesus walked the earth, God had a bit of a bad reputation—what with zapping people dead on the spot (2 Sam. 6:6–7) and sending killer plagues (Exodus 7–12). But when Jesus arrived on the planet, he helped people see God's nature up close and personal—a nature that was not only holy but also full of unending grace and kindness (John 1:14).

4. Jesus told great stories. Yes, sometimes people were confused by his stories (Matt. 13:10–18). Sometimes his stories made people over-the-top angry (Matt. 21:33–46). But huge crowds still showed up to hear Jesus tell a great story (Matt. 13:1–9). His stories are still loved today because they stir up the imagination; they put flesh, blood, and feelings onto spiritual truths; and they challenge people to think better thoughts and live in a better way.

5. Jesus was smart. Luke 4:32 tells us that people "were surprised and impressed—his teaching was so forthright, so confident, so authoritative" (Message). His words were meant to help people think about what mattered most. Someone would ask him a tricky question and he'd come back at them with an even better question—one that would dig deep into dark hearts and messed-up motives (Matt. 21:23–27). His teaching

33

was also easily understood by the uneducated and by those who lacked formal religious training (John 4:4–30). Imagine having a conversation with a very smart person who, while occasionally humbling you, never makes you feel worthless and stupid. That was Jesus.

6. Jesus had a big, forgiving heart. He forgave and forgave and forgave again—and instructed his followers to do the same (Matt. 18:21–35). Remember that amazing prayer he prayed during his execution? "Father, forgive them, for they do not know what they are doing" (Luke 23:34). He prayed that prayer for those who'd jammed a crown of thorns on his head, pounded nails into his hands and feet, and bloodied his back with a whip. And today—two thousand years later—here's what continues to attract people to Jesus the Forgiver: his loving forgiveness is the kind that wipes away our wrongs, makes us morally clean, raises our own souls from the dead, and gives us eternal life (Eph. 1:7–14; Col. 2:13–15; 1 John 1:9).

—Chris

What do you like about him?

* Think about what you like most about Jesus. What has he done for you that you really appreciate? Jot down the first three things that come to mind.
    1.
    2.
    3.

DAY 26 The Best Superhero Ever!

Why are superhero stories so popular? Maybe it's because we know superheroes can do for us what we can't do for ourselves. When things look impossible, we want heroes to help us, save us, and give their all for us. This is exactly what superheroes do: they step in when we can't go on.

In *X2*, the X-Men are about to drown in a tidal wave until Jean Grey decides to save them, no matter what it means for her. She holds her arms out, telekinetically lifting the X-Men's powerless jet with one hand and holding back the water with the other. As the waters rush over her, the X-Men regain their power and fly away to safety.

When all looks hopeless for a runaway train in *Spider-Man 2*, Spidey sacrifices himself—arms outstretched and with gashes in his side—to save the train's passengers.

In *The Dark Knight*, Batman self-sacrificially takes the blame for the sins of Harvey Dent. He was willing to be distrusted and even wanted by the police so that the people of Gotham could have hope.

Such selfless acts of heroism appeal to us because they reflect something bigger than just a comic book story or a superhero action movie. They mirror the story of a different kind of superhero, the Son of God, who gave his all for us. As we enjoy the amazing feats of our favorite superheroes, let's see them as reminders that we have a God who helps us, saves us, and gives his all—no matter the cost.

—Todd

My personal superhero

* Do at least one of the following:

Write out five character qualities of your favorite superhero, and then think about how Jesus does or doesn't model each quality.

Make a superhero. With modeling clay, Play-doh, paints, or pencil, create your own superhero.

Draw a picture of your favorite superhero rescuing you.

Write a story, a poem, or lyrics to a song that shows your favorite superhero saving the day.

DAY 27 My Best Friend Needed Jesus

I punched Rick. He punched me. We ended up in detention together. As we walked out of detention, we got to talking about how stupid our fight had been. Before we knew it, we were best friends. After that, we only

35

fought for fun, like when we watched pro wrestling together. That was way back in fifth grade.

Then something happened in middle school that totally turned my life around. I asked Jesus to be my Lord and Savior. God totally changed my life.

The bad thing was that Rick didn't feel the same way about God as I did. That really bothered me. After all, he was my best friend in the whole world. I wanted him to find out how cool life could be with Jesus Christ at the center of it.

One night during the summer before eighth grade, we camped out in his backyard. As we stared upward at the star-dotted darkness, Rick started asking me a lot of questions about religion. Soon I was telling him about everything I knew at the time. No big theological insights. I just knew the basics: Without God, we're sinners bound for hell. With Christ, we're saved and that means heaven. Most of all, I told him how Jesus had changed my life.

"I don't know too much, dude," I remember saying. "But I do know that without Jesus we're lost. Just try asking God to change your life. If it doesn't work, forget it. But at least try it."

He told me that what I'd said seemed to make sense and that he'd like to give God a try. So I asked him to repeat a prayer: "God, I know I'm a sinner. Please change my life for the better. Take away my sin. I want to give my life to you."

God did change Rick's life that night. Now he's one of the strongest Christians I know. He's even shared Jesus with his mom and now she's a Christian.

Sometimes people wonder why I'm so into letting others know about my faith. I like to tell them something like this: "If you understand what Jesus did for you on the cross, why wouldn't you want to share it with others?"

—Jarrod

Fill-in-the-blanks prayer

* Dear Jesus,

My friend ___(name of friend)___ needs you so badly because ___(something your friend struggles with)___. One thing I'd really like my friend to understand about you is ___(a trait or characteristic)___. One way I will show your love for ___(name of friend)___ this week is by ___(an action)___. Amen.

DAY 28 Talk and Listen

Go to a quiet place. No iPod. No computer. No TV. No distractions. Now, talk to Jesus. Tell him what you're thinking. Be totally honest. Maybe thank him for the changes he's made in your life. Or ask him questions about stuff that's bothering you. You might want to talk about your struggles or confess your sins. Then spend as much time listening in the silence as you did praying.

DAY 29 Why I Believe in Jesus

I grew up in Sri Lanka where my family and friends were into Buddhism and New Age thinking. Since that was all I knew, I believed it too. Then I came to the United States to attend a small state college.

At college I met plenty of Christians. I even read the Bible, just so I could argue with them. For example, my biophysics professor was a Christian. He would tell me about the miracles in his life, the ways he supposedly saw God's work in the world. I'd argue with him and try to convince him he was foolish to believe in Jesus. His faith was a joke to me.

During my junior year of college, everything in my world started to fall apart. My girlfriend broke up with me, I ran out of money, and I knew I'd have to drop out of school. I thought about going back to my family in Sri Lanka, but I didn't want to face them when I'd failed so miserably.

One night, I sat in the college library, trying to come up with ways to get out of my situation. The only solution that seemed "reasonable" was suicide. But then I heard a voice say, "Have you ever asked me for help?" I looked around and couldn't see anyone. I thought I was going crazy. Then I heard the voice say, "I'm Jesus, and I'm right here next to you."

I know this sounds strange. Believe me, I was pretty freaked out by it too. But I honestly heard Jesus talking to me.

I suddenly had this strong urge to go see my biophysics professor—the guy I'd been arguing with all year.

I walked across campus to the science building and found him working in his office. As I walked in, he said, "I'm so glad you're here. God has put you on my heart and I've been hoping you'd come and talk to me." We talked a long time. I told him how empty my life had become.

I told him what I'd experienced in the library. As he talked to me about Jesus's power to change lives, I knew I was ready to follow Jesus. He prayed with me. That was the day I became a Christian.

I was no longer worried about the future, because I knew the Lord was in control, not me.

The people around me saw the changes too. Before I became a Christian, I was arrogant, selfish, and manipulative. I had done things to intentionally turn people away from their Christian faith. But after my conversion, I felt humbled by God's power to change me. I wanted people to see Jesus in my life, not me or my accomplishments. I was almost grateful for my struggles, because I knew God was using them to keep me humble and focused on him.

So why do I believe in Jesus? Because he's real. That night in the library, when I hit the bottom, my New Age thinking didn't help me. Buddha wasn't there for me. It was Jesus who saved me.

—Shamitha

Think about it

* Read Acts 9:1–22. How is Shamitha's story similar to Paul's conversion? How is it different? How did Jesus change both men's lives?

* Jesus obviously doesn't always reveal himself in such dramatic and miraculous ways. But he does change people's lives. How has he changed the life of someone you know? How has he changed your life?

DAY 30 Stretch Your Brain Muscles

Christ is the visible image of the invisible God. He existed before anything was created and is supreme over all creation, for through him God created everything in the heavenly realms and on earth. He made the things we can see and the things we can't see—such as thrones, kingdoms, rulers, and authorities in the unseen world. Everything was created through him and for him.

—Colossians 1:15–16 NLT

* Go back and read that passage again—*slowly*. OK, read it a third time and underline the words and phrases that jump out at you, and circle the ones that make no sense at all. Now try to answer this question: what does Colossians 1:15–16 tell you about Jesus? Unsure? Stumped? Baffled? Take your questions—and your circled words and phrases—to your youth pastor, pastor, or small group leader.

DAY 31 Getting in God's Face

Don't nag. Don't mouth off. Be respectful. Those are pretty much the three commandments for getting along with authority figures, whether they're parents, teachers, or Doberman pinschers.

Surprisingly, it doesn't seem to be the way God wants us to act toward him.

Check out Matthew 15:21–28 (Message). One day Jesus and the disciples find themselves in foreign territory. They're minding their own business when a local woman starts pestering them. "Mercy, Master, Son of David!" she yells out. "My daughter is cruelly afflicted by an evil spirit."

What does Jesus do? He ignores her. But apparently she *really* wants her daughter healed, so she keeps at it. And keeps at it. Finally the disciples complain, "Would you please take care of her? She's driving us crazy."

So what does Jesus do? He refuses. And he tells his disciples, "I have my hands full dealing with the lost sheep of Israel." Meaning, it appears, that this foreigner is just not a priority. But this is not meant for the disciples' ears as much as for the woman's.

Now this woman runs in front of Jesus, falls on her knees, and insists, "Master, help me!"

What does Jesus do now? He says to her directly, "It's not right to take bread out of children's mouths and throw it to dogs."

This could easily be interpreted as an insult. Jesus seems to be calling this non-Jewish woman a dog. Ouch.

But, really, there seems to be some playful banter going on here. It's like when you're teasing your little brother to get him to take out the garbage for you: "You're too weak to carry this!" To which the little brother says, "Oh yeah?"

And this woman gets it. She's not insulted, because she knows this comment is to see if she's just whining or really wants her daughter healed. She replies, "You're right, Master"—and I imagine a wry smile crosses her face—"but beggar dogs do get scraps from the master's table." A little attitude, a little humor, and right to the point. To put it another way: "You came to minister to Jews first? Fine. But you know as well as I that your mission is bigger than that. Even we non-Jews need what you have to offer."

That seems to be enough for Jesus. First, he praises her: "Oh, woman, your faith is something else." And then he heals her daughter.

A lot of times God doesn't answer our prayers immediately. Will we give up? Or will we approach him even more boldly and intimately? Maybe like we would if a friend refuses to do us a favor at first:

"What do you mean you won't give me a ride to school—you forgot how to get there?"

"Give me a break! OK, I'll drive you."

When we hear God's silence, there's nothing wrong with responding, "And I don't want to hear any excuses. You're God. You can do this. And remember, you love me!"

In short, when we pray, God wants us to care passionately enough to stick with it, and to be honest and intimate enough to tell it like it is from our perspective.

This isn't a formula for getting all your prayers answered. It's a description of the life of faith.

—Mark

* Have you considered that "pestering" God could be a good thing? Why or why not? Are there any prayers you've given up on? Why not start praying those prayers again? And this time keep praying them until you receive an answer.

DAY 32 Stuck in a Prayer Rut?

Try these different ways to pray:

Journal your prayers. But don't just journal requests. Write out questions, heartaches, and struggles. Don't forget to journal praises too. Be creative. Put your prayers into poems. Write a letter to God. Then go back and read your journal entries in a week or a month. There's a good chance you'll be reminded of how God has answered your prayers. And when you're feeling down, your past praises remind you of God's goodness and love for you.

Take a prayer walk. Hike in a forest preserve and praise God for his beautiful creation. Walk around your neighborhood and pray for the family in each home you pass. Or take a "prayer walk" on the sidewalk around your school.

Keep a prayer on your lips. Dozens of thoughts pass through your mind daily. You daydream. You may think bad or gossipy thoughts. Turn those daydreams and not-so-great thoughts into prayers. Ask God to help a person hurt by gossip. Ask him to forgive you for thoughts that take your mind places it shouldn't go. Turn daydreams and other passing thoughts into moments to recognize God's presence in your life. As you learn to keep a prayer on your lips, you'll come a little bit closer to understanding what it means to "pray continually" (1 Thess. 5:17).

Pray over your calendar and schedule. Got a test coming up? Pray for peace of mind. Pray for the players of Friday night's basketball game— both sides. Ask God to bring non-Christians to your winter youth retreat.

Pray about the news. When you read or hear about a troubling issue, pray for the people involved. Pray for politicians and other national and community leaders who make the news.

—Rebecca

DAY 33 Is God Listening?

Q: I feel far from God right now. I pray and hear nothing. How do I know he's listening, or even there? I'm afraid I'm missing his answers or that he's not hearing me.

—Anonymous

A: You're not alone. Almost every Christian feels this way sometimes. Read Psalm 22:1–2. King David, who certainly knew God, wrote: "My God, my God, why have you forsaken me? . . . I cry out by day, but you do not answer." We often feel God is distant or disconnected. Even Jesus felt this way—and quoted this Psalm—when he was on the cross.

But despite how you feel, God hasn't gone anywhere. He created you, and he loves you so much that he made arrangements for you to live with him forever (Rom. 8:32). Since God is so deeply committed to you, he's not going to walk away from you.

In fact, he's watching over you. Right here. Right now. You may not see him or hear him, but you're on his mind, and he loves you. Keep your eyes open, and watch for God's presence in your life. You may not see him all the time, but like the wind, you can see the effect he has. Maybe you see him in how he provides. Or comforts. Or the people he sends into your life.

God wants you to keep looking for him by praying, reading his Word, and living out your faith. "Come and pray to me, and I will listen to you," God says. "You will seek me and find me when you seek me with all your heart" (Jer. 29:12–13).

—Marshall

DAY 34 Good Words on Prayer

Prayer is not a convenient device for imposing our will upon God, or bending his will to ours, but the prescribed way of subordinating our will to his.

—*John Stott*

Prayer is the spiritual gymnasium in which we exercise and practice godliness.

—*V. L. Crawford*

The great tragedy of life is not unanswered prayer, but unoffered prayer.

—*F. B. Meyer*

* **Bring these quotes to your small group. Go around in a circle and read each quote. Share which was your favorite quote and why. Discuss any additional thoughts on prayer. Then, put those thoughts into practice—take prayer requests and pray together.**

DAY 35 I Wanted to Help . . . Tim Said Pray

"Pray, pray, pray," Tim, my youth pastor, told my youth group at one of our meetings.

I zoned out because I'd heard his message before. Tim was constantly telling us that prayer could change a person's life. I'd already spent a lot of time praying during church and youth group. Now I wanted to do something—which was why I'd signed up for my youth group's upcoming weeklong mission trip.

We were headed to Tim's hometown because the church he'd attended as a kid had fallen on hard times and badly needed repairs. I didn't mind cleaning up and painting, but what I really wanted to do was connect with people—especially kids.

When we finally arrived at Tim's old church, I was excited to hear that we were going to spend a lot of time at a park with neighborhood kids. Tim explained that everyone was getting a "little buddy" to spend the day with. He told us this was a great chance to tell these kids about Jesus. I couldn't wait.

43

But only thirteen kids showed up—and there were fourteen of us. I ended up as the only one in my youth group not paired up with a child. So just to keep busy, I filled water balloons and cleaned up after everyone. I tried not to let it show, but I was feeling totally down. It seemed like I wasn't needed. I started to feel even worse on the ride back to the church. My friends talked nonstop about what an amazing day they'd had. They were sure God had worked through them to impact the lives of their "little buddies."

"I felt completely useless all day," I blurted out. "I didn't do a thing."

"It may not feel like you're doing important stuff, but God is using you," Tim said gently. "He's using you in ways that you can't imagine."

Yeah, right, I thought.

Then he said, "Whitley, I am really glad you want to do things to help out. But don't forget you should also be praying for the people here. And then once you get home, keep praying for them."

Maybe Tim was right. Maybe I really did need to spend more time in prayer. So for the rest of our mission trip, I started spending time in the church's prayer room. I asked God to use me in any way he wanted. I also prayed that the people in the town would get to know him. As I prayed, it hit me: praying for people went hand-in-hand with helping them.

When I focused on prayer, I started to feel like God *was* using me. One afternoon, a bunch of kids from the neighborhood were headed to the town pool. I noticed one little girl was staying behind. She told me that her parents didn't have any extra money for things like the pool. It didn't cost much, so I gave her money so she could go swimming. She smiled and happily went on her way.

I knew I probably wouldn't see her again. And the money wouldn't change her life, but what could change her life was prayer.

When it was time for us to go home, I couldn't help but feel like there was so much more that needed to be done. I didn't feel helpless, though. I felt like I could do something really powerful for my new friends—even though we were hours apart. I could pray for them.

I hope that my youth group's next mission trip gives me a chance to work hard, to meet and help others, and to spread God's love. But I know through prayer God can use me in ways I never imagined—even when I'm right here at home.

—Whitley

* Whitley felt useless because all she could do was pray. Have you ever felt that way? How can a different view of prayer change your attitude?

DAY 36 The Word on Prayer

And we are confident that he hears us whenever we ask for anything that pleases him. And since we know he hears us when we make our requests, we also know that he will give us what we ask for.

—1 John 5:14–15 NLT

Don't fret or worry. Instead of worrying, pray. Let petitions and praises shape your worries into prayers, letting God know your concerns. Before you know it, a sense of God's wholeness, everything coming together for good, will come and settle you down. It's wonderful what happens when Christ displaces worry at the center of your life.

—Philippians 4:6–7 Message

The prayer of a righteous man is powerful and effective.

—James 5:16

Pray in the Spirit at all times and on every occasion. Stay alert and be persistent in your prayers for all believers everywhere.

—Ephesians 6:18 NLT

In certain ways we are weak, but the Spirit is here to help us. For example, when we don't know what to pray for, the Spirit prays for us in ways that cannot be put into words.

—Romans 8:26 CEV

Be joyful always; pray continually; give thanks in all circumstances, for this is God's will for you in Christ Jesus.

—1 Thessalonians 5:16–18

45

When you ask, you do not receive, because you ask with wrong motives, that you may spend what you get on your pleasures.

—James 4:3

* *Pick a passage* that speaks to you the most and write it on a note card. Put it on your bathroom mirror or in your locker to remember what God says about prayer—and to remind you to pray!

DAY 37 Don't Suffocate Your Faith

To be a Christian without prayer is no more possible than to be alive without breathing.

—Martin Luther

* Hold your breath for as long as you can.

* What was the experience like? How desperate were you for oxygen? Now compare it to your desperation for connection to God through prayer.

* *Look up Psalm 42:1–2.* What do these verses tell us about our greatest need?

DAY 38 I Was Too Busy for God

With my evenings taken over by play practice and other activities, I missed a few weeks of youth group. Joel, my youth pastor, called me a few times to see why I wasn't making it to church. I always gave him an excuse about being way too busy.

One night, during a break at play practice, I found a quiet spot backstage to practice my lines. As I scanned the script, I felt a tap on my shoulder. It was Daniel, one of the guys from my youth group. He had a lead in the play and knew how stressed out I'd been at practice recently.

"You doing OK?" he asked, plopping down next to me.

I gave a quick nod to say yes, but Daniel looked at me in a way that said he wasn't buying it.

Then I admitted, "I feel like I'm sinking from all I have to do." Daniel asked if he could pray for me. When I said OK, he bowed his head and said a short prayer.

Daniel then said, "Ben, you need to make time for God first. Then I really believe everything else will fall into place."

I knew deep down inside that Daniel was right. I did need to put God first. And I needed to connect with God every single day. So the next morning, before I left for swim practice, I stuffed my Bible in my backpack. I got out of the pool ten minutes early and read a chapter of the Bible and prayed in the locker room. Later, when I felt overwhelmed with a hard assignment, I bowed my head at my desk and said a quick prayer.

I also started making youth group a top priority. I knew that going helped to keep me focused on Christ.

Spending time with God during school and going to youth group regularly didn't make all of my stress magically disappear. But when I began making God a priority in my everyday life, I started to feel a whole lot better. I also made a promise to myself: in the future, I will say no to some activities. Doing that will not only help me avoid a lot of stress; it will also open up more opportunities to say yes to God.

—Ben

> * *Why is it?* Why is time with God often the first to go when our lives get busy? Why should time with God be the last to go?

DAY 39 Do Something Small

Don't assume that the snippets of time you spend with God don't count. Sure, you wouldn't want to get into the habit of only devoting minutes a day to your spirituality. But on crazy days, get creative when it comes to grabbing time with God. Do a ten-minute devotional during lunch. Or attend half of the youth group meeting. Hey, it's better than missing the whole thing! And don't forget to make the most of travel time. When I was on long bus rides to and from cross-country meets, I'd put on my headphones, listen to some worship music, and tune into God by praying or journaling during the trip.

—Christy

DAY 40 A Tale of Two Sisters

As Jesus and the disciples continued on their way to Jerusalem, they came to a certain village where a woman named Martha welcomed him into her home. Her sister, Mary, sat at the Lord's feet, listening to what he taught. But Martha was distracted by the big dinner she was preparing. She came to Jesus and said, "Lord, doesn't it seem unfair to you that my sister just sits here while I do all the work? Tell her to come and help me." But the Lord said to her, "My dear Martha, you are worried and upset over all these details! There is only one thing worth being concerned about. Mary has discovered it, and it will not be taken away from her."

—Luke 10:38–42 NLT

* *What's wrong with this picture?* Martha was just trying to make her house look nice for Jesus. So why did he scold her?

* *What's right with this picture?* At a quick glance, Mary seems like the lazy sister. Jesus apparently didn't see it that way. Why not?

* *Some deeper thinking, please:* How is being busy for God just as bad as being busy with other stuff? How is worship and spending time with God different from just being busy for him?

DAY 41 Where Worship Happens

I was leading worship. Standing on that stage, singing with as much passion as I could muster, I really felt like I was worshiping God. But when the night was over—when the music had stopped, the emotions had leveled, and the people had gone home—I couldn't help thinking, *God, is this it? Is this what it means to worship you?*

God placed an answer to my questions in the first commandment: "You shall have no other gods before me" (Exod. 20:3). It seems crazy at first, but there's a whole lot about worship packed into that little sentence. So let's go back to the time when this sentence first appeared on a tablet of stone.

When God gave the Ten Commandments to Moses (Exod. 19:1–20:17), the nations around Israel believed their gods held power only over the land they owned.

And why is this significant? Because since the days of Abraham, the people of Israel were nomadic—wandering from place to place. They had no homeland. But it got even worse for the Israelites. For the four hundred years before God gave them the Ten Commandments, they'd been slaves in Egypt. So it makes sense that other nations assumed Israel's God was a pushover. A failure. A God to a bunch of landless losers. So when this wimpy God issued a command to "have no other gods before me," it sounded ridiculous! Why would Israel, who'd been enslaved in someone else's land, obey this command?

The verse that comes right before the first commandment holds the answer: "I am the LORD your God, who brought you out of Egypt, out of the land of slavery" (Exod. 20:2). God reminds Israel that he freed them from slavery. And he did it with more than a dozen miracles in Egypt—a land Israel didn't own.

It was a whole new way of thinking: God was not limited to certain pieces of land, like the other nations believed about their own gods. He was present and powerful wherever Israel went.

I think many of us are sometimes like those nations who believed their gods roamed only certain places. We expect God's presence and power in special locations—a sanctuary, a retreat center, a small group Bible study. We call our actions in these places "worship" because we believe God is there. But there are no buildings or boundaries that tie God down. He's present and powerful in every place. So we can worship him in every place.

This one and only God we worship wants so much more than our Sundays, youth group nights, and special events. He wants us to worship him in our schools, our homes, our churches, our jobs, and anywhere in between.

49

How do we worship God in all these places? Obviously, it's not simply about singing praise songs in youth group. It's also about reaching out to the loner in the cafeteria, obeying our parents and loving our siblings (even if they're driving us nuts), working hard at our part-time jobs, standing up for our faith in hard situations, and so much more.

The first commandment reminds us that God is supreme—and he's still right there with us wherever we are. So every day, in every place, we are called to worship him.

—Jason

Fill in the blank

* I will worship God today by _____.

DAY 42 8 Places to Worship: Pick One

1. Take a walk in a park or forest with a friend. Or even walk down a tree-lined street. Look for things God has created. Take turns pointing out how God is like his creation. For example: "God is like this oak tree because he's sturdy and strong."

2. Sit down in your yard with your Bible and pick a blade of grass. Turn to Isaiah 40:7–8, which says: "The grass withers and the flowers fall. . . . Surely the people are grass. The grass withers and the flowers fall, but the word of our God stands forever." Read the passage a few times, then think about what it means to you. Use the blade of grass to bookmark the passage. Read the passage periodically throughout the next few weeks, watching as the blade of grass withers.

3. Start each day of school by reciting this verse: "In all the work you are doing, work the best you can. Work as if you were doing it for the Lord, not for people" (Col. 3:23 NCV). Memorize this verse and then recite it before you begin your first class, repeat it during times of frustration, and repeat it again at the end of your school day.

4. *On a still, windless day, stand at the end of a pier and toss a rock into the water.* Watch the ripples roll outward. Try to count them. Now think about God's love. How is it like those ripples? How can you be a "ripple of God's love" today?

5. *As you play a sport or work out, thank God* for the ability to run, throw, kick, swim—or whatever it is you do to participate in your sport. Try to stay aware of his presence with you each time you play. You can also do this with any extracurricular activity—thanking God for the gifts related to your specific activity.

6. *Worship God and bring praise to him through helping and serving others* (1 Peter 4:11). Play ball with the neighbor kid. Shovel snow for an elderly neighbor *for free.* Help out with the children's Sunday school at your church. And whenever possible, do your serving in secret so that God gets the glory. Just look around you and you're sure to discover simple, everyday ways to worship through serving others.

7. *Plan a small group worship service around a backyard fire pit.* Sing praise songs, read Scripture, pray, and share stories about Christ working in your life. And don't forget the marshmallows!

8. *Find a quiet place to watch the sunset.* As you watch the sun sink beneath the horizon, sit very still and think about your day. Recall the good and the bad moments. Thank God for being with you throughout everything that happened that day. Thank God for being present with you during these quiet moments.

—Chris

DAY 43 My Day

Sunup

Alarm. Snooze. Alarm. Snooze. Mom. Knock. Groan. Stretch. Feet. Floor. Bathroom. Wait. Wait. Bang. Finally. Relief. Shower. Hot. Awake. Sing. Jeans. T-shirt. Pray. Protein? Grains? Late. Pop-Tart. Rush. Car. Radio.

51

Tardy. Sigh. Friends. Laugh. Argue. Learn. Lunch. Sandwich. Tuna. Trade. Cupcake. Class.

Midday

English. Beowulf. Who? Notes. Scribble. Doodle. Lecture. Doze. Drool. Bell. Biology. Paper. Ugh! Forgotten. Excuse? Dog? Brother? Martians? No. Zero. Bell. Practice. Run. Sweat. Shower. Home. Smile. Love. Accepted. Warm. Dad. Hug. Dog. Lick. Good. God. Remember.

Dusk

Air. Crisp. Dinner. Family. Laugh. Talk. Blockbuster. Movie. Couch. Popcorn. Share. Honest. Love. Remember. Midnight. Stars. Shimmer. Bed. Quiet. Rest. Good. God. Good.

—Winn

From the rising of the sun to its setting the name of the LORD is to be praised.

—Psalm 113:3 NASB

Your day

* How has God moved and worked through the rhythms of a single day in your life? Write a few words describing your day.

Pray

* God of the rising and the setting sun, I want to encounter you in each hour, each day, throughout it, intertwined with it. I don't want to be content to give you only portions of it. I want all of you in all of me.

DAY 44 Doodle

* In the space provided, do one or more of these worshipful doodles:

Ask yourself: What image or symbol comes to mind when I think of God? Draw it.

Draw a maze and think about the things that keep you from reaching God.

Use your coolest handwriting to write "God loves me!" Then think about what that means.

Draw a quarter-sized circle and then fill it with tiny dots—pretend that these dots represent God's thoughts about you in the last second.

Look back at your circle of dots and thank God for all his thoughts of you.

DAY 45 When God Hit Pause

Sometimes I wish I had a universal remote control for time. I'd skip through life's bad and boring parts, and play the best parts over and over.

Strangely enough, something kind of like that happened twice in the Old Testament.

The first incident occurred when Joshua was on a mission to defeat five wicked kings. In a moment of deep faith, he prayed out loud for God to hit the Pause button on the sun and the moon so he could defeat his enemies:

The day GOD gave the Amorites up to Israel, Joshua spoke to GOD, with all Israel listening: "Stop, Sun, over Gibeon; halt, Moon, over Aijalon Valley." And Sun stopped, Moon stood stock still until he defeated his enemies. . . . The sun stopped in its tracks in mid sky; just sat there all day. There's never been a day like that before or since.

—Joshua 10:12–14 Message

The lesson found in this exercise of holy time control? The God who created time itself was still Lord over it, and he could use his control over creation to bring victory to his people and glory to himself.

The second time we see God mess with time is in Isaiah 38. King Hezekiah was at death's door and begged God not to let him die. God was moved by the king's prayer and decided to let him live fifteen more years. God gave Isaiah this message for King Hezekiah:

"Watch for this: As the sun goes down and the shadow lengthens on the sundial of Ahaz, I'm going to reverse the shadow ten notches on the dial." And that's what happened: The declining sun's shadow reversed ten notches on the dial.

—Isaiah 38:8 Message

God actually caused the shadow on a sundial to move backward, "adding" more hours to the day and more years to the life of King Hezekiah. In doing so, God proved he was in control of everything, including that crazy little thing called time.

Now I don't think God will stop the sun anytime soon so that you can have more time to study for your history test. But I do know that not a second passes without God allowing it to pass. God didn't put the sun, moon, days, hours, and minutes into motion, set the timer, and then go on vacation. He's actively engaged and in charge of every second. And he still cares about every second he creates.

We, on the other hand, often do not. We either rush busily through our days with very little to show for the time we've been given, or we sluggishly stumble through them, missing and even wasting divine moments given to us by God. The truth is, you've been given an amazing opportunity to engage with the Creator of time. Each day, each hour, each moment is a chance to engage with God. Right now, in this very moment, you

54

can be with God. And he can be with you in every one of the seemingly insignificant moments of your life.

While he might not stop the sun to help you avoid telling your parents you flunked that history test, you just might discover something better— a day filled with the loving presence of God . . . every minute . . . every moment.

—Jarrett

DAY 46 Times Change

There is a time for everything, and a season for every activity under heaven: a time to be born and a time to die, a time to plant and a time to uproot, a time to kill and a time to heal, a time to tear down and a time to build, a time to weep and a time to laugh . . . a time to be silent and a time to speak, a time to love and a time to hate, a time for war and a time for peace.

—Ecclesiastes 3:1–8

A time for rewriting

* Write these verses in your own words. What do these words mean to you? How do you see change in your daily life?

DAY 47 Times Change, God Doesn't

I am God—yes, I Am. I haven't changed.
　　　　　—Malachi 3:6 Message

God isn't a mere man. . . . He doesn't change his mind. He speaks, and then he acts. He makes a promise, and then he keeps it.

—Numbers 23:19 NIrV

Before you created the world and the mountains were made, from the beginning to the end you are God.

—Psalm 90:2 NIrV

The grass withers and the flowers fall, but the word of our God stands forever.

—Isaiah 40:8

* *So what?* Why is it important for God to be unchangeable?

* *Imagine this:* What might the universe be like if God could never make up his mind?

DAY 48 Michael's Prayer

Lord, sometimes I don't understand the changes that happen in life. To me. To the world.

I fear change because I'm not sure where it will lead or what it will bring. How can I prepare for something I know nothing about? Not having control is scary.

I'm not just changing schools, or making new friends. My changes aren't just superficial. I'm changing the way I feel inside: my opinions, my sense of who I am. I'm becoming a different Michael. I'm not like anyone else. I'm me. And sometimes I don't even know who that is.

Who am I, Lord?

I don't understand the total me. I understand that I'm a Christian. I understand that I go to high school and that my parents love me. But I don't always understand the choices I make. I don't understand all my actions or what I say. Lord, I'm not even sure of who I am. But I do believe that right now, I'm doing the best I can. I am trying to change into the me you want me to be.

Lord, help me understand my changes. Every change in who I am brings new opportunities and wonders—but also new problems. New risks. New things I cannot control. But in the end, I know you are in control of everything, Lord. I guess I just have to accept that I won't understand everything that you allow to happen. After all, you said some things are not for us to know.

—Michael

Your turn

* In what ways can you relate to Michael?

* How do you react to change and lack of control?

* Spend three minutes in prayer about change—change in the world, change in your heart, change in your relationships, and so on.

DAY 49 Why Doesn't God Just Change the World?

We long, maybe desperately at times, for heaven. A place where there's no violence. No hatred. No abuse. No divorce. No in-group. No out-group. No suffering. No Satan. No evil.

Yet we imagine this paradise as some distant place we won't see for a very long time. So what about *the present*? Well, maybe we can experience heaven right here, right now. Sounds kind of crazy, doesn't it? There's just so much wrong with the world. Yet two thousand years ago, Jesus said this: "The kingdom of heaven is near" (Matt. 4:17). Jesus himself said heaven was so close you could reach out and touch it.

Just read John 1:14: "The Word became flesh and blood, and moved into the neighborhood" (Message). God landed on this planet, took on the name of Jesus, and brought a touch of heaven with him. He healed the sick. He gave sight to the blind. He fed the hungry. He raised people from the dead. He chased evil spirits from the possessed.

But not everything was perfect during Jesus's lifetime. When he walked around in his well-worn sandals, there was still war and poverty and plenty of evil—just like now. Well, it wasn't just like now, because Jesus is back in heaven. So it's all even worse now that his heavenly touch is gone, right?

Wrong. Jesus not only changed the world but also sent out his disciples to continue what he started. Following in Jesus's footsteps, his broken

57

human disciples (like us!) brought a good dose of God's love and truth into the world. In doing so, they gave everybody a glimpse of heaven.

And then, before Jesus went back to heaven, he told his disciples: "For John baptized with water, but in a few days you will be baptized with the Holy Spirit. . . . You will receive power when the Holy Spirit comes on you; and you will be my witnesses" (Acts 1:5, 8).

The Spirit came and now lives inside every believer (2 Tim. 1:14). In fact, a Christian's body is called the temple of the Holy Spirit (1 Cor. 6:19). Wherever we go, we take a touch of heaven with us.

Yes, we still make mistakes. We still sin. But we don't have to be discouraged by everything that's wrong with us. Change is possible. We can straighten things out by confessing our sins to God and to each other (James 5:16; 1 John 1:9). And when we do live out our faith, we also experience some truly heavenly qualities, like those found in Galatians 5:22–23: "But the fruit of the Spirit is love, joy, peace, patience, kindness, goodness, faithfulness, gentleness and self-control."

And as Christians we are called to take this touch of heaven to the world around us. Is a friend hurting? Lend a listening ear. Do you know someone who's lonely? Reach out and make a new friend. Do your non-Christian friends feel hopeless? Tell them where they can find real hope. Show everyone around you a little bit of heaven in the very real world. You can, with God's power, help change this world and bring heaven to earth.

—Chris

Pray

* Thank God for sending the Holy Spirit and for changing this broken world.

Do

* Brainstorm practical ways you can bring Christ's kingdom to earth this week.

DAY 50 You Can Change, Just Not by Yourself

You were saved by faith in God, who treats us much better than we deserve. This is God's gift to you, and not anything you have done on your own.

—Ephesians 2:8 CEV

God rescued us from the dark power of Satan and brought us into the kingdom of his dear Son, who forgives our sins and sets us free.

—Colossians 1:13–14 CEV

Everyone has sinned. No one measures up to God's glory. The free gift of God's grace makes all of us right with him. Christ Jesus paid the price to set us free.

—Romans 3:23–24 NIrV

Thank you!

* Write God a thank-you note expressing appreciation for the gift of salvation.

DAY 51 I Can Do It Myself!

I stood on the edge of the high, snowy ski slope. I hadn't skied for two years. And even then—my last ski retreat with my youth group—I had only gone down three or four hills and had just barely learned enough to not kill myself.

But surely, I thought, *I'll be able to figure it out.*

I pushed off and built up speed. I lasted about fifteen feet before collapsing into the snow. I fell another seven times before I finally came to a stop at the bottom by hitting a small tree. My second and third tries went about the same.

I rode up the ski lift for another try with my friends Jen and Mike. We were chatting when—all of a sudden—I realized we were at the lift ramp! I struggled to get my feet under me so I could hop off. But before I could get my footing, I was knocked in the rear by the lift chair. I tumbled over a line of traffic cones and landed in a snow bank.

"Todd, you might really hurt yourself," Jen said gently. "I think you should take a lesson."

I don't need help! I screamed in my head. I knew I could improve if I just worked harder. So I stood up and rocketed down the hill. Near the bottom of the hill, my left ski flew out from under me. My upper body flew forward. My entire weight landed on my face, and I skidded down the hill about ten feet.

My face hurt. My glasses were three feet away. My head throbbed. My right eye was swelling shut. There was blood all over the snow.

As I got up, I finally admitted I couldn't keep doing this. I was a danger to others and myself. Jen was right; I needed lessons. *If this is going to change,* I thought, *I'll need help.*

At my lesson, the instructor watched how I skied and offered advice. Before I knew it, I could turn. I could stop. Instead of fear and panic, I felt confidence and enjoyment. I could actually ski—not just careen downhill!

After my lesson, I went down the hill and completely mastered it. At the bottom, Mike said, "I couldn't believe that was you. You're completely transformed!"

As the two of us rode the ski lift up to go down again, I thought about my day. I thought about how much I'd fallen. I also thought about how stubborn I'd been through it all. Only after I'd really hurt myself had I finally admitted I needed help. I realized that this doesn't just happen with skiing.

When I've faced tough problems or wrestled with sin, I've often thought, *I can do it. I can handle this.* But whenever I think like that, my problems only get worse. Real transformation comes only when I give up doing it all by myself and let God help me change.

—Todd

I went down to the potter's house, and I saw him working at the wheel. But the pot he was shaping from the clay was marred in his hands; so the potter formed it into another pot, shaping it as seemed best to him. Then the word of the LORD came to me: . . . "Like clay in the hand of the potter, so are you in my hand."

—Jeremiah 18:3–5

DAY 52 To-Do Lists

Don't be like the people of this world, but let God change the way you think. Then you will know how to do everything that is good and pleasing to him.

—Romans 12:2 CEV

I will sprinkle you with clean water, and you will be clean and acceptable to me. I will wash away everything that makes you unclean, and I will remove your disgusting idols. I will take away your stubborn heart and give you a new heart and a desire to be faithful. You will have only pure thoughts, because I will put my Spirit in you and make you eager to obey my laws and teachings.

—Ezekiel 36:25–27 CEV

You were told that your foolish desires will destroy you and that you must give up your old way of life with all its bad habits. Let the Spirit change your way of thinking and make you into a new person. You were created to be like God, and so you must please him and be truly holy.

—Ephesians 4:22–24 CEV

* *List what these verses say* are your roles and God's roles in changing your heart:

What I do: *What God does:*

DAY 53 Change That Matters

I was surfing online this week when I found an article about how some wealthy girls in New York give themselves a new look for a new school year. But these girls aren't simply buying some new clothes. Instead, they go to the nail salon for manicures and pedicures, to the dentist for teeth whitening, to the beach or the tanning bed for tanning sessions, to the hair stylist for chemical hair straightening and coloring, and to the plastic surgeon for nose jobs!

When the writer of the article asked one of the girls why everyone was spending so much time and money on their appearances, she said, "You want everyone to be like, 'She looks good or different.'"

I can understand wanting to look nice. But I try to remind myself that what's more important is the person I am inside—not outside. I'm hoping people will notice that the person inside is changing, slowly looking different, more like God's Son.

Sure, I hope someone will notice when I'm wearing a new outfit. But I also want them to say, "LaTonya's more generous than she used to be." Maybe they'll say, "She's closer to God than she was before," or "She's a lot more willing to forgive others now."

Little by little, I'm seeing God use situations in my life to make me more beautiful—but in the ways that really matter.

—LaTonya

Anyone who belongs to Christ is a new person. The past is forgotten, and everything is new.

—2 Corinthians 5:17 CEV

DAY 54 I Am Not a Robot

Where do my values come from? My parents. My friends. School. Church. But I've noticed something else has shaped my view of life: the media. All those hours absorbing life as portrayed on TV. Every film viewed. Every song heard. Every newscast watched. Every blog or book read. Every image that meets my eyes. Every sound in my ears. Everything that enters my head has the potential to challenge my thinking. Or change it.

I once heard someone say, "You are whatever enters your mind."

This makes me sound like a robot that's programmed to behave in certain ways. But I have two things a robot doesn't: (1) the ability to evaluate, to weigh one idea against another; and (2) the gift of choice. I decide what I will do with the information I receive—and in many cases, whether I even receive that information in the first place. I discern right and wrong, good and bad.

But how do I know what is right and what is bad? Thankfully I don't have to guess at it. I am not on my own in deciding. There is a standard against which I measure all things. That standard is the Word of God.

—James

* How can you compare what you see in the media with the Word of God? What does that mean to you?

* Do you take the time to evaluate the messages that enter your head? Spend a minute in prayer about what you do with what you see and hear.

DAY 55 It's Just Entertainment!

Q: I recently gave my life to Christ. I'm surprised that my church makes such a big deal about what I watch or listen to. What does it matter? Entertainment is just that: entertainment. I don't see how it affects my mind at all. And I haven't seen it distract me from God. How could it?

—Anonymous

A: If what you watch and listen to doesn't touch your mind or emotions, why bother? Why not just watch paint dry? We watch TV shows and listen to music precisely *because* they engage our thoughts and feelings. That's what entertainment is all about. I don't think most people realize how many messages they can pick up from what they watch and listen to.

For those of us who have given our lives to Christ, the important question isn't whether something is OK or not. Instead, we need to ask whether it helps or hurts our goal of becoming more like Jesus. In 1 Corinthians 10:23, Paul says, "Some of you say, 'We can do whatever we want to!' But I tell you that not everything may be good or helpful" (CEV). Deciding what is good and helpful requires brutal self-honesty. Does violent or aggressive content cause you to feel angry or fearful? Do sexual images or content drag your mind toward lustful thoughts? Does swearing make it tougher for you not to spew it?

Following Jesus means killing off our "old ways" of living. That's hard to do when you're still playing around with music, movies, or TV shows that depict those temptations. God's Word turns your question of "why not?" back on you: Why watch? Why listen? How is it helping you live like Christ?

—Mark

Put to death, therefore, whatever belongs to your earthly nature: sexual immorality, impurity, lust, evil desires and greed. . . . You used to walk in these ways, in the life you once lived. But now you must rid yourselves of all such things as these: anger, rage, malice, slander and filthy language from your lips.

—Colossians 3:5–9

DAY 56 The Dictionary Says

dis·cern, verb: to perceive by sight or some other sense or by intellect; to exhibit keen insight and good judgment.

* **What does discernment mean to you personally? How does your understanding of discernment relate to entertainment?**

The Bible says

A discerning man keeps wisdom in view, but a fool's eyes wander to the ends of the earth.

—Proverbs 17:24

Put everything to the test. Accept what is good and don't have anything to do with evil.

—1 Thessalonians 5:21–22 CEV

Your definition

* With these verses in mind, write your own definition of discernment.

DAY 57 Can't I Decide?

Q: I'm sixteen and have always obeyed my parents' rules about what movies I may watch. But I want to make decisions for myself. I really want to be responsible. I take it seriously. I read about movies I'd like to see to evaluate if I should see them. But how can I get my parents to hear me out?

—Anonymous

Your turn

* How would you respond to this question?

How IYF's expert answered:

A: My parents used to forbid me from listening to punk rock—even if by Christian bands. Without disrespecting them, I asked if we could discuss the lyrics and the lives of some of these bands. Using reason rather than emotion, I made my case for why this was important to me. Slowly, my parents gave me more and more responsibility for choosing my music.

65

They did this because they believed I was very thoughtful about what I chose to listen to.

It sounds to me like you also are really trying to figure out what's best for you in entertainment choices. Prove to your parents that you take your decisions seriously and want to honor them and God with your choices. For instance, show them the sites you visit to read about movies. (I'd recommend PlanetWisdom.com and ChristianityTodayMovies.com.) Ask your parents what conditions would be needed for you to gradually get more and more decision-making responsibility.

Two helpful attitudes: First, realize that your parents know you well and may have good reasons for their decisions. Be sure you listen to them as much as you want them to hear you. Second, make the choice to believe that God is directing your life through your parents' decisions. Proverbs says, "Good leadership is a channel of water controlled by GOD; he directs it to whatever ends he chooses" (21:1 Message).

One last thing: make sure you are using this time of your life to understand what entertainment choices are helpful or not helpful to your walk with Christ. I don't know any Christian who regrets *not* seeing things their parents said no to, but lots of us regret some things we've chosen to watch on our own.

—Mark

DAY 58 Movies Are Evil?

Seeing my first *Star Wars* movie gave me a taste for an experience that I later came to crave more and more: escaping for at least a while into a world of excitement and emotion and action.

By the time I was fourteen, I watched movies constantly—any movies. I'd realized by then that I could easily buy tickets to R-rated movies even though I was underage. There was nothing I couldn't, and didn't, see. The violent movies didn't attract me so much; what I wanted was to see some skin.

At first I had my limits. For instance, when I saw a movie at a friend's house that featured a violent rape, I was sick to my stomach. I made my friend turn it off and I tried to erase the images from my mind. But eventually I didn't care what I saw. I liked any movie that scared or stimulated me. I liked seeing my fantasies play out on screen. And I just liked escaping the rules, pressures, confusion, and criticism of real life.

One week at youth group, I realized I had some pretty bad thoughts floating around in my head. I couldn't deny that movies fed a lot of those bad thoughts. I felt ashamed of myself. I needed to talk to someone, so I pulled a youth counselor aside. He said God loved me, forgave me, and had already taken away those sins that made me feel so guilty and ashamed.

Somehow, it all sank in. I wanted to dedicate my life to Christ in a real, everyday way. I couldn't help but see a connection between the things I saw on screen and my vulgar language, horrible thoughts, and suggestive remarks. I finally knew what I had to do: give up movies completely. *They are the work of Satan*, I thought. I went further and threw out all my movies, secular albums, violent videogames, and sci-fi books.

It seemed easy—fiction was evil; films were evil. Stay away from them. I could do that. But then something happened that confused me. A Christian movie came out in theaters. My church asked me to be part of a team that would be available at showings to pray with audience members. At first, I said, "No way!" I had made a vow to never step foot into a movie theater again. After all, this is where evil resides, in these nasty movies! However, over a couple of weeks I had a growing desire to accept the responsibility. I said yes.

After my first viewing of this movie, I prayed with a woman and her son. Each of them accepted Christ. I was so excited. I thought, *I'm feeling this incredible joy in a movie theater, the place I said I'd never go to again as a Christian!*

That experience showed me that theaters and movies aren't evil by definition. Film can be used for good just as much as for evil. There is good, noble, beautiful stuff in many, many films. I didn't have to legalistically deny myself from seeing every movie. There was a balance.

I started going to movies again—but now, I was picky about what I saw. I'd read reviews online. I'd think through the message, why I really wanted to see it, and what it would do for me. I looked for well-done movies that said something important, that were worth the time and money I'd spend on them. And sure enough, I found them.

—Sean

"Everything is permissible"—but not everything is beneficial. "Everything is permissible"—but not everything is constructive.

—1 Corinthians 10:23

DAY 59 Whatever . . .

Finally, brothers, whatever is true, whatever is noble, whatever is right, whatever is pure, whatever is lovely, whatever is admirable—if anything is excellent or praiseworthy—think about such things.

—Philippians 4:8

* *Do one of these:*
  Turn this verse into a prayer about how you choose what you absorb from the media.

  Memorize Philippians 4:8.

DAY 60 Don't Forget to Think

Some Christians only watch G-rated movies. Other Christians watch anything and everything.

But there's one thing that can be missing from both approaches: thinking. I'm convinced that what matters most in entertainment choices is *how* we consume our entertainment. Too often we swallow it whole. We don't chew it up and break it down. Instead of watching anything or only "safe" things, we need to learn to make wise decisions.

There are two reasons to think about what we watch: (1) to protect our minds and hearts; and (2) to not get confused about the truth.

Movies, music, and TV are powerful teachers. Often what they teach contradicts God's Word. Obvious examples of false messages: Two people in love should have sex. People who are wronged should get even. Obedience to parents is optional.

If we don't take time to compare what we're watching to what is true, our entertainment may start telling us what to believe. If we're honest about comparing our entertainment with the truth, though, we might get irritated with all the lies and choose not to waste our time with some things. As the apostle Paul wrote, "I pray that . . . you will fully know and understand how to make the right choices. Then you will still be pure and innocent when Christ returns" (Phil. 1:9–10 CEV).

—Mark

* Write the name of a movie, video game, or TV show you've seen or played: _____

* In the left-hand column below, write some false messages you notice in it.

* Now, think about its positive themes or messages. How does it show glimpses of God or his work in the world? Of hope or love? Of redemption? Write these things in the right-hand column.

DAY 61 Your Guide to Truth

When the Spirit of truth comes, he will guide you into all truth.
—John 16:13 NIrV

* Spend three minutes in total silence asking God to reveal what this verse means for you in terms of discernment, entertainment, and making choices.

DAY 62 Ready to Date?

Q: I've never had a girlfriend. Some books I've read say you should wait until your twenties to date, because that's when your character is fully developed, and that's when you can get married. As I've read these books, I've also kept a list of mistakes to avoid. Now I think I'm ready to date, but I guess I'm afraid of doing something wrong—I'm afraid I'll mess up or marry the wrong person and end up divorced. Recently I met a girl while I was volunteering at a Christian camp, and I think she liked me. But it totally scared me, and I ended up avoiding her as much as I could. Am I normal? How can I get ready to date? How do I get over this fear?

—Anonymous

A: A lot can be said for the "no dating" as a teen philosophy, but it does often lead to a problem: you don't get to know the opposite sex. You haven't experienced the strong feelings that come with romance (or even potential romance); and then when you do get these feelings for the first time, they can scare you. In situations like that, shy people can be terrified and paralyzed. More outgoing people might make hasty or irrational decisions.

The other thing I noticed in your question is that you are concentrating very hard on "doing" dating right. Reading and studying up on dating "dos and don'ts" is fine, but it can also make us think too much about it. Honestly, there's no cut-and-dried way to date. Every human interaction and relationship is different. Because of that, don't worry too much about making mistakes.

Here's the truth: you will make some mistakes. So will the girls you date. Don't fear them. Don't worry about saying or doing something dumb once in a while. That will happen. And God can use those mistakes to teach you and help you grow. It comes down to trusting him to guide you through relationships and to help you make wise and godly choices.

To me, it sounds like right now you probably need friends who are girls more than a girlfriend. You need to be around girls so you learn to feel comfortable relating to them. I'm glad to hear that you volunteered at a Christian camp. That's a good idea—and the type of activity that would allow you to meet girls who can be friends. Get involved with activities that put you close to girls. Make yourself say hi to them. Think in advance of a question you can ask them. Gradually your fears will fade.

—Tim

DAY 63 Feeling Sleepy?

Promise me, O women of Jerusalem, not to awaken love until the time is right.

—Song of Solomon 8:4 NLT

* What are some ways—whether you're a girl or a guy—to avoid awakening love before the time is right?

* What would that mean if you're in a dating relationship right now?

* How does it apply if you're not dating anyone?

DAY 64 About a Boy

The picture didn't show the guy's head, but I knew it was Will. No, I didn't know him. We'd never even said hi in the halls. But when I found a photo of this cute boy from the neck down, I hung it in my locker. I looked at it all year and planned ways we could meet.

I was obsessed with trying to find him after class. He didn't even know my name, but I wasted my entire sophomore year obsessing over this guy.

Looking back, I really regret spending so much time in high school obsessing over boys like Will. When I didn't have a boyfriend, I was busy looking for one. But I wasn't mature enough to really know what I wanted. So I was making some bad decisions.

This wasn't just a waste of time—it was also bad news. When I would try too hard, wear revealing clothes to impress guys, or base choices on popularity and looks, I'd attract the wrong type of guy who'd try to get me to do things I knew were wrong.

71

If I had set my mind on my friends, activities, God, and enjoying high school instead of making sure I had somebody to date, I would have been so much happier. I wish someone had told me that the best years were still to come and to make high school a fun time, a time to discover who I am—not a time of finding someone to marry.

—Chrissy

* It's hard to trust that God has the right person waiting for you. You may have many years of being single ahead of you, and your wedding might be a long time away. What is your motivation for making wise choices right now? Whether or not you're dating, or even if you end up never getting married, how can you honor God in your relationships?

DAY 65 Happily Ever After?

* Write down three romantic comedies or dramas that come to mind.
    1.
    2.
    3.

* What do each of these movies seem to say about dating, romance, love, sex, and marriage?

* Now look up these three Bible passages:
    1 John 3:16
    Proverbs 5:15–19
    1 Corinthians 13:1–8

* What does the Bible say about love and relationships? How is this different from how Hollywood often portrays them?

DAY 66 My Boyfriend Wasn't a Christian

From the beginning, I knew Paul wasn't a Christian. I knew he didn't go to church. I knew he drank and partied on weekends. I knew the girl he'd dated before me had a reputation for sleeping around. On the other hand, I was a Christian. I went to church regularly. I didn't drink or party. And I had no intention of sleeping with anyone before marriage.

While my eyes were wide open about what kind of guy Paul was, I was blinded to what I was getting involved in when I agreed to go out with him. Within a few months of our first date, I had moved way beyond liking Paul and felt that I really loved him. When we were apart, I thought about him all the time. When we were together, I couldn't think about anything else—not God, not my family, not anything but him.

There was something exciting about being with him. This attractive, talented, popular guy cared about me. He didn't think I was in any way ordinary or plain or boring. I got caught up in feeling important, loved, special. Besides, Paul was a great guy. He was compassionate, caring, funny, kind. If only he believed in God.

"But I do believe in God," he'd insist. "Just not the same way you do."

By then I was so caught up in our relationship that I missed the obvious: Paul just wasn't interested in Christ.

Once, Paul and a group of our friends were headed to a party. I desperately wanted to be there with Paul, so I told my parents I was going to a movie with a girlfriend. At the party, I thought about how great Paul was because he never once tried to get me to drink. I never thought about the fact that I'd lied to my parents about where I was going.

On the outside, I hadn't really changed. I still went to church, still read my Bible, still did well in school. I still didn't drink or have sex. I still loved God, still loved my parents, still cared deeply about trying to follow the values I believed in.

But deep down, things had changed, and it took me awhile to realize it.

One thing that helped was meeting a good Christian guy friend. We could talk openly about our faith and even pray together. That never happened with Paul. Also, some other friends helped me see that Paul had

73

become the focus of my life. I'd given our relationship more importance than my family and my faith.

Finally, I realized Paul and I didn't share the most important thing in life—a deep love for Christ. What Paul and I had wasn't at all what God had in mind for a dating relationship.

I knew I had to tell Paul it was time to put God back in the center of my life. I couldn't do that and still be Paul's girlfriend.

It wasn't easy. I still really cared about Paul. But I knew my emotions couldn't lead me any longer. It was time to let God have control again, and time to start making decisions based on what I knew, not on what I felt.

—Crystal

Do not be yoked together with unbelievers. For what do righteousness and wickedness have in common? Or what fellowship can light have with darkness?

—2 Corinthians 6:14

DAY 67 Sounding Off on Dating

There's a big difference between wanting to be with someone and needing to be with someone. I don't want to go out with a girl because I need her. That's not good for me, and it sure puts a lot of pressure on her to be the person in charge of my happiness. I want to be with her because I enjoy her company, because she's a great friend, and because I care about her. The best thing I can do for me and for her is to get closer to my friends from church and to God.

—Jim

We long for approval and definition. And while that need is designed to draw us to God, we are quick to pass our hearts to anyone who will complete, define, or love us. But our hearts weren't meant to be passed around and treated carelessly.

—Alyssa

I need to let God be the one who defines me. We put so much importance on what people—especially the opposite sex—think of us. We let that determine our worth. But what God says about me is worth so much more.

—Lauren

I understand the pressures of wanting to date, but I believe with all my heart that Christians should date only Christians. Be friends with non-Christians. Get this friend interested in God before you get him or her interested in you.

—Robert

Every once in a while, we need to stop and think about how it felt when we first fell in love with God. But that's not enough. We also need to keep this love alive and growing by talking to God, turning to him with all of our needs, and showing our love for him by the way we live. When this begins to happen, everything else will fall into place—including our desire for romance.

—Jaci

Your turn

* Sound off with your own words about why it's smart to be wise about dating:

DAY 68 Time-Traveling Prayer

Today, take some time to pray about:

Your future: Include everything from college plans, to a career, to ministry, to a possible future spouse. Spend time with God dreaming big.

Then surrender those plans to God, and ask for his wisdom to make the best choices.

Your present: Pray that all your relationships—guys and girls, friends and dating relationships—will be pleasing to God. Tell God you're putting him first in your life, whether or not you're dating.

Your past: Confess any ways you've fallen short in your relationships. Thank God for the ways your relationships have helped you grow. Praise God for the gift of friendship.

DAY 69 Is Church Relevant?

I slid into the pew next to my family, glanced at the bulletin, and sighed. The sermon was on marriage. I knew it would be just another Sunday where the church service went right over my head.

When the pastor got up to preach, I zoned out. I woke up when the choir started singing the last hymn.

I was relieved to go home, but felt a little disappointed. Lately I'd been feeling like church wasn't really for me. None of it seemed to matter to my life and my day-to-day struggles. On the ride home, I flipped through the bulletin again and noticed that the youth group was starting up later in the week. I'd just started seventh grade and I was finally old enough to join.

By Wednesday night, I was totally pumped. When I got to youth group, I was surprised at how many people I already knew. I fit right in. It wasn't long before Ron, our youth pastor, introduced himself. I could tell he was on fire for Christ and wanted people like me to feel that same excitement.

After a while, the praise band started singing. Ron encouraged us to focus on what the songs meant and to see singing as a way to worship God. As we sang one song after another, I really started to feel connected to Christ.

The night got even better when Ron got up to talk. He told us about David and Jonathan's friendship in 1 Samuel 18. It was a story I'd heard a million times before, but Ron actually made it relevant to my life.

"They were true friends," Ron said. "You need to choose your friends wisely too. Your closest friends should be people who help build up your faith."

After youth group, I thought about Ron's words. I had a good friend, Tim, who wasn't the best influence. Over the next few months I stopped spending so much time with him. Instead I hung out with friends from youth group and invited Tim to join us.

Although Tim never took me up on my offer, I kept going back to youth group. Ron seemed to make every story from the Bible mean something to my life. Like the story about Abraham and Sarah. I'd always thought it was just a story about two old people who had a kid. But Ron asked us to imagine what it would be like to have the kind of faith God wanted Abraham and Sarah to have.

I wanted that kind of faith. Although I'd been reading my Bible for as long as I could remember, I'd never really taken time to understand it. I started reading only a few verses at a time. If I had questions, I asked Ron or my parents. Over time, my understanding of the Bible grew. So did my faith.

I've been going to youth group for three years. My attitude about church has changed. I stopped tuning out when I thought the sermon wasn't going to matter to me. I was surprised at how much I could learn just by paying attention to the verses my pastor used. Sure, not every sermon directly relates to my life, but I know I can always learn something. And now I know that I really do belong at church and especially at youth group.

—Danny

* Danny's involvement in youth group didn't eliminate his need for church—it actually helped him enjoy Sunday church service. Write about your own experience with church and youth group. If you're able to go to both, how do they relate? What are some ways you can use one to get more out of the other?

DAY 70 Do We Really Need Church?

Q: Do you really need to belong to a church to be a Christian? Faith is a personal thing, so why can't you just have an individual relationship with God?

—*Anonymous*

A: Lots of people wonder about that, usually after a bad experience with Christians. The best answer I know is in the story of a fourth-century Egyptian soldier named Pachomius.

Determined to grow in his faith, Pachomius did what many serious believers did in those days. He became a hermit: living by himself in the desert, fasting, praying, and having visions.

But after a while, Pachomius began to question this approach: How can you learn to love if no one else is around? Can you learn humility living alone? Is it possible to learn patience, kindness, or gentleness in isolation?

He realized that developing spiritual fruit requires being around people. Pachomius quit the hermit life and formed one of the first monasteries. "To save souls," he said, "you must bring them together."

Let me take it a step further. Building spiritual strength requires other people, but not just people you *choose* to hang with. God's kind of love is best learned when we have to be around people we haven't specifically chosen as friends. Living around people we like is fairly easy. Doing life with just anybody is more challenging and forces us to grow. We have no choice about who our parents or brothers or sisters are; yet we are expected to love them. Neither can we choose who will or will not be in our spiritual family. Anyone who professes "Jesus is Lord" is to be welcomed in the church, where we encourage and challenge each other to grow in the faith. Living in this challenging but rewarding environment helps us grow and learn about love, humility, and the very fruits the Lord calls us to produce (Gal. 5:22–23).

The Bible says Christians are each like a different member of a body (Rom. 12:4–8). Can you be an eye without a neck, or a foot without a knee? I suppose it's possible to be a disconnected member without a body, but that's hardly what God has in mind for you (Heb. 10:24–25). You won't function right. Being a Christian means contributing to the

78

body, letting it contribute to your life, and submitting to the teaching and correction of others.

Can you be a Christian without the church? I suppose so. But what kind of Christian would you be?

—Marshall

Quick, grab a pen . . .

Like it!

* Write down three things you like about church:
1.
2.
3.

Now, talk to God

* Turn each "Like it!" item above into a prayer of thanksgiving. (Example: "Dear God, I'm thankful for my great youth pastor.")

Hate it!

* Write down three things you don't like about church:
1.
2.
3.

Think and pray

* Ask God to help you think through your reasons you don't like church. Why do you feel that way? Be honest. Admit any bad attitude about your church or the people you serve and worship with. Close your prayer time by asking God to help you do something to make your church a better place to serve and worship.

DAY 71 What's Your Role?

In the church, people have lots of different roles and gifts. Read the passages below to find out more:

> We all have different gifts, each of which came because of the grace God gave us. The person who has the gift of prophecy should use that gift in agreement with the faith. Anyone who has the gift of serving should serve. Anyone who has the gift of teaching should teach. Whoever has the gift of encouraging others should encourage. Whoever has the gift of giving to others should give freely. Anyone who has the gift of being a leader should try hard when he leads. Whoever has the gift of showing mercy to others should do so with joy.
>
> — Romans 12:6–8 NCV

> To one person the Spirit gives the ability to give wise advice; to another the same Spirit gives a message of special knowledge. The same Spirit gives great faith to another, and to someone else the one Spirit gives the gift of healing. He gives one person the power to perform miracles, and another the ability to prophesy. He gives someone else the ability to discern whether a message is from the Spirit of God or from another spirit. Still another person is given the ability to speak in unknown languages, while another is given the ability to interpret what is being said.
>
> —1 Corinthians 12:8–10 NLT

Apply it

* In your church, who has a gift of teaching? Who is serving? Who offers mercy? Who has the gift of discernment? Think of some people who match the gifts in these passages. Write them down.

* So how do you fit in? What gifts do you have? Write 'em if you know 'em. What gifts do you think you have that aren't on the list? How are you using them?

* If you're unsure of the gifts you have, talk to your friends, parents, and youth leader about what gifts they see in you. You can also talk to your youth pastor about taking a spiritual gifts inventory test, or look online for one.

* Remember: no matter who you are or what gifts God has given you, you have a role to play. Paul writes in Ephesians 4:12–13 that God gave us roles "so that his people would learn to serve and his body would grow strong. This will continue until we are united by our faith and by our understanding of the Son of God" (CEV).

DAY 72 The Cure for Loneliness

When I was in college I faced one of my deepest times of loneliness. I had friends and I had a family. I had a roommate who was always around. I had people who called me, and I had buddies to chat with online. People were always around me. But what I didn't have was a community of people I was honest with about the things happening in my life. That's what I really needed. I discovered the church offers us a cure for the kind of loneliness I experienced.

The church is a place for all people who claim Christ as Lord and Savior. It's a place of acceptance, no matter who you are or what you are going through. It's a place where you can take care of those deep, gnawing feelings of loneliness. Maybe if I had understood this better when I was in college, life would have been a little easier.

The church isn't a group of superhumanly good people. It's the fellowship of all Christians—even those who are often less than "saintly." It's all about a community of believers doing life together (Heb. 10:24). It's about helping each other get through times of hurt and loneliness. It's also about helping each other grow and mature in the Christian faith.

We must also be willing to take a risk to trust others in our Christian community. This is a challenge. To grow in love, to live out real community, we must be honest with each other about our struggles. We must also do what we can to make our community a safe place to share struggles. Can't do that with everybody? That's OK. Start small. Start with your small group leader or youth pastor—just someone in your church you really trust.

When we commit ourselves to love as Jesus loved, church can become the cure for loneliness—not only for us but also for our hurting and lonely friends who need Jesus. So are you ready to live the cure?

—Grady

* *Make a fist* with each hand and bang your fists together. Ask yourself: *How is church sometimes like two fists banging together?*

* Now, *fold your hands* together as if you're getting ready to pray. Look at your folded hands for a moment. How do you think your folded hands represent the best a church has to offer?

* Since your hands are folded, *take some time to pray* that your church and youth group would be a true cure for lonely and hurting people.

DAY 73 The First Church

* *Read Acts 4:32–37.* After you're done, jot down your answers to these questions:

* What are some defining characteristics of the early church?

* How is your church similar to this church?

* How is it different?

* What can you and your youth group friends do to help your church become more like the one described in Acts?

DAY 74 Why We Need Each Other

Matt admits: "Sometimes I don't want to go to church. Some weeks it's just hard for me to get up and go. Yeah, laziness is no excuse for missing church, but it has happened. Other times, my reason for not going starts with nagging thoughts about some of the people who've hurt me. Or people I've had bad experiences with at churches. I think about some of the people who don't seem to represent the name of Christ too well. Thinking about those experiences makes me want to stay home."

* Have you ever felt like Matt? What advice would you give him?

Matt continues: "It hit me that maybe I wasn't really giving the people around me much of a chance. Maybe my attitude was messed up. Maybe I misunderstood the purpose of church. Having all those people together is important. Why? We have to love and support our brothers and sisters in Christ. It's how we show God's love. This realization helped me see that I'm often so concerned with loving the lost and reaching out to the unsaved that I forget my own Christian brothers and sisters. I don't support them as much as I could, I don't spend enough time with fellow believers, and I even use some of them as excuses not to go to church! It's easy for me to let small hurts stand in the way of loving my brothers and sisters in Christ."

* **Think of one fellow believer you could do a better job of supporting, loving, or caring for.**

Matt concludes: "I've realized the love I show fellow believers will help those who don't believe to understand that Christ's love is for everyone, no matter what we've done or what we struggle with. I am also reminded that I should be happy to have opportunities to be with other Christians in church. By learning to love other believers as they are, I am modeling the love of God."

DAY 75 Your Big Toe Matters

* Try one or two of these experiments:

Type with your hands tied behind your back.
Pick up a coin without the use of your thumb.
Carry this book across the room without the use of your hands.
Walk across the room on the heels of your feet. No cheating. Your toes must remain off the floor!
"Walk" across a fifty-foot stretch of grass or sidewalk with only one leg.
Try to find your algebra or biology book in your locker or on your shelf with your eyes closed.

* How did you cope? What did these activities tell you about how your body functions as a whole? And how does that relate to you and your church?

DAY 76 "Have You Hooked Up Lately?"

"Hey Jason!" Luke shouted across the locker room as he changed for gym class. "Did you score with Chelsea last night?"

"You know it!" Jason boasted, reaching out for a high-five.

The room erupted with whistles and applause. All year long Luke, Jason, and some of the other guys in my gym class had been bragging about who they had sex with. I wasn't sure if they were telling the truth or just full of hot air. Either way, it bothered me to hear them talk about girls with such disrespect.

"How 'bout you?" Luke asked me as he laced up his gym shoes. "Have ya hooked up lately?"

"Nah," I said, shaking my head.

"Seriously, dude," Luke prodded. "Have you ever gotten laid?"

I had a split second to decide whether to tell the truth or simply say something to get them off my back. My gut told me to be honest. I cleared my throat and said, "No. I'm not having sex until I'm married."

As the words fell from my lips, my heart started thumping hard and fast. I couldn't believe I'd just announced to everybody that I was a virgin.

"Wait until marriage," Luke scoffed. "Oh, that's code for 'can't get any.'"

My cheeks burned hot with anger as I blurted out something about how I didn't have to worry about picking up nasty STDs or getting some girl pregnant. I then took a deep breath and continued in a calmer voice.

"I've chosen not to have sex yet because I'm a Christian and God wants me to wait. I want to share something that personal only with my wife."

"Oh great," Jason groaned. "Preacher Boy is gearing up for a sermon."

"Listen," I said, "you may think you're a stud for getting so much action, but I'm proud of my virginity."

Suddenly the room got really silent. As I turned to close my locker I heard someone snicker, "He's gotta be gay."

"Or totally crazy!" another added.

The rest of the morning I replayed the locker room scene over and over in my mind. By lunchtime my head was throbbing. When I walked through the cafeteria line I was mentally kicking myself.

Why did I let them drag me into their stupid conversation? I thought. *Why didn't I just walk away instead of blurting out my views?*

As I made my way to a table, a guy from my gym class named David tapped me on the shoulder. "You know, Harrison, I, uh, think it's great you had the guts to stand up for your beliefs in front of all those guys. I'm a Christian too, but I don't say much about it. I guess I'm afraid of being made fun of."

He told me he agreed with my views about sex, and apologized for not backing me up. He then added, "It's cool to see someone who's just as open about his faith at school as he must be at church."

"Thanks, man," was all I could manage to say.

Suddenly I felt really good inside. *If nothing else,* I thought, *at least what I said meant a lot to David.*

And maybe I had gotten through to some of the other guys too. But even if I hadn't, I'd done something just as important. I'd expressed and defended my Christian values. And in doing so I had stayed true to myself, to my future wife, and to God.

—Harrison

* **How has "hook-up culture" affected you? Have you been ridiculed for your standards? Tempted to give in?**

* **How do you stay strong and remain pure in light of the pressure from friends, dates, classmates, and the media?**

* **How can you reverse the pressure—challenging others to guard their purity without judging them?**

* **If you struggle with sexual purity, seek guidance and accountability from a caring Christian friend or youth leader.**

DAY 77 What's Wrong with Sex Songs?

Q: The Bible's Song of Songs is about erotic love. It's essentially an explicit love song. If Solomon could write that in the Bible, then what's wrong with sexual lyrics in secular love songs?

A: Song of Songs definitely contains explicit and erotic imagery, and it certainly proves the Bible isn't anti-sex. God created sex—and all the passions that come along with it. But there are three problems with connecting Song of Songs to sexually explicit secular love songs: context, motive, and audience.

First, scholars say the couple in Song of Songs is married. So it addresses sex within the context God designed—marriage. Are the explicit songs you're thinking about describing sex within marriage, as God intended it?

Second, what's the point of most sexually explicit love songs today? Is it to capture the beauty of God's creation of sex between husband and wife—or to represent sex as something fun, carefree, and casual? Does it lead your mind toward God or toward immoral and impure fantasies?

Third, who is the intended audience for Song of Songs—and who is the intended audience for today's sexually explicit songs? Do you honestly think reading Songs of Songs will warp your view of sex the way that large doses of sexually explicit secular lyrics will?

Yes, there is room even in Christian art to capture the beauty of sexual love, but it takes maturity and wisdom to appreciate that beauty. Even the young woman in Song of Songs warns that love should not be aroused until the time is right (2:7; 3:5; 8:4).

—Mark

* *Think about* your favorite movies, TV shows, websites, and songs. How can you determine what's OK for you to watch and listen to? How can you know if certain lyrics or images erode your purity?

DAY 78 All Kinds of Pure

Being pure isn't just about sexual purity. God's Word says we're to be pure in three specific ways:

Thoughts

And now, dear brothers and sisters, one final thing. Fix your thoughts on what is true, and honorable, and right, and pure, and lovely, and admirable. Think about things that are excellent and worthy of praise.

—Philippians 4:8 NLT

Nothing is pure for an unbeliever with a dirty mind. That person's mind and conscience are destroyed.

—Titus 1:15 CEV

The Lord detests the thoughts of the wicked, but those of the pure are pleasing to him.

—Proverbs 15:26

Actions

Don't let anyone think less of you because you are young. Be an example to all believers in what you say, in the way you live, in your love, your faith, and your purity.

—1 Timothy 4:12 NLT

For God did not call us to be impure, but to live a holy life.

—1 Thessalonians 4:7

Religion that pleases God the Father must be pure and spotless. You must help needy orphans and widows and not let this world make you evil.

—James 1:27 CEV

Heart

Blessed are the pure in heart, for they will see God.

—Matthew 5:8

The purpose of my instruction is that all believers would be filled with love that comes from a pure heart, a clear conscience, and genuine faith.

—1 Timothy 1:5 NLT

Come near to God, and he will come near to you. Clean up your lives, you sinners. Purify your hearts, you people who can't make up your mind.

—James 4:8 CEV

Having purified your souls by your obedience to the truth for a sincere brotherly love, love one another earnestly from a pure heart.

—1 Peter 1:22 ESV

* How do your thoughts, actions, and heart all relate to each other? When it comes to purity, how can one affect the other?

* *Idea:* Make a copy of Day 78 and hang it on your bedroom or bathroom mirror.

* *Another idea*: Choose your favorite verse and memorize it.

DAY 79 | I Thought We Were in Love

I started dating John in high school. It was the first serious relationship either of us ever had, and we were absolutely crazy about one another. We decided pretty early on that we were made for each other, and everyone in our small town agreed. They all thought we'd end up getting married and living happily ever after. I thought so too.

John and I had our lives planned out. After high school we'd go to the same college. Then as soon as we graduated, we'd get married. We knew what kind of house we'd live in and the cars we'd drive. We even decided how many kids we'd have and what we'd name them. Both of us were convinced that nothing could ever come between us.

That's how we justified our physical relationship. When we started having sex, we figured it was OK since we knew we would marry each other eventually. When we went away to college, we used the same reasoning to justify our living together.

Deep down I knew what we were doing was wrong. I could see how far we'd drifted from the habits we'd practiced in the beginning. When we first started dating, we made a big deal about making sure God was the center of our relationship. We went to church together and encouraged one another to read the Bible and pray daily. But by the time we got to college, we had pretty much stopped going to church. We never opened the Bible, and we only prayed when there was a crisis. I told myself everything would change as soon as we got married.

Then came Jessica. I had met her before and knew John studied with her occasionally, but I never thought much about it. I could hardly believe it when he told me there was more than studying going on between them. He said his love for me had faded and that we had no future. He expected me to just forget about him, about the plans we'd made and the six years we'd spent together.

That time in my life was the deepest and darkest valley I have ever known. It was also, strangely enough, a time of great hope. I say that because in the midst of my despair, Jesus found me. Until then, I had never known what it meant to need him. I had never felt so empty and broken, so hurt and alone. When I cried out to God, he came and wrapped his arms around me.

I'm forever grateful for God's unbelievable grace. Through it, he continues to heal me. But even so, I still bear the scar of a deep wound. I heard someone compare premarital sex to pieces of paper being glued together and pulled apart. I can't think of a better way to describe it. John and I were joined together like that. When the relationship ended, we were ripped apart, and I left part of myself with him that I can never get back. I'm talking about more than my virginity. I was joined to him emotionally and spiritually too.

I tell my story because I want to keep others from making the same mistake. I'm a living testimony of how unexpected nightmares can come true. Please believe me: the pain is real, and it's not worth it.

—LeAnne

* The author of this story doesn't mention any accountability partners or conversations with her parents or youth leaders. How could these

have helped her? How can you best use the resources and people in your life to help you stay pure?

DAY 80 Throwing It Away

Go check out the nearest garbage can. No, really. What's in there? Used tissues? Old homework? A banana peel? Something you can't (and don't want to) recognize?

Now think about what occupies your brain. How could your mind become like that garbage can? And what would it mean to regularly "take out the trash"? Better still, what can you do to keep garbage from getting in your mind in the first place?

DAY 81 10 Ways to Practice Purity

1. Keep innocent expressions special. Rather than making the innocent expressions a mere prelude to the "heavier stuff," make the most of them. Let holding hands mean something. Express tenderness by simply putting your arms around each other. Make sure a kiss communicates true feeling and isn't just the first step to further physical involvement.

2. Pace your passion. Every marathon runner knows that you don't use up your energy at the beginning of the race; you need most of it at the end. Pacing your passion means that you realize you're trying to remain pure all the way to your wedding day. It's OK to express your love in little ways, but don't start messing with the package that is sex. To get real practical, avoid French kissing and petting—anything that is sure to ignite the fires of passion.

3. Don't feed your fantasies. It's normal to think about sex sometimes. In fact, with the way advertising and Hollywood exploit sex, it is impossible *not* to think about it. So choose your entertainment carefully. Certain songs, books, television shows, movies, and websites only turn up the pressure. Feeding your mind junk only makes it harder to remain pure in your actions.

4. Remember whose property you're touching. You do not own the person you're dating. That person belongs to God. And so do you.

5. Make a promise to God, and renew your commitment daily. Decide where you're going to draw the line, and tell God that with his help, you're not going to cross that line until marriage. Don't commit to it unless you mean it, though. The Bible says it's a serious thing to make a promise to God. At the same time, realize that you can't stick to your promise without his help. That's why it's important to renew your commitment *daily*.

6. Acknowledge Jesus's presence on every date. Before a date, make sure you're spiritually prepared. Spend at least as much time in prayer as you spend getting ready in front of the mirror. As God's Word says in Proverbs 3:6, "Seek his will in all you do, and he will show you which path to take" (NLT).

7. Agree on your standards. Before sex becomes an issue in the relationship, talk about your standards with your boyfriend or girlfriend. Don't dwell only on the negative—what you *won't* do. Hebrews 10:24 tells us to "motivate one another to acts of love and good works" (NLT). Discuss ways your friendship can help each of you become a better person.

8. Don't always go it alone. Sure, you want to be alone with your date; that's only normal. Yet too much time alone can lead you to do things you'll regret later. Your relationship will be a lot healthier if you spend time with each other's families and friends.

9. Put real love first. Genuine love always respects the other person. It never says, "If you love me, you'll . . ." Real love says instead, "Since I care about you so much, I will respect you, treat you with kindness, and never ask you to do something you know or feel is wrong."

10. Declare a new beginning. If you think you've already given away too much, don't give up. The beauty of Christianity is that sins are forgiven and erased. You can start over today.

—Ron

* Think of two more ways to practice purity. Write them below.
   1.
   2.

DAY 82 God = Purifier

Purify me from my sins, and I will be clean;
wash me, and I will be whiter than snow.
                    —Psalm 51:7 NLT

* Spend some time with God in prayer. Follow the suggestions below:

Confess

any less-than-pure thoughts,

words,

or actions.

Ask for

strength to stand up under temptation,

discernment in choosing what you watch and listen to,

and desire to please God in all that you do.

Praise God that Jesus's blood

cleanses your sins,

gives you a fresh start,

and makes you pure!

DAY 83 Handle with Care

There's a beautiful gift inside this package.
It's wrapped for protection.
Tied for security.
Stamped:
"Fragile!"
"Handle with Care!"

It's easy to loosen the strings,
to let anyone tear away
the wrapping,
to give the gift without commitment—
offer it to the
highest bidder,
or hand it out as
a prize for a game.

There's a gift wrapped
inside this brown paper.
It's for keeps—
not to be exchanged.
It's a surprise,
to be
opened by the person
to whom it's addressed,
on the date marked
"Forever."

—Ruth

* In the space provided below, write a poem or a letter to your future spouse about your desire to remain pure until marriage. Think about purity in terms of your mind, heart, and body.

Dear future husband or wife,

Love,
Me

DAY 84 God's Plan

God always wanted to be your friend. He created you—and all people—so he could love us. He even built a place to live with all his creations, and life was good in the Garden of Eden. Then something went wrong.

Satan knew that if humans were sinners, they'd be separated from God because God is holy and can't stand sin. So he started tempting Adam and Eve to break Eden's one rule. When they gave in to Satan's tempting and doubted God's goodness, sin moved into the garden.

God still loved us, but now he couldn't be around us. But God had a plan. As he handed Adam and Eve their suitcases, he looked at Satan (in the form of the serpent) and said, "I will cause hostility between you and the woman, and between your offspring and her offspring. He will strike your head, and you will strike his heel" (Gen. 3:15 NLT).

No, God wasn't talking about gardeners using shovels to kill snakes who get in their tomato plants. He was talking about Jesus.

—Todd

* In what way or ways did Satan strike Jesus on the heel? (See Isa. 53:3–5; Mark 15:16–37.)

* What does "he will strike your head" refer to? (See John 12:31; Col. 1:13–14; Rev. 20:10.)

* Think about this: God's ultimate plan appeared way back in Genesis. What does this fact tell you about God?

DAY 85 God Orders Curtains

In Exodus, God told Moses to build a tabernacle where he could live among the Israelites. But because of sin, this wasn't an open hanging-out place like the garden. God instructed Moses to put a curtain down the middle. This curtain represents the barrier sin created between humans and God.

The Lord stayed on one side of the curtain, humans on the other. If anyone with sin walked onto God's side of the curtain, they'd die (Lev. 16:1–2).

* *Take a look:* Use a pencil to draw a square room. Add a line down the middle to represent the curtain. Write *God* on one side of the room, *Humans* on the other.

There will be blood

One time a year, the high priest Aaron could cross the curtain to pay, or "atone," for all the sins of the Israelites. How could he cross and not die? He had to perform a long list of cleansing rituals that involved a whole lot of bull and goat blood. Why blood?

The Bible is clear that the "wages of sin is death" (Rom. 6:23). This means that when we sin, we deserve to die. Death is required. But instead of killing people left and right when they sin, the merciful God allows them to replace their own death with the death of a pure, unblemished animal: "Life is in the blood, and I have given you the blood of animals to sacrifice in place of your own" (Lev. 17:11 CEV).

Christ is often referred to as a sacrificial lamb. This terminology would make a lot of sense to the Israelites who sacrificed pure, unblemished animals. This sinless, pure, unblemished Son of God was sent so that his sacrificed blood wouldn't just cover up sin for a year or just allow one man to cross the curtain. This sacrifice would bridge the gap that sin created between humans and God. For good. Take a look at what Luke says happened the instant Jesus died: "The curtain of the temple was torn in two" (Luke 23:45).

—Todd

* *Take another look:* **Erase the line you drew down the middle of your room drawing. Without that sin curtain, humans and God are no longer separated.**

Now the dwelling of God is with men, and he will live with them.

—Revelation 21:3

DAY 86 Say Thanks

Set a timer for ten minutes. Then think about these verses and pray with thanksgiving until the alarm goes off:

But God demonstrates his own love for us in this: While we were still sinners, Christ died for us.

—Romans 5:8

He himself carried our sins in his body on the cross. He did it so that we would die as far as sins are concerned. Then we would lead godly lives. His wounds have made you whole.

—1 Peter 2:24 NIrV

DAY 87 I'll See Dave Again

Dave was the kind of kid everyone liked. He was cool and athletic. Everyone loved how crazy-funny he was. And Dave loved God. A lot.

One day during our junior year, Dave didn't show up for astronomy class. He had a brain tumor. There was nothing the doctors could do for him. Dave got worse and worse. Before the end of our senior year of high school, Dave died. None of us could believe it happened.

I would like to see my friend again. I'd like to see the joy on Dave's face when he played volleyball—and beat me bad. I'd like to see him whole again. Strong, athletic, and crazy-funny.

I believe I will.

I believe that Jesus rose from the dead so that my friend Dave could too. The resurrection of Jesus assures me that God has indeed conquered death. He physically walked out of the tomb. With his for-real body.

It's because of Jesus's victory over death that we have hope in the life everlasting. But if there's no resurrection, there's no hope, and Christian belief is just plain lame. Sound a little harsh? Well, check out something the apostle Paul said: "And if Christ wasn't raised to life, our message is worthless, and so is your faith. If the dead won't be raised to life, we have told lies about God by saying that he raised Christ to life, when he really did not" (1 Cor. 15:14–15 CEV).

I believe in the resurrection and the life everlasting because it's a very important fact of my faith. But it's also way more than just a fact.

I believe in the resurrection and the life everlasting because I'm looking forward to meeting Jesus and spending eternity talking to him, learning from him, and just being with him.

I believe in the resurrection and the life everlasting because in heaven there will be no backstabbing, no gossip, and no cliques. There will be no more sin—the very thing that brought death into the world in the first place.

I believe in the resurrection and the life everlasting because I will live in a heavenly world full of real, honest love and compassion.

And I believe in the resurrection and life everlasting because I will be able to see my friend Dave. He will be walking. He will be whole. I don't know exactly what his resurrected body will look like—or mine. But I do know our resurrected bodies won't grow old and will never die. So I have hope that someday I will get to challenge Dave to a game of volleyball. He'll destroy me once again, but who cares? It'll be Dave!

—Grady

> That's how it will be when our bodies are raised to life. These bodies will die, but the bodies that are raised will live forever. These ugly and weak bodies will become beautiful and strong. As surely as there are physical bodies, there are spiritual bodies. And our physical bodies will be changed into spiritual bodies.
>
> —1 Corinthians 15:42–44 CEV

DAY 88 4 Truths about Death

1. Everyone dies. The Bible makes it clear that all of us will die one day. In Psalm 89:48, a poet named Ethan asks, "What man can live and not see death, or save himself from the power of the grave?" Solomon says it this way in Ecclesiastes: "Death is the destiny of every man; the living should take this to heart" (7:2).

2. Death is scary. Psalm 55 is a poem David wrote during a very tough period of his life. Even though he loved God, here's what he writes in verses 4–5: "My heart is in anguish within me; the terrors of death assail me. Fear and trembling have beset me; horror has overwhelmed me."

3. Death is not the end. In *The Lord of the Rings: The Return of the King*, Gandalf and Pippin are about to be overrun by orcs when Pippin says, "I didn't think it would end this way."

Gandalf shrugs. "End?" he says. "No, the journey doesn't end here. Death is just another path—one that we all must take."

He's right. Death isn't the end. Yet the Bible makes it clear we won't all walk the same path after death. Hebrews 9:27 says, "Man is destined to die once, and after that to face judgment." In Matthew 25:46, Jesus declares the wicked "will go away to eternal punishment, but the righteous to eternal life." How do we make sure our next adventure is on the right path?

4. Death has been conquered. Everyone can experience eternal life because Christ died for our sins and then conquered death. That's something God promised way back in the Old Testament: "I will ransom them from the power of the grave; I will redeem them from death" (Hos. 13:14; see also 1 Cor. 15:54–55).

Jesus conquered death. The best part is that we too can conquer death if we put our trust and hope in Christ.

—Sam

Memorize this

God raised him from the dead, freeing him from the agony of death, because it was impossible for death to keep its hold on him.

—Acts 2:24

DAY 89 Jesus Feels Your Pain

Jesus, the Son of God, not only became a man but also suffered at the hands of other men and willingly submitted himself to death. And not just any death, but death on a cross—public crucifixion and humiliation. There is something powerful and too deep for words about this suffering and killing of God.

But things aren't always as they seem. As the saying goes, the darkest part of the night is the moment before dawn. We have all experienced some sort of crisis. We have all been through times when things seemed so dark and despairing that we were ready to call it quits—thinking the game was over and we had lost everything.

But the story of the crucifixion shows us that the game was not over. Jesus would return. And that fact is so important—and gives us great hope for our own resurrection and eternal future. It also gives us hope for getting through our current crises. Good can follow bad. The resurrection teaches us that. But in looking at the resurrection, we must also remember the great good that came out of Jesus's suffering, crucifixion, and terrible death. All this showed just how much God loves us. That death also became the means of forgiveness of sins and threw the doorway wide open to heaven. His death became our hope and healing.

As we look at Jesus's suffering, however, we need to remember something. His suffering wasn't just about his painful death on the cross. It wasn't just about all the whippings and beatings, and that crown of thorns crushed down on his head.

Have you ever had a friend betray your confidence? So did Jesus. Have you ever had a friend deny you at a moment when you needed someone to stick up for you? So did Jesus. Have you ever been misunderstood? So was Jesus. Have you ever had people accuse you of things you never did? It happened to Jesus too. Have you ever felt alone in this world? Jesus knows the feeling. He experienced it too.

Jesus's suffering is really incredible once you stop and think about it. Perhaps we often easily turn to him for help because, way down inside, we know we are praying to someone who understands what we're going through. Sometimes there's great comfort in having our sadness understood by someone else who knows how we feel.

—Jerry and Grady

Pain into prayer

* What are you or a friend going through right now that seems too difficult to handle? Turn this pain into a prayer. Ask God to help you see how much he understands your deepest hurts. Ask him to help you communicate his love to hurting friends.

DAY 90 The Plunge

A diver stands rigid on the tip of a high board;
he bounces once and then leaps into the air
he stretches his arms outward
and glides into an effortless fall;
his outstretched arms gracefully
sweep over his head
and he cups his hands firmly;
his arrow-straight, muscled body
rushes downward then slips
into the clear-as-glass surface,
barely leaving a watery wrinkle.

God once stood on the edge of the universe;
arms spread wide, he leapt into space (and time),
falling blur-like into the sea of humanity;
barely noticed, his body soon sank
into the breathless depths—
silence, frightening, awful, deadly silence—
then God exploded to the surface
and wave after wave after wave
rippled outward,
and continue to ripple outward,
washing and cleansing the soul
of anyone who willingly
wades into the water.

—*Marie*

DAY 91 When the Good Is Hard to See

Every year my parents and I attend a Good Friday service that ends sadly. The lights go out, no one talks, and there's a gloomy mood to capture what it must have been like the day Jesus died. Every year I try to grieve, but I just can't feel real sadness about his death because I know Jesus didn't stay dead.

101

While I know the happy ending to come out of Jesus's death, his disciples sure didn't. They had dedicated their lives to Jesus, and now he was gone. Dead. Without him, they could see no hope. Nothing made sense.

Jesus repeatedly tried to convince his disciples to keep hope. Jesus said, "I am on my way to the One who sent me. Not one of you has asked, 'Where are you going?' Instead, the longer I've talked, the sadder you've become. So let me say it again, this truth: It's better for you that I leave" (John 16:5–7 Message).

In John 16:19–23 (Message), Jesus tries explaining again:

> You're going to be in deep mourning while the godless world throws a party. You'll be sad, very sad, but your sadness will develop into gladness. When a woman gives birth, she has a hard time, there's no getting around it. But when the baby is born, there is joy in the birth. This new life in the world wipes out memory of the pain. The sadness you have right now is similar to that pain, but the coming joy is also similar. When I see you again, you'll be full of joy, and it will be a joy no one can rob from you. You'll no longer be so full of questions.

The disciples were missing the big picture. But it wasn't their fault. They weren't God. They couldn't comprehend his whole plan. Most of the time, I'm just like the disciples. I know God has a plan for the world. I know he has a destination for me. And I know it's good (Jer. 29:11). But when things aren't going according to my plan, it sure doesn't feel like this is for the best. I complain and cry and even fight against the hard times that are actually necessary to bring about God's way.

God knows we cannot see past the current bad stuff to see his full plan. And that's why he doesn't leave us to do it alone. In John 16, Jesus explains that because he is leaving, God is sending the Holy Spirit to help believers find their way. Jesus says the Holy Spirit will "take you by the hand and guide you into all the truth there is" (John 16:13 Message).

Thanks to God's Holy Spirit working in each of us, we know he's guiding us, even when things look hopeless. Even when I feel lost and forgotten, I know from the resurrection that I can trust God to bring a bright dawn from even the darkest night.

—Todd

* *Spend three minutes in prayer* about any doubts, confusion, or future worries you have. End with this prayer by Thomas Merton:

> My Lord God, I have no idea where I am going. I do not see the road ahead of me. I cannot know for certain where it will end. . . . But I believe that the desire to please you does in fact please you. . . . And I know that if I do this, you will lead me by the right road, though I may know nothing about it.

DAY 92 | I Was a Silent Christian

Like the other guys on my college football team, each year I signed an athletic pledge stating that I wouldn't drink alcohol—even in the off-season. As a Christian, I felt signing the pledge should be taken seriously. If I signed it, I would live by it.

But most of my teammates didn't feel that way. At the end of every season, the guys on the team held a big end-of-season beer party. Even worse, the coach knew what was going on. He'd even told us, "Just don't get caught." And he was the one who had us sign the pledge.

Each year, I always felt like I should say something to the team about why I felt it was wrong to break the pledge. But I wasn't sure how to talk about my beliefs and values with them. I also felt intimidated by what they might think. So each time the end-of-season party rolled around, I kept quiet.

God was slowly working on me, though, helping me not only grow in my faith but also become bolder in talking about what I believed and valued. By the time I started my junior year, I felt ready to take another step forward in my Christian walk. So I started talking to some of my teammates about joining me in studying the Bible. I believe God honored my efforts. After a few weeks, about six guys were coming to the Bible study.

I think these small steps in my Christian growth led me to make a very big decision near the end of my junior year. I decided I'd take a stand against the end-of-season drinking party.

On Thursday afternoon, we had our last practice before the game. At the end of practice, I jogged over to the team captain and said, "After you and Coach talk to the team, I'd like to say a few words."

The team captain said OK and called everyone into an all-team huddle. The coach gave us a typical pep talk and then said, "We have a big game to focus on. We now have the opportunity to fulfill a lot of goals we've set for ourselves. . . . As for drinking afterward, I don't want you to have any part of it. No excuses. I don't want it to happen!" And I could tell he meant it.

The coach's words caught me off guard. I don't know why he'd changed his attitude about the drinking party. Knowing the coach had a change of heart made me less nervous about speaking out.

Here's pretty much what I ended up saying:

"After the game tomorrow, the season is over and the seniors are no longer obligated to keep the pledge. But my encouragement to you is to set a good example for the underclassmen, especially the freshmen. To be the best athletes we can possibly be, we need to get rid of partying and drinking. It's just not helpful for us."

When I stopped talking, the team was pretty quiet. Some guys actually thanked me. As for the party, I don't know how many guys went. I just hope some chose not to go because of what I said.

One thing I do know is that the whole experience changed me. It made me feel better about myself, because I took a stand for something I believed in.

—Jason

* When have you taken a stand for something you believe in?

* When did you wish you'd taken a stand and didn't?

* When is it hardest for you to take a stand?

* What small steps helped Jason to eventually talk to the team?

* What small steps can you take that might prepare you to take a big stand?

DAY 93 Amy's Quiz: Got Courage?

Do you take a courageous stand in everyday ways? Take this quiz to find out.

1. You're hanging out with your friends when they flip on a cable show. The opening sex scene makes you feel uncomfortable. You:
   A. Get comfortable. It's just TV—not real life.
   B. Feel stuck. So when the show heats up you volunteer to get popcorn and pop.
   C. Say it's not your thing and ask if anyone wants to go shoot hoops.

2. You arrive at class early. Everyone is gossiping about the new guy at school. You:
   A. Refuse to listen. Refuse to spread it.
   B. Jump in with another rumor you heard about him.
   C. Eavesdrop. You won't jump in, but you can listen.

3. It's your birthday and one of your friends gives you a shirt with a beer logo on it. You:
   A. Say thanks, but privately ask if you can exchange it for a retro TV show T-shirt you like.
   B. Think it's awesome! You'll wear it when Mom isn't around.
   C. Laugh—you figure it's a joke; then you tuck it away in your drawer.

4. Your little sister just found out she made the cheerleading squad. Excitedly she shouts, "Oh my God! I can't believe it!" How do you react?
   A. Give her a hug. You didn't even notice she said anything wrong.
   B. Say congratulations. Later, you gently ask if she realizes what she said.
   C. Cringe, but don't say anything.

5. Your English class reads a poem about homosexuality. The discussion centers around "judgmental Christians" who say gay people are evil. You:

  A. Say you're a Christian and also dislike it when some believers are hateful and judgmental. After all, homosexuality is a sin—but we all have sin. Your faith is about Christ's love.

  B. Side with those who put down all Christians as judgmental.

  C. Keep quiet.

Scoring

  1. A (1), B (2), C (3)
  2. A (3), B (1), C (2)
  3. A (3), B (1), C (2)
  4. A (1), B (3), C (2)
  5. A (3), B (1), C (2)

13–15 points: You have courage. You try to stand up for what you believe. Keep it up, but make sure your courage comes with kindness and respect for others (1 Peter 3:15–16).

9–12 points: Be bold. Sure, it takes guts to live like Christ, to step out of your comfort zone, but people will notice there's something different about you. Go ahead—let your faith shine through.

5–8 points: Take a stand. An important question to think about: does your life seem any different from the lives of the non-Christians at your school? If not, please talk with your youth pastor about what it means to be a courageous Christian.

DAY 94 Would You Say No to Rolling Stone?

As a member of the biggest group of their day, former Backstreet Boy Brian Littrell had many opportunities to stand up for his faith. One of them made big headlines.

For a *Rolling Stone* magazine cover shoot, the photographer had arranged for the Backstreet Boys to stand in front of fifty nude women. "That's not me," Brian says. "I didn't want to be represented that way. That's not my heart."

Brian sat out of the photo shoot—thus, not appearing on the cover. "That ruffled some feathers in the group and with our record label," he says. "But the *Rolling Stone* article became a chance to explain *why* I didn't stand in the photo. That bad situation became a great witness. God has truly used me in magnificent ways like that over and over."

—Todd

* What do you think of Brian Littrell's boldness?

* What might he have sacrificed because of his stand?

* List three reasons why boldness could be better than backing down:
    1.
    2.
    3.

DAY 95 A Prayer Exercise

Stand up

* Really, stand up where you're at right now. Pray: *Lord, help me to stand up for what I believe in.*

Sit down

* Pray: *Lord, I am sorry when I stay seated and should stand up for you.*

Stand up

* Pray: *Lord, help me to be bold for you even when I'd rather run and hide.*

Sit down

* Spend one minute in silence, listening for God to speak to you (maybe with just a gentle "mind nudge") about one way you can take a bold stand for him.

DAY 96 God's Brave Spy (Todd's fake interview with a for-real Bible character)

The subject of this fake interview is a scout Moses sent to check out the land that the Lord was giving to the Israelites. He and eleven other scouts were told to see if this really was the "land of milk and honey" promised to them.

Q: So did you take this mission just to get your Milk and Honey Merit Badge?

A: Merit badge? What? Umm, I wasn't a *Boy Scout.* I was an actual scout—you know, doing reconnaissance, gathering intelligence. I was like a Bible spy.

Q: Oh. So why were you spying on milk and honey?

A: When God told Moses he was going to free the Israelites from their slavery in Egypt, he said he was going to give them some good land flowing with milk and honey [Exod. 3:8]. But that didn't mean actual rivers of the stuff. I made that mistake too. I was looking forward to kayaking down a honey rapids. Instead, God meant we'd have a booming economy with plenty to eat.

Q: Ah, so you were checking to see if this was good land?

A: Exactly. On God's orders, twelve of us explored the land of Canaan. And God was right: this *was* great land! When we got back, we told Moses all we'd seen and showed off the fruit we found. But ten of the scouts—real party poopers—pointed out that we also discovered very powerful people living on this land. These ten scouts were full of fear. They just wanted to go live somewhere else. Quickly I said, "We should go up and take that land because that's God's plan! We can certainly do it with God behind us!"

Q: How did the scared scouts react?

A: Not well. They whined, "The land devours those living in it. All the people are of great size. We were like grasshoppers compared to them!" They were a bit dramatic. I mean, the residents of Canaan were big, but like pro wrestler big—not Godzilla big. But still, their nutty lies and gossip about what we'd seen worked. Our entire community was scared out of following God's plan!

Q: What did you do?

A: I took a stand with Joshua, one of the other scouts. We said, "If God is pleased with us, he'll lead us into this land. But please don't rebel. Don't be afraid, because the Lord is with us. What can't we do if God is on our side?"

Q: How'd they take that advice?

A: Not well. They talked about stoning us. But that's when God showed up. He said, "How long will these people refuse to believe in me despite all I've done for them?" He wasn't happy. The ten scouts who spread the gossip fell dead. And then he declared that no one there except Josh and me would ever step a foot in the Promised Land. He had asked them to do something, promising to be with them—and they declined. Because of their lack of trust, he cut them off from the milk and honey.

Q: What did you learn from all this?

A: Three things: First, God is mighty. Our paths won't be free of obstacles, but with God leading us, we can overcome anything. Second, God is faithful. I never doubted God could make good on his promise. Because of that, Josh and I were among the Israelites who eventually entered the Promised Land. And third, a good home always has milk and honey!

* *Read the real story:* **Who is the real Bible character behind Todd's fake interview? Find out in Numbers 13–14.**

DAY 97 A Prayer

Lord,
I used to think taking a stand for you
meant arguing with people who didn't
believe in you or in your Word
or who mocked your name.

But lately, Lord, I realize
if I want people to see
how great you are,
I need to let your greatness
shine in and through me.

By loving the unlovable,
being kind to the unkind,
and blessing those who
curse me (and you),
I'm taking a stand for you.

By doing what you've called me
to do (no matter what criticism
or callousness I face),
I'm battling against
the lies of Satan.

Taking a stand starts with
embracing this truth:
If I want you to be real to others,
I must allow you to be real in me.
Then I'm truly standing up
for you—not just with words,
but with my life.

—Elaine

Your turn

* Write a prayer expressing your own fears and/or desires about taking a stand for your values or beliefs.

DAY 98 Afraid to Speak Up

During my sophomore year, I had a class in comparative religions. I took this class thinking I was going to learn about other religions. It turned out to be very different from what I expected.

We would sit with our desks in a circle. Then our teacher would throw out questions for discussion. We were to answer the questions in a way that supported the specific religion we each believed in. Fearful of how others might respond, I always slouched in my desk. I wasn't alone in my fears; usually the room was filled with uncomfortable silence.

One day, the teacher asked a question that shook me up: "Why does God let a child molester get away with his actions, but a six-month-old baby dies of cancer?" Suddenly the class was no longer so silent—this question started a huge discussion. The two answers I remember most went something like this:

"Maybe God is trying to get revenge on us for our sins."

"I think God wants us to be Buddhist because they believe in happiness."

I looked at two other Christians in my class, realizing they were fearful and not going to speak at all. My heart started pounding as I glanced nervously at a few students who appeared to be sleeping. Some of them probably thought they were too cool to answer.

Intermission

* What would you have done if you had been in this person's shoes?

111

. . . the rest of the story

Out of nowhere I heard my voice saying, "I don't believe any of that."
I sucked in my breath, realizing that all heads had turned toward me. I
contemplated not explaining myself as my teacher just looked at me.
I was risking becoming "that Christian freak." But suddenly I felt the
courage to continue.

"I don't think God chose to have the world filled with evil, but Satan
and humans have shaped the world into the way it is."

"What about the baby? Shouldn't God have ordered one of his
heavenly angels to come save it?" my teacher asked, waving his arms
dramatically.

I cautiously answered, trying not to anger the teacher. "To be honest, I
don't have an answer, but I know God doesn't enjoy the pain we experience.
And he doesn't enjoy it when people get away with doing wrong things.
I don't really know how to explain, but God didn't make the world this
way. It's broken by sin, so maybe the question should be stated differently.
I don't think we can judge God on the evil of this world. Instead, I just
have faith he is in control and will one day right the wrongs."

As the teacher glared at me and moved on to a different question, I felt
a rush of happiness. I had a sense that God was proud of what I had just
done, and that he was smiling over the courage and the faith I showed
in this tough moment.

—Brooke

Try one

* Imagine you were in the class when Brooke spoke up. What would
  you have been thinking? Feeling? Would you have joined in the conversation? If so, what would you have said?

* Have a Christian friend read Brooke's story. Ask your friend what he
  or she would have done in this situation.

DAY 99 Stretch Your Brain Muscles

Honor Christ and let him be the Lord of your life. Always be ready to give an answer when someone asks you about your hope. Give a kind and respectful answer and keep your conscience clear. This way you will make people ashamed for saying bad things about your good conduct as a follower of Christ.

—1 Peter 3:15–16 CEV

* Go back and read the passage again—*slowly*. OK, read it a third time and underline the words and phrases that jump out at you, and circle the ones that make no sense at all. Now try to answer this question: what does 1 Peter say to me about speaking up for Jesus? Take your questions—and your circled words and phrases—to your pastor, youth pastor, or small group leader.

DAY 100 Rahab the Prostitute Hero

My friends and I used to love to pretend we were superheroes. This involved running as fast as we could with our arms out in front of us and also jumping off the swings at the highest possible point. Everyone would always pick their favorite superhero, and I, without fail, would pick Aquaman.

Aquaman isn't the greatest of heroes. After all, his superpowers were swimming and talking to fish! Now, I realize I hadn't chosen the most impressive superhero around. But do you realize the Bible is filled with my kind of heroes? People who, at first glance, don't seem so much like heroes. Rahab is one such hero. Her story is found in Joshua 2.

Rahab had a couple of things working against her as a hero. First off, she was a prostitute—not really what we'd expect from a hero of our faith. Second, she lived in Jericho, a city about to be attacked by Joshua and the army of Israel. But out of nowhere, the craziest thing happened to her.

Joshua had sent two spies into Jericho to check things out before Israel attacked. The spies decided to hide out for a while in Rahab's "house of

113

business." However, the king of Jericho heard about their hideout and sent his troops after them.

When the troops got there, they questioned Rahab about the spies. She responded: "Yes, the men came to me, but I did not know where they had come from. At dusk, when it was time to close the city gate, the men left. I don't know which way they went" (Josh. 2:4–5 TNIV). Nice alibi, but totally not true. She was actually hiding the spies under a pile of dried plants up on her roof! So at this point in the story, Rahab's list of immoral or illegal activities included: prostitution, perjury, aiding and abetting criminals, and treason against the king. Not a great resumé (or rap sheet) for a superhero, is it?

When the soldiers left, Rahab made a deal with the spies: if she helped them escape, in return, they would spare her and her family when the attack on Jericho began. The spies were true to their word, and Rahab left her former life of prostitution and went to live among the Israelites. Rahab's amazing story and influence doesn't end there. Matthew 1:5 lists her as a part of the royal lineage of Jesus. She shows up again in Hebrews 11:31 as one of the great heroes of the faith. That's quite a legacy for a woman with such flaws.

—Jarrett

Super you

* You may not think of yourself as a superhero. Odds are, you probably relate more to someone like Rahab (minus the prostitution part). You know there are things about yourself that aren't right. You know every one of your issues. You may think you're nothing special. In fact, there are probably days when you feel pretty far from God. But if God used Rahab to play a part in history and to pave a way for Jesus, why couldn't he use you?

* Thank God for using imperfect people, and surrender yourself to be used by him.

* What ways could God want to use you right now, as is? Write 'em down:

DAY 101 "I Have a Bigger Weakness than You!"

To keep me from becoming conceited because of these surpassingly great revelations, there was given me a thorn in my flesh, a messenger of Satan, to torment me. Three times I pleaded with the Lord to take it away from me. But he said to me, "My grace is sufficient for you, for my power is made perfect in weakness." Therefore I will boast all the more gladly about my weaknesses, so that Christ's power may rest on me. That is why, for Christ's sake, I delight in weaknesses, in insults, in hardships, in persecutions, in difficulties. For when I am weak, then I am strong.

—2 Corinthians 12:7–10

10 Questions

1. What is a "thorn in my flesh"?
2. What would you consider a thorn in your flesh?
3. Is it cruel of God not to remove something if a believer asks?
4. If God is all-powerful and loves us, why would he not remove an obstacle or cure a weakness?
5. What does it mean to say God's grace is sufficient?
6. Why would someone boast about a weakness?
7. What good could come out of a weakness?
8. What does "For when I am weak, then I am strong" mean?

9. How have you seen God use a weakness of yours in a good way?

10. What don't you understand about these verses? Take your questions to a parent or youth leader.

DAY 102 Heroes Hate Baths?
(Todd's fake interview with a for-real Bible character)

Q: I've heard you're a big hero, a great man.

A: You could say that. I'm the commander of a great army. Everybody looks up to me. After I led us to victory over Israel, my reputation skyrocketed. And I bought the hype that I was hot stuff. That is, until I realized everyone has a weakness.

Q: Oh, what's your weakness?

A: Well, leprosy.

Q: Yikes! Isn't that a really infectious skin disease?

A: Can be, yeah.

Q: Say, maybe we can continue this interview over the phone.

A: It's OK. I've been healed. Do you know who helped me with my problem?

Q: A dermatologist?

A: No. A young servant girl I captured when I raided Israel. One day, she told my wife, "If your husband went to the prophet in Israel, he could be cured."

Q: Wow. You're a big heroic soldier and a little girl helps you. That's humbling.

A: Tell me about it. But I was forced to swallow my pride even more. You see, the Israelites were my biggest enemies. I didn't want to go to them for help! It's like the mighty Lord Voldemort going to a house elf for help. It's crazy.

Q: What did you do?

A: Well, I thought, *A great man like me can't have a flaw! I need to get rid of this.* So I sucked up my pride and went to Israel. There, the prophet Elisha told me to go wash myself seven times in the Jordan River. This made me so mad.

Q: *Why? Do you hate baths?*

A: No. I was angry because this "cure" seemed stupid. And easy. I was a military hero. I was a big shot. I was ready to do some great act to be cured. I wanted to earn it. But taking a bath? In an enemy's river? Bah. To humbly obey isn't heroic. To just accept a gift isn't daring.

Q: *So what happened?*

A: My servants encouraged me to forget my pride and just accept the free gift I was being offered. I went into the Jordan, and I was healed. It was miraculous.

Q: *What did you learn from all this?*

A: From the actions of that servant girl to God's simple gift of healing, I realized that money and power and reputation are nothing when it comes to God. Only God's love and strength help me overcome human weakness—not my own power at all.

* *What about you?* How has pride or embarrassment kept you from seeking help for your weaknesses? How have you had to rely on God's power and not your own?

* *Read the real story:* Who is the real Bible character behind Todd's fake interview? Find out in 2 Kings 5:1–19.

DAY 103 Tough Question

Q: *I keep reading in the Old Testament that people—even heroes of our faith like Abraham and David—had more than one wife or slept with their servants and stuff. How is that OK? How come we can say we should be virgins until marriage when these guys were sleeping around and having multiple wives?*

—Anonymous

Your turn

* How would you answer this question?

How IYF's expert answered:

A: Lots of people in the Bible are described doing things God doesn't approve of. Even "good" people, heroes like Abraham and David, at times behave in ways God never intended. The Bible doesn't whitewash their bad decisions, but presents these people authentically, flaws and all. They were people of great faith, but they were also people who sinned in significant ways, with horrible consequences.

Even though polygamy was common in ancient culture, and having sex with partners outside of marriage was (and continues to be) frequent, God desires his followers to be different—both then and now. He wants sex to be expressed in a one-and-only relationship between a husband and wife. In the very beginning, God said, "A man will leave his father and mother and be united to his wife, and they will become one flesh" (Gen. 2:24). That was true way back in the beginning of Genesis and it remains true today.

—Jim

DAY 104 4 Common Weaknesses

No hero is perfect—not even those amazing, save-the-day movie heroes or the great heroes of faith in the Bible. In fact, here are pairs of similar movie and Bible characters who faced—and overcame—four common weaknesses:

Flaw #1: Deceitfulness. Both Captain Jack Sparrow and Jacob (Genesis 25–50) are tricksters who exploit others to get what they want. The *Pirates of the Caribbean* captain's motto is "Take all you can! Give nothing back!" Not a very heroic motto. And Jacob's very name means "he grasps the heel," a phrase indicating he's a deceiver who takes advantage of others. Both men's deceptions came back around to haunt them before they learned better. But in the end, Jack sacrificially saved his friends, freed the Caribbean of a tyrant, and was regarded as a hero. Likewise we remember Jacob as a hero of our faith. He humbly sought his brother's forgiveness and depended on God alone.

Flaw #2: Fear. In *The Incredibles*, Violet is a shy, insecure teenager who fears rejection. She's worried she's not worth much, so she stays—literally—invisible. Eventually, she has to overcome her fears with courage to become the heroine she's meant to be.

There's a young girl in Bible times very much like Violet. Through a series of fateful circumstances, Esther became the queen of Persia. When she learned of a plot to destroy her people, the Jews, she was afraid to go to her husband, the king. Eventually, she overcame her fear and saved the Jewish nation from annihilation.

Flaw #3: Anger. In *Spider-Man 2*, Harry Osborn blames Spider-Man for his father's death. He wants revenge. His anger consumes him, even when he discovers Spider-Man is his best friend Peter Parker. Harry is like Jonah (Jonah 1–4), God's prophet chosen to tell the sinful people of Nineveh that the city would be destroyed in forty days unless they repented. Jonah was all for Nineveh's destruction. Like Harry, he wanted the guilty to get what was coming to them. Both Harry's and Jonah's anger blinded them from seeing what really mattered: compassion, forgiveness, truth, and mercy. God showed Jonah he had no right to be angry. In *Spider-Man 3*, Harry's anger subsides in the face of truth, compassion, and forgiveness.

Flaw #4: A Dark Past. Aragorn in *The Lord of the Rings* is a lot like Moses in Exodus. Both Moses and Aragorn were in self-imposed exile, trying to escape dark pasts. When Aragorn is asked why he's afraid of his forefather's legacy, Aragorn says, "The same blood flows in my veins—the same weakness." He fears the past will repeat itself. But Aragorn eventually overcomes the shadow of the past. He rises up, becomes king, and delivers his people from the forces of darkness.

In Exodus 2, Moses also exiles himself, because of his own dark past. He had killed an Egyptian whom he had seen beating an Israelite. In Exodus 3, God speaks to Moses and tells him to return to Egypt and deliver the Israelites out of Pharaoh's hand. Moses is afraid. Like Aragorn, his past weakens him. However, he eventually overcomes his fears and delivers his people from bondage. Once again, a flawed human becomes a great hero.

—Tom

119

* Write down some movie, TV, or book characters with these weaknesses:
    Pride
    Jealousy
    Physical or mental challenges
    Low self-image

* How could God be glorified by these specific flaws?

DAY 105 Take Time to Pray

Set a timer for four minutes and go into quiet prayer based on this outline:

Praise God for how he uses human weakness to shine a light on his divine strength. Think about how you, an imperfect being, are in the presence of a perfect God.

Confess to God the places where you are weak. Honestly tell him where you've fallen.

Thank God for your weaknesses. Name them and try to feel real joy and gratitude that you have them.

Pray about the weaknesses of others.

List your needs. Tell God how you'd like him to work through your weaknesses. Think about how much his will matters more than your own needs.

DAY 106 Samson's Weakness

When I was a kid, I thought it was cool to go to Sunday school and hear stories about a really strong guy who fought a lot. When I got older, I read the story of Samson myself and discovered the unrated director's cut. Samson wasn't the squeaky-clean hero for God I thought he was.

Sure, Samson was truly special. Before Samson was even born, God made it clear that Samson would one day take the Nazirite vow. This was God's way of marking people who were completely devoted to him. Some of the basics of the vow included not cutting your hair, not drinking wine or even eating grapes, and not going near anything dead. (Read more about this vow in Numbers 6:1–21.)

However, Samson had a little trouble keeping all the fine details of this vow. You see, with all his super strength, Samson had a super weakness: he made a lot of bad choices when it came to women.

In Judges 14:1–3, Samson met a Philistine girl, the daughter of his worst enemy. And despite his parents' protests, he insisted on marrying her. But Samson left his bride waiting at the altar. So how did Samson get over that relationship? He slept with a prostitute (Judg. 16:1).

Later, Samson started dating another Philistine named Delilah. Here's the bad news: she had been paid off by the Philistine Mafia to discover the secret to his strength. She asked him over and over why he was so strong. "Finally, he was fed up—he couldn't take another minute of it. He spilled it. He told her, 'A razor has never touched my head. I've been God's Nazirite from conception. If I were shaved, my strength would leave me; I would be as helpless as any other mortal'" (Judg. 16:16–17 Message).

Delilah hired a barber to cut Samson's hair while he slept and—*whoosh!*—Samson's strength was gone. He was captured by his enemies, had his eyes poked out, and was chained to columns in the Philistine temple. But Samson would have his grand finale. He prayed to God for the strength to bring down the columns. In one final act of strength, Samson killed more Philistines than he ever had in his whole life. It is a heroic ending to a complicated and messy story. In fact, this story raises more questions than it answers. Did Samson have any idea how truly unique he was? If so, then why didn't he live up to the Nazirite vow he made with God?

Instead of criticizing Samson, I need to stop and take a look at my own less-than-perfect story. How often do I stop to think about how unique I really am to God? How easy is it for me to sell out my own God-given strength so that I can gain acceptance from people who don't have my best interests in mind? Why do we, like Samson, so often give in to our own weaknesses?

—Jarrett

121

What are your gifts?

* Take time right now and think through your strengths—the unique gifts, talents, and abilities God has given you. Write a few here:

Make a vow

* Write out your own vow to God, promising that you will not sell out these strengths to anyone or anything.

One last thing

* When you do mess up on your vow, know that God is there to forgive and help you to do better the next time (1 John 1:9). Don't give up, and always remember the true source of your strength. (No, it's not your hair.)

DAY 107 Messengers from the Invisible World

My friend Tim thinks he may have had a close encounter with an angel.

While on a winter ski trip, Tim was driving along an ice-covered road in the Colorado Rockies. "Suddenly my car went into a skid," Tim says. "I hit the brakes. No action. The car spun around backward and kept sliding downhill and was about to drop off the side of the mountain. But my car came to a stop *right on the edge of the cliff.*

"It was like somebody had ahold of my back bumper. And there was no way my car stopped just because I was slamming on the brakes. *No way.* Too much ice. . . . It was weird."

Tim believes God was watching over him in some supernatural way. As he puts it, "I really think it was an angel."

Now, Tim's not the type of guy who makes up stuff. He's a sane, sensible guy who thinks he might have had an angel's arms (if angels have arms) wrapped around the bumper of his car.

And Tim's not alone.

People all over the place claim to have crossed paths with supernatural beings. And a lot of the encounters are pretty bizarre. Some people believe angels are spirits that reside inside them, offering them guidance. Others claim the helpful angels they've encountered are beings from other planets.

Tim has a much different view of angels. He's very quick to point out that God is *The One* to thank for keeping him from falling off the side of that mountain, not the angel that grabbed the bumper.

Actually, angels like it that way. What I've read in the Bible tells me these spiritual beings are not into getting pats on the back (if they even have backs). What they like to do is point us to God.

Their chief purpose, in fact, seems to be about delivering messages from our Creator. The word *angel* actually means "messenger."

Here's an example of what I'm talking about, taken from Matthew's version of the resurrection story (28:2–7).

With earthquake-like power, an angel shoves aside the huge boulder that blocked the entrance to the cave holding Jesus's body. Two women show up and are terrified by the angel's awesome appearance, which, Matthew says, "was like lightning, and his clothes were white as snow."

Then the angel tells the women, "Don't be afraid. I know that you are looking for Jesus, who has been crucified. He is not here. He has risen from the dead as he said he would. Come and see the place where his body was. And go quickly and tell his followers, 'Jesus has risen from the dead!'" (vv. 5–7 NCV).

No doubt about it. The supernatural being in white with the lightning look was a fearsome and incredible messenger. And even more incredible than the messenger was the message itself: *Jesus is alive!*

It's a message worth remembering—whether or not an angel ever grabs the bumper of my car.

—Chris

123

Try one

* Draw what you imagine a real angel to look like.

* Write a poem about an angel.

* What do you think are the most important qualities or characteristics of angels? List them.

DAY 108 Facts about Angels

What do angels look like? Theologians generally believe angels are invisible spirits that can take on appearances to fit their purposes. If they need to reflect God's glory (as in Ezekiel 1), they look awesome and scary. On the other hand, Hebrews 13:2 says some of us have helped angels without even knowing about it. Angels can look like humans too.

Angels are not spirits of dead humans. Contrary to what many movies and TV shows tell us, angels are not human souls who have earned (or are trying to earn) their wings. Angels are altogether separate creations from humans (Ps. 8:4–5).

Angels are not wimps. They can form powerful armies (2 Kings 6) and demonstrate superhuman strength (Matt. 28:2–4).

Good angels are very good. The Bible even calls them "holy" (Luke 9:26; Acts 10:22).

Bad angels are very bad. Christians call them "fallen angels," and they include Satan and all of the demons. For a glimpse into their evil activities, see Genesis 3:1–5 and Mark 5:1–5.

Don't call them for help—or for anything. Angels have a habit of showing up when they want to show up (or at least when God wants them to). But nowhere in the Bible do we find people calling on angels for help or guidance. On the other hand, we see tons of examples of God's people going directly to him for the help they need.

Angels are never to take the place of God. Angels are not to be worshiped (Col. 2:18).

So, what's the purpose of angels? In the Bible, the word *angel* means "messenger." The idea is that angels deliver messages from God (Luke 2:8–12). Angels also are known for saving people from harm (Ps. 91:11–12), carrying out God's wrath and judgment (Rev. 16:1), and praising God (Rev. 4:6–8). Oh, and they also get pretty excited when even one person repents from sin and turns to God (Luke 15:10).

—Chris

* *Want to know more?* Go to the index, subject guide, or topical concordance in your Bible and look up every "angel" reference. Need more? Then go to biblegateway.com and drop "angel" or "angels" into the keyword search option. This will keep you busy for a long time. There are also some good books on angels written from a Christian perspective. Here's one you may want to check out: *Angels* by Billy Graham. And be sure to talk to your youth pastor or visit your church library for other good reads on angels.

DAY 109 Interview with an Angel

Imagine that you're an angel. Really, imagine it. Let's say you've dropped down to earth and a reporter catches up with you and starts asking you a bunch of questions. How would you answer them?

So, you're an angel. What's your name and what exactly are you doing here?

What do you usually do in heaven—just sit around and play a harp?

What's the most fun you've ever had?

What are the toughest kinds of assignments you've ever been given?

What are Satan and his demons like? What do you hate most about them?

So, tell me about God. What's he *really* like?

One final question: if you could give one important message to humans, what would you like to say?

DAY 110 Think about This

Remember to welcome strangers, because some who have done this have welcomed angels without knowing it.

—Hebrews 13:2 NCV

Angels . . . do I know any?

* How would it change your attitude toward strangers—toward the homeless guy downtown, the lonely kid in the cafeteria, the needy girl in gym class—if you thought they were supernatural beings from God?

DAY 111 Two Real Worlds

Even after all God has done for me, I still have doubts. I will always believe he is real. But often my prayers seem like hollow, sleepy words that bounce off walls and rise no higher than my ceiling. It's still sometimes hard for me to believe—*really* believe—that there is another world out there beyond trees and rocks and people and cars and buildings. A world of angels and demons and God and heaven and hell. If only I could see that other world, just once, perhaps that would solve all my doubts.

When these doubts surface, I always try to think back to some of Jesus's teachings about the two worlds. One incident (in Luke 10) especially pulled the two worlds together. Jesus sent out seventy-two of his faithful followers to the towns and villages he planned to visit later. He warned them sternly that they might be mocked or even persecuted for representing him. "You are like lambs among wolves," he said.

The seventy-two disciples trudged away in the dust, certainly expecting the worst after Jesus's pessimistic warnings. But they returned exuberant. People had accepted them. Towns were eagerly awaiting the visit of Jesus. They had healed sick people. "Even the demons submitted to us in your name," they reported breathlessly.

Jesus, who had been waiting for their return, gave a unique summary of what had happened. He said, "I saw Satan fall like lightning from heaven!"

Jesus brought the two worlds together. The world of the disciples had been one of walking over hot sand, preaching to mixed crowds, knocking on doors, asking to see the sick, announcing the coming of Jesus. All their actions took place in the visible world, which they could touch, smell, and see. But Jesus, with supernatural insight, saw that those actions in the visible world were having a phenomenal impact on the invisible world. While his disciples were grinding out spiritual victories in the visible world, their victories had caused Satan to fall in the invisible world.

Jesus was, of course, the ultimate example of the two worlds working as one. He was a man with sweat glands, hair, fingernails, lips, and all the other characteristics that define humans. Yet the Bible tells us that in him "all the fullness of the Deity lives in bodily form" (Col. 2:9).

All of us who are Christians believe in the invisible world; we merely forget it. We get consumed by our world of arguments, relationships, jobs, school—even the "religious" world of church and small group meetings. Perhaps if Jesus were standing beside us murmuring phrases like "I saw Satan fall" whenever God uses us for good, we would more easily remember.

—Philip

Jesus saw Satan fall when . . .

* Satan suffers a great loss in the invisible world when good things happen for God in the visible world. Write a story, a poem, or simply a list that demonstrates how you've seen God doing good things through you and through other believers. After you finish your story, poem, or list, write these words underneath your work: "And this was something that caused Satan to take a good, hard fall."

DAY 112 I Saw the Invisible (Todd's fake interview with a for-real Bible character)

Q: So, you saw the invisible supernatural world?

A: I did. It was cool. I now know for a fact that the trees, circus chimps, and plywood we see around us are not all there is. There's an entire

127

unseen spiritual world all around us—demons and angels, and big battles between them. We aren't alone.

Q: Do you have super X-ray vision or something?

A: Ummm, no.

Q: A special pair of infrared goggles?

A: Nope.

Q: Were you exposed to radiation or a mutant spider bite?

A: Not that I know of.

Q: Then how did you get this ability?

A: It all started with a war between Israel and a king named Aram. Aram's strategy was to sneak attack Israel in random places. But it never worked because of a prophet named Elisha. I knew this prophet pretty well because I was his servant. Anyway, God would tell Elisha where Aram was about to attack so Elisha could warn Israel's king. Of course, King Aram didn't like this one bit. And so he ordered his army to track down Elisha.

Q: When are we gonna get to the exciting "seeing angels" part?

A: Soon. So, Aram's mighty army swooped in to snag Elisha in the middle of the night. I woke up and looked out the window. I saw all these soldiers storming the city. I freaked out. I ran into Elisha's room—still in my Spider-Man PJs—and yelled, "My master! What can we do?" Elisha was all calm. He's like, "Don't be afraid. Those who are with us are more than those who are with them."

Q: "Those who are with you"? What's that mean?

A: That's exactly what I wondered. But since I knew Elisha loved God, I figured he meant that we have God on our side and he's greater than this army. But seriously, that didn't comfort me all that much. I didn't see how God up in heaven was gonna help us out of this. We needed a S.W.A.T. team or, at the very least, Jack Bauer.

Q: How'd Elisha react to your doubt?

A: He prayed, "Lord, open my servant's eyes so he can see."

Q: And that's when he gave you the special angel-vision goggles?

A: No, there were no special goggles. Instead, it was like a curtain was pulled back on the world. I saw protective horses and chariots of fire surrounding the town. We were being protected by the unseen spiritual forces of God! I suddenly had to believe in God's presence and protection.

Q: So, was there a massive war between Aram's army and the Super Angel Army?

A: No. Instead, the Lord made Aram's men blind. Then Elisha said to them, "Hey, you're in the wrong place. Follow me!" He led them out of town and into the stronghold for Israel's army. When Aram's men could finally see, they were sitting right in the middle of all of Israel's troops! We were safe! Elisha told the king of Israel not to kill these men, but to feed them and let them go. And with that, the armies of Aram stopped attacking Israel's territory!

Q: Wow! That's incredible.

A: Yep. And it was all because of God's unseen, but constant, presence and power.

Q: Are God's spiritual forces surrounding us right now?

A: I can't see them anymore. But I really believe they are.

Q: Oh, did you lose your special goggles?

A: Ugh. I never had any goggles!

* *Read the real story:* Who is the real Bible character behind Todd's fake interview? Find out in 2 Kings 6:8–22.

DAY 113 Stretch Your Brain Muscles

Our fight is not against people on earth but against the rulers and authorities and the powers of this world's darkness, against the spiritual powers of evil in the heavenly world. That is why you need to put on God's full armor. Then on the day of evil you will be able to stand strong. And when you have finished the whole fight, you will still be standing. So stand strong, with the belt of truth tied around your waist and the protection of right living on your chest. On your feet wear the Good News of peace to help you stand strong. And also use the shield of faith with which you can stop all the burning arrows of the Evil One. Accept God's salvation as your helmet, and take the sword of the Spirit, which is the word of God. Pray in the Spirit at all times with all kinds of prayers, asking for everything you need. To do this you must always be ready and never give up. Always pray for all God's people.

—Ephesians 6:12–18 NCV

* Go back and read the passage again—*slowly*. OK, read it a third time and underline the words and phrases that jump out at you, and circle the ones that make no sense at all. Now try to answer these questions: What types of "armor" do we need to fight spiritual battles? What do these verses tell us about spiritual battle? What do you think prayer has to do with spiritual warfare? Not sure how to answer these questions? Take your questions—and your circled words and phrases—to your pastor, youth pastor, or small group leader.

DAY 114 Too Busy to Be Sick!

The annoying buzz of my alarm clock jolted me from my deep sleep. I groaned and stared at the all-too-bright numbers: 6:30.

It seemed like it had only been a few minutes ago that I'd closed my textbooks and thrown down my pencil. In truth, it had been a few very short hours. My head throbbed and my forehead felt like it was on fire.

My tired, aching body sent one message to my brain: *Don't you dare get up!*

I was determined not to listen. I had too much to do. I dragged myself out of bed in total slow motion, got myself ready as best I could, and started for the door.

"Wait one minute, Allison," Mom said before I could even turn the doorknob. "Look at yourself. You're sick. You can't possibly go to school."

"But, Mom, I can't miss school today!"

For dramatic effect, I held my school calendar above my head—it felt like it weighed a ton—and started rattling off a long list of things I had to do.

"No wonder you're sick," Mom cut in, interrupting my to-do list. And my whining. "You've overcommitted yourself and are too stressed out. Take it easy today. Those things can wait."

I wanted to argue. I wanted to get up and run out the door. But all I managed to do was drag my aching body back up to bed. I fell asleep counting all the stuff on my to-do list instead of sheep.

Sometime later I woke up in a panic, my mind cluttered with all those unfinished tasks, assignments, and responsibilities. I felt like I was about to explode. I even wondered if I was having a nervous breakdown.

My mom walked into the room. She placed a tray on the stand next to my bed and left quietly. On the tray, next to the bowl of soup, was a slip of paper with a Bible verse written on it:

Cast all your anxiety on him because he cares for you. —1 Peter 5:7

Mom's timing was incredible. I leaned back, and then I prayed silently and simply, *God, give me the strength to get through this stressful week.*

Getting everything done suddenly didn't seem to matter much anymore. I knew I needed some rest. I also knew I couldn't live with such a jammed schedule. I would have to deal with that. But right then, all of that didn't matter. What mattered was just giving my worries to God.

I read the verse again, sipped a little soup, and then drifted off into a dreamless, peaceful sleep uncluttered by any thoughts of everything I had to do.

—Allison

DAY 115 Grab Some Loose Change . . .

Find ten coins. Pick up a coin and look at it. Imagine that it's something in your life that either causes you stress or gives you great stress-free joy. OK, got something in mind? If it creates stress, place it in circle 1. If it brings you joy, put it in circle 2. Leave the coin there and do the same for each coin—stacking one coin on top of the other. When finished, look at the stack of coins in circle 1. Imagine giving those "anxieties" to

God. Sit quietly for a moment, repeating 1 Peter 5:7 at least five times. Now, look at the stack of coins in circle 2. Sit quietly for several seconds and then read Psalm 106:1, thanking your loving heavenly Father for the stress-free joy in your life.

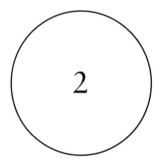

Cast all your anxiety on him because he cares for you.
—1 Peter 5:7

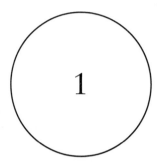

We will celebrate and praise you, LORD!
You are good to us, and your love never fails.
—Psalm 106:1 CEV

DAY 116 Amy's Quiz: Is Busyness Destroying Your Joy?

Take this quiz to see if you need to put on the brakes and smell the roses.

1. How often do you take a walk, just for the fun or enjoyment of it?
   A. Every once in a while.
   B. Pretty often. It's a good way to clear your head, relax, and just enjoy God's creation.
   C. Um, why would someone do that? If you're outside, it's because you're on your way somewhere.

2. Your goal this summer is to save a lot of cash for college. So the first week of summer you:
   A. Set the pattern for the summer by combining plenty of work with plenty of time for picnics, youth group activities, staring into space, and some serious time around the pool. After all, you need to recharge too.
   B. Immediately pick up as many hours as possible at work.
   C. Take a few days off, then kick it into work mode.

3. When you eat ice cream, you:
   A. Slurp the first few bites quickly, then slow down and enjoy it.
   B. Eat it so fast you get a headache. Ouch!
   C. Take time to savor every bite.

4. When you sit down to have your devotions, you:
   A. Read a verse, figure out what it must mean, say a quick prayer, and are done with it.
   B. Relax and calm down long enough to feel like you've really spent meaningful time with God.
   C. Don't have much time, but you try to spend at least a few moments just quietly opening your heart to God.

5. You are driving home from school when a large family of ducks waddles across the road, blocking traffic. You:
   A. Take advantage of the moment to just watch the babies hustle along after Mom.
   B. Slow down for a moment, then gently swerve around the fowl family.
   C. Get irritated and honk loudly for them to hurry up.

Scoring

1. A (2), B (3), C (1)
2. A (3), B (1), C (2)
3. A (2), B (1), C (3)
4. A (1), B (3), C (2)
5. A (3), B (2), C (1)

13–15 points: A+ for taking time out to stop and smell the roses. You know how to enjoy and celebrate life, and how to worship God in everyday ways. Good for you. Keep it up!

9–12 points: Sounds like you're learning how to balance going with the flow of life with stopping to enjoy special moments along the way. You know how to get things done, but you're willing to slow down in order to celebrate a special occasion with your friends and family. Keep enjoying the joys of life that God gives you, and remember there's more to come!

5–8 points: You may be missing out on life's little pleasures. You have a very hard time just relaxing and enjoying the life God has given you. Don't let life and God's little whispers pass you by.

DAY 117 Striving to Do Less

With only so many hours in the day and lots of demands on those hours, singer/songwriter Jeremy Camp admits that his time with God has sometimes gotten pushed to the back burner.

"I'm a very passionate person who wants to go out and serve God as much as I can," Jeremy says. "To do that as a musician, you have to put in a lot of work and lots of traveling. Sometimes, the work of serving the Lord gets in the way of spending time with the Lord."

This was exactly what happened as Jeremy was trying to get his music career up and running.

"Instead of enjoying what God was doing in my life, I spent too much time trying to do more for him," he says. "I got too busy and burdened by things that distracted me from spending time with God. By working so hard at my career, I was also not trusting God enough—I was trying to take control by doing it all alone."

In addition to nonstop touring and recording, Jeremy got married (to solo artist Adie) and started a family. As life continued to get busier and busier with family and career, Jeremy finally hit a wall and realized he was doing too much.

"I just got to a point where I called out, 'Help me, Lord,'" says Jeremy. "I cried out for forgiveness. I'd let serving God get in the way of just being with him. When I did, I felt like God said, 'Jeremy, you cannot steer this ship alone. Let me give you true peace, joy, and rest.' I learned that unless we find our contentment in Christ, we'll just feel empty after a while."

Now Jeremy strives to "wake up and smell the coffee" every day. He tries to enjoy the little things, to relax, and to give God control. He's extremely careful when filling his calendar. He commits to a daily quiet time. And he's very conscious of not letting anything—even work for God—keep him from time with God. He says this is also a danger for anyone who loads up their days with youth group, serving at church, and outreach projects.

"People think the more they are doing for the Lord, the better, and that he'll be more pleased with them," says Jeremy. "But God is more concerned with our relationship with him. If we're spending time with him, those activities should come as a natural outpouring—not the other way around."

—Andy

Think about it

* Am I busy doing so much stuff that I'm missing out on what's really important?

* Is "time with God" just another item on my to-do list?

* Do I need to slow down and spend a little extra time with God today?

Pray about it

* Spend at least a minute talking to God about your:

schedule

priorities

relationship with him

DAY 118 You Can't Do It All! (Todd's fake interview with a for-real Bible character)

I was very busy interviewing dozens of Bible characters, when one figure from Scripture called me out of the blue. "We need to talk," he said. I had twenty other interviews to do and a deadline coming. But I squeezed him in.

Q: So, what did you want to talk about today?

A: You, actually. What you're doing is not good.

Q: Fine, jerk . . . I don't like your haircut.

A: Oh, I'm not trying to insult you. I want to help. I've seen how busy you are with everything you think you need to do. You need to relax a bit. Give yourself a break. You'll only wear yourself out.

Q: But all this work has to get done.

A: Maybe. But *you* don't have to do it all. Ask others for help. God asks us to serve him, but that doesn't mean we have to do it all by ourselves. In fact, God knows we can't handle things alone and he gives us others to work with and to help us see how to work in the best way. And taking on too much is *not* the best way. When we do too much, we burn out. That's not a good way to manage the time, abilities, and talents God gives us.

Q: You seem to know a lot about this.

A: Well, I once noticed a very similar thing with my son-in-law. He's one of those people everyone turns to in order to get stuff accomplished. He also has a way of knowing how God wants things done. So he was very busy helping people and doing God's work. That's

136

all good. But the problem was that he would do all the work himself. He wouldn't ask for help. He just assumed he needed to do it all. And he overloaded himself.

Q: That sounds like me.

A: It sounds like a lot of us. For instance, we may feel God nudging us to help our neighbor. But because of everything else we have going on, we either don't do it or we stress out and take on too much so we can help. However, it'd go much easier if we just looked for someone else—who maybe has free Saturdays—who could help instead. So that's the kind of advice I gave my son-in-law. I told him, "The work is too heavy for you; you cannot handle it alone." I suggested that he find some good folks around him to help him serve others.

Q: What'd he do?

A: He took my advice—without insulting my hair, by the way—and found some good people who also wanted to serve God by serving others. He discovered that being a godly leader doesn't mean doing all the work himself.

* *Read the real story:* **Who is the real Bible character behind Todd's fake interview? Find out in Exodus 18.**

When I need help . . .

with homework, I can go to _____.

organizing my time, I can go to _____.

with issues I'm dealing with, I can go to

_____.

getting my priorities straight, I can go to

_____.

with stuff I'm committed to at church/youth group, I can go to

_____.

getting my relationship with God right, I can go to

_____.

137

DAY 119 5 Ways to Beat the Clock

1. Start at the top. You can't do *everything*, right? That's why you have to figure out what's really important, what's kind of important, and what's not so important. Here's how: make a list of ways you spend your time. Include homework, watching TV, sports, time with family and friends, texting, time online, Bible study, youth group, and other things you do during a typical week.

Next, rank each item on the list with a number, from most important to least important. The next time you must decide between two activities, think about your priority list. Another important tip: if you play on two sports teams and are in three different clubs, take a hard look at all five activities and decide which of the five are most important.

By the way, this isn't about getting rid of all the fun stuff. An hour of TV after three hours of homework is probably not a bad thing. But notice what comes first: homework.

2. Get organized. "I forgot!" "I'm late again!" "I can't be in two places at once!" Sound familiar? Then you need some serious organization in your life. Want a little organizational secret? It's called a personal digital assistant (PDA) or a day planner. You need something to help you keep a detailed schedule of your assignments, appointments, and responsibilities—as well as an up-to-date list of important phone numbers and email addresses. A PDA or day planner will help keep you from double-booking; it will also help keep you from losing assignments and important phone numbers. If PDAs or day planners are simply not your style, then find something that is your style. Talk to an adult who knows you well. Work with this person to figure out a system that matches your personality.

3. Be nice to yourself. The next time you're tempted to pull an all-nighter or skip another meal because you're late for play practice, think again. And think priority list. Decent eating habits, sleep, and exercise should be near the top of the list. Here's the thing: when you're healthy and well rested, you feel better and you usually end up making the best use of the time you have.

4. *Don't waste small spaces.* Every day is the hiding place for small spaces of time. Search them out and put them to work. Let's say you're waiting in line at the mall. You can tap your foot impatiently over that terribly slow sales clerk. Or you can pull out small note cards and work on Spanish vocab. What about those spaces of time you spend waiting for a friend to arrive? Make good use of those five or ten minutes: clear your floor of dirty clothes, write a note to a friend, pray for a family member.

5. *Say no.* If you're constantly overcommitting, you must learn to say no. Possible problem: you overcommit because you're a people pleaser. That's a tough one, but try working on this area of your life. Practice saying no in a mirror. Repeat this sentence over and over: "I'm important not because of what I do, but because God loves me!" If saying no continues to be hard, talk to your youth leader or another trusted adult. Along with holding you accountable for how you use your time, this caring friend can also affirm your self-worth.

—Cherissa

Think about it

> Without good advice, everything goes wrong—it takes careful planning for things to go right.
>
> —Proverbs 15:22 CEV

DAY 120 Give It a Rest

To keep from burning out, we gotta find time to rest. God thinks rest is so important that he wrote it into the fourth commandment: "Remember the Sabbath day by keeping it holy" (Exod. 20:8).

A "Sabbath" is a time of rest. The words "Remember the Sabbath day" point back to the first Sabbath in history. On that day, the Bible says God "blessed the seventh day and made it holy, because on it he rested from all the work of creating he had done" (Gen. 2:3). Now, let's be realistic: God's strength is unlimited. So why did God rest?

I think God was setting an example for us to follow. He wants us to take time to rest, and he wants that rest time to be, as the verse says, "holy."

Whenever the word *holy* appears in the Bible, it means "set apart just for God." In other words, totally devoted to God. A holy Sabbath, then, isn't just any old time of rest, and it's not just rest for our physical bodies. God didn't give us the fourth commandment as encouragement to zone out while watching TV or to spend an entire weekend playing Rock Band. Doing those things might help recharge our batteries physically, but a Sabbath is more than a time of physical rest. It's also a time of spiritual rest—rest devoted totally to God.

Most of us know that nonstop busyness can wear us down and cause major physical problems or illnesses. What we so easily forget is that our spiritual lives work that way too. As Christians, we're called to represent Christ wherever we go and to share his Good News through our words and actions. If we're trying to live up to that calling every single day, it can really wear us out! If we're pouring out our faith all the time, we need to eventually get filled back up. Taking a Sabbath and resting with God can revive us spiritually with the energy and encouragement we need to live each day as messengers of the Good News. Even Jesus, our Lord and Savior, repeatedly devoted time to rest with God, far away from the busyness of his life (Matt. 14:22–24; Mark 1:35).

As we try to keep a Sabbath, however, we need to remember something: it's not about just keeping another rule. When the Pharisees confronted Jesus about breaking the Sabbath, he made one thing clear: "The Sabbath was made to meet the needs of people, and not people to meet the requirements of the Sabbath" (Mark 2:27 NLT).

So how can the Sabbath best meet our needs?

Intermission

* **List three ways a Sabbath rest can meet your needs:**
   1.
   2.
   3.

. . . the rest of the story

The key to taking a Sabbath is finding a way to be with God that doesn't include or feel like work. Along with participating in a church worship service and youth group, keeping the Sabbath could mean taking more time than usual to read your Bible, journaling your prayers to God, listening to Christian music, or enjoying God's creation on a walk outdoors. Find your own unique way to be with him.

Then, with your faith reenergized, you'll be ready to reenter our crazy world with the strength to share the gospel with others who also need the rest God offers.

—Jason

Epilogue

* How can you worship in your own unique way? Write down three ideas:
    1.
    2.
    3.

* Try out one of your ideas this week . . . or right now.

DAY 121 | Benched God

"Three, two, one!" the crowd chanted. The final buzzer blared through the gym. My entire basketball team raced onto the court for a championship huddle. My school hadn't won a regional tournament in ten years. Everyone went crazy. Except me. I wasn't happy.

This was our biggest game of the season and I'd sat on the bench the entire time. I felt like I didn't really matter to my team. That was hard to handle—I'd always thought basketball was my thing. My high school basketball career started out pretty good too. After a great freshman season, my coach moved me up to varsity.

As a sophomore, I didn't play a lot but got to contribute in a few crucial games. But everything took a turn for the worse the summer before my junior year. I had surgery because of a nose injury, and I wasn't allowed to play—no summer leagues, no pick-up games, no one-on-one. And so for that whole season, I was the guy who sat on the bench and only got to play when the game was a shutout. Then came that big tournament win. I wanted to be excited for my team, but deep down I felt empty and alone. *If only I could get in the game and play ball,* I told myself over and over. *Then I'd feel better and have something to live for.*

Then one night, shortly after the season ended, I went to youth group and heard my youth pastor say something pretty simple: "We need to slow down, listen to God, and let him work in our lives." That struck me. I had been a Christian most of my life and went to church every Sunday, but I'd stopped reading my Bible and praying. I knew I needed to reconnect with God.

I loved playing ball, but I'd put so much hope into basketball only to be disappointed by my awful season. I needed something that would never disappoint me. And I knew in my heart that God would never let me down. So I started reading my Bible and praying. After talking to my small group leader and reading a lot of Scripture, I realized that I needed to depend on God more too.

I was so focused on performing on the basketball court that I forgot what it meant to depend on God for strength when things got tough. Looking back, I wish I'd prayed about my struggles. I don't think praying about basketball would have made me a star player, but I know it would have helped me find peace through it all.

I've also realized something else. I can't let basketball consume me so much that I forget about what's really important. I've made a commitment to do my best at basketball, but to give my all to Christ.

—Shane

Your turn

* What activity have you thrown yourself into only to end up disappointed?

* What do you think God was trying to show you or teach you through your disappointment?

* What does it mean to give your all to Christ?

* What's something you're willing to change so that you can follow Christ more closely?

DAY 122 Lord over To-Do Lists

If Jesus really is our Lord, he is not one priority on a long list of many priorities. He is not merely a name at the top of the to-do list of life. He is *The One* Christians have always believed can make sense of all of life. The fact that Jesus Christ is Lord means we can look to him for direction and guidance.

Stop a moment and think about areas of your life where Jesus needs to have more influence. List three of them here:
 1.
 2.
 3.

Ask Jesus to come into each area you listed, and then do something to show you're really serious about committing each area to him. Now, think about those places where Jesus really is Lord. List three of them here:
 1.
 2.
 3.

Thank him for helping you make decisions that please him and help you grow in your faith. Most importantly, thank him for being both Lord and Savior of your life.

—Jerry and Grady

DAY 123 Who's in Control?

Imagine a guy (we'll call him Fred) puts on a T-shirt. Across the chest, in huge letters, it says, "Jesus is Lord." Fred has just labeled himself a Christian.

Yet when it comes to the way Fred acts, Jesus is definitely not in charge. When Fred misses a shot in tennis, he goes ballistic. And he just can't remember to take out the garbage—even though he's been told a dozen times. When he's with his girlfriend, he's always pushing her physical limits.

Who's in control? Certainly not Jesus. Fred's shirt is just that: a shirt. The statement is empty. He's labeled himself a "Christian," but he sure doesn't act like one. Instead, Fred's feelings rule. He does what feels good—that is the controlling factor over all he chooses.

Fred's way of looking at faith would have been unimaginable to believers in the early church. To them, faith was not just something a person *believed*; it was something that had to be *lived*.

It meant a radically different way of life. They had to put their feelings in second place and put Jesus first—right where a person called "Lord" belongs.

These early believers worked so hard at following Jesus's example that people began to call them "Christians"—which means "little Christs" (Acts 11:26). And theologians generally believe it wasn't a compliment either. You can almost hear it said with a sneer and a laugh: "You people are just a bunch of 'little Christs.' A bunch of *Christians*." But what could be better than being named after the person you most want to be like?

With the name, however, comes the responsibility to live in a way Jesus would be proud of. And that means living a life of self-control. It's not easy, because sometimes your desires fight God's will. But you don't have to struggle alone.

God is at work in and through your life. Even in the middle of temptation, he opens a door to give you a way out (1 Cor. 10:13). You do not have to fall. You can have self-control.

—James

Don't forget

You are tempted in the same way that everyone else is tempted. But God can be trusted not to let you be tempted too much, and he will show you how to escape from your temptations.

—1 Corinthians 10:13 CEV

So, before you're tempted . . . again

* Think back to the last time you gave in to temptation. Walk through
  the experience step-by-step. Do you see where God has provided a
  way out? It's there. Keep looking until you see it, then look for it next
  time you face temptation—*before you fall.*

DAY 124 How They Prayed

Putting Jesus first has always been an important part of Christian prayer.
Read these prayers by some famous dead guys, and then write a prayer
that expresses your own desires, and even struggles, to put and keep
Jesus first.

My God,
I give you this day.
I offer you, now,
all the good that I shall do
and I promise to accept,
for love of you,
all the difficulty that I shall meet.
Help me to conduct myself during this day
in a way that pleases you.
  —Francis de Sales (1567–1622), French church leader

Lord Jesus,
I give you my hands to do your work.
I give you my feet to go your way.
I give you my eyes to see as you see.
I give you my tongue to speak your words.
I give you my mind that you may think in me.
I give you my spirit that you may pray in me.
  —adapted from Lancelot Andrewes (1555–1626),
      English clergyman and scholar

Most high and glorious God,
come and enlighten the darkness
of my heart.

Give me right faith,
certain hope,
and perfect love,
that everything I do
may be in fulfillment of your holy will;
through Jesus Christ my Lord.
 —Francis of Assisi (1182–1226), Italian monk

* **Dear Lord Jesus,**

Amen.

DAY 125 No Time for Funerals

When I told my band director I'd be missing a few practices, he asked why.

"Well, my father just died," I said, "and I need to go to the funeral."

He looked me straight in the eye and said, "What's past is past. You need to be at all my practices."

If your jaw dropped when you read this, I've accomplished my goal. I made up the band director story to show how shocking some of Jesus's words were.

When crowds were pressing in on Jesus, he told his disciples to go to the other side of the Sea of Galilee. One of his disciples said, "Lord, first let me go and bury my father."

To this Jesus replied, "Follow me, and let the dead bury their own dead" (Matt. 8:21–22).

Sure, Jesus is Lord, but doesn't this still seem a bit over the top? I mean, why not let the guy attend the funeral and then rejoin Jesus in a few days?

Well, as he often did, Jesus was exaggerating to make a point. He wasn't telling people to reject their families.

Instead, Jesus was trying to make it clear that being a loving son or daughter isn't the point. While it is part of life, it is not the ultimate purpose of life. He was saying that sometimes duty to family conflicts with obedience to God.

Robert Morrison was the first Protestant missionary to China. But for a long time, his powerful call to be a missionary was put on hold because his mother told him she didn't want him to leave home while she was still living.

After she died, he excitedly prepared to go overseas. But then he received a heartbreaking letter from his family begging him to care for his sick father. At this point, Morrison was in his midtwenties and sensed he had to make a tough choice.

"Honored father, brother, and sisters," he wrote back. "What can I do? I look to my God and my father's God. You advise me to return home. . . . But I have no inclination to do so; having set my hand to the plough, I would not look back" (see Luke 9:62).

The way God has ordered things, it's clear that the younger we are, the more we are to obey our parents. But as we get older, we sometimes have to weigh obedience to anything—including our parents—against obedience to Jesus. Sometimes honoring your parents is the way to obey Jesus—like Morrison's submitting to his mother's plea. Other times, these two loyalties conflict, and Jesus must be followed—like Morrison going off to China.

The difference is hard to figure out sometimes. Such decisions should be made in prayer and with godly counsel from many Christian people. But make no mistake, Jesus sometimes will ask us to do something that seems over the top. So don't let your jaw drop when it happens.

—Mark

Think it through

* **When was a time you felt God calling you to do something difficult? How did you respond? How could you tell if God really was talking to you?**

Talk it through

* Have a conversation with someone—your youth pastor, a parent, a
mature Christian friend—about how to know whether or not God is
calling you to do something difficult.

DAY 126 My Choice

Today I choose to let go
of trying to be better,
of trying to do more,
of trying to earn God's love
rather than depending completely
on the blood of Jesus to cleanse me.

Today I choose to let go
of the things of this world
which I believe can comfort me
and make me whole—
my car, my money, my friends,
my achievements, my successes.

Today I choose to let go
of my desires,
my plans,
my demands,
my will.
I am willing to die to all of these
and to my very self,
so Christ can live more fully in me.

—*Elaine*

I was put to death on the cross with Christ, and I do not live anymore—it is
Christ who lives in me. I still live in my body, but I live by faith in the Son of
God who loved me and gave himself to save me.

—Galatians 2:20 NCV

DAY 127 What Does It Really Mean?

What do Christians really mean when they call Jesus "Lord"?

They mean that he is in control of significant things. And positive experiences. And all that's good. When the timing and events seem most right, God is in control. He is Lord.

They mean that he is in control of insignificant, little things.

They mean that he is in control of negative experiences. And even in control over all that is evil. No matter how bad things seem, God is still in control.

They mean that he reigns, kinglike, over friendships and families, successes and good times, laughter and joy, lightheartedness and smiles. But he has not relinquished control when we face grief and sadness, disappointment and discouragement, strife and brokenness, failure and depression.

Christians may wonder about the mysteries of good and evil in the world. But they hold on to the idea that God has an agenda to make everything right. No experience happens and no power operates outside the circle of God's influence and power. Nothing will frustrate his ultimate purpose. Nothing will destroy his flawless timetable.

—James

Don't move . . .

* Sit in silence for one minute. No distractions. No noise. No music playing. After a minute of silence, thank Jesus for being in control of all things, and especially of your own life.

DAY 128 Love's True Definition

If I speak in the tongues of men and of angels, but have not love, I am only a resounding gong or a clanging cymbal. If I have the gift of prophecy and can fathom all mysteries and all knowledge, and if I have a faith that can move mountains, but have not love, I am nothing. If I give all I possess to the poor and surrender my body to the flames, but have not love, I gain nothing.

149

Love is patient, love is kind. It does not envy, it does not boast, it is not proud. It is not rude, it is not self-seeking, it is not easily angered, it keeps no record of wrongs. Love does not delight in evil but rejoices with the truth. It always protects, always trusts, always hopes, always perseveres. Love never fails.

—1 Corinthians 13:1–8

A rusty gate?

* **Read these verses again, this time in the Message paraphrase:**

If I speak with human eloquence and angelic ecstasy but don't love, I'm nothing but the creaking of a rusty gate. If I speak God's Word with power, revealing all his mysteries and making everything plain as day, and if I have faith that says to a mountain, "Jump," and it jumps, but I don't love, I'm nothing. If I give everything I own to the poor and even go to the stake to be burned as a martyr, but I don't love, I've gotten nowhere. So, no matter what I say, what I believe, and what I do, I'm bankrupt without love.

> Love never gives up.
> Love cares more for others than for self.
> Love doesn't want what it doesn't have.
> Love doesn't strut,
> Doesn't have a swelled head,
> Doesn't force itself on others,
> Isn't always "me first,"
> Doesn't fly off the handle,
> Doesn't keep score of the sins of others,
> Doesn't revel when others grovel,
> Takes pleasure in the flowering of truth,
> Puts up with anything,
> Trusts God always,
> Always looks for the best,
> Never looks back,
> But keeps going to the end.

Love never dies.

Your version

* Rewrite 1 Corinthians 13:1–8 in your own words. Make it personal. Be creative.

DAY 129 Real Love

What is Real Love? Real Love loves everybody. We have a responsibility to love everybody, but that doesn't mean having the same relationship with everyone. However, as we begin to love everyone, we discover a whole new dimension to our special, close relationships. For instance, the kinder we are to strangers, the kinder we become to our parents, siblings, and romantic interests.

How does Real Love act? That depends. What does the other person need? Does he or she need your attention? Your listening? Practical help? Correction? Warning? Real Love acts unselfishly to give whatever is needed.

How is Real Love measured? How do we know when we are getting good at loving? Real Love is measured in difficulty. The true test does not come in loving someone who loves us. It comes when we appropriately meet the needs of a stranger who does not return our love. Or how loving are we when we feel crummy? How gracious are we when someone wrongly accuses us, or someone we love betrays our trust or acts unkindly?

How do we develop Real Love? Observe. We will make mistakes as we try to love. When we act selfishly or indifferently toward others, people will give us clear clues that will teach us a lot about how to act or not act. In time, we will get better. We also learn by watching people who are good examples. Of course, there is no better example than Jesus. As we copy his self-sacrificing spirit, our capacity to love will surely deepen.

What is the reward for Real Love? When we practice love in its purest form, we are acting like God. People are more inclined to believe there is a God when they see Real Love in us. In fact, the Bible suggests our expressions of Real Love make the invisible God visible.

—James

Real love's traits

Patience: When you make a mistake, Real Love never rolls its eyes and gripes. Real Love allows you time to grow.

Kindness: Real Love offers a strong shoulder to lean on. Its words are gentle and packed with care and encouragement.

Loyalty: Real Love is there for you when others walk away. It stands up for you.

Honesty: Real Love is no liar. It has no fronts. Real Love keeps promises.

Forgiveness: Real Love doesn't hold grudges or build walls of bitterness.

DAY 130 Why Love?

Dear friends, since God so loved us, we also ought to love one another. No one has ever seen God; but if we love one another, God lives in us and his love is made complete in us.

—1 John 4:11–12

For God so loved the world that he gave his one and only Son, that whoever believes in him shall not perish but have eternal life.

—John 3:16

Here is the command God has given us. Anyone who loves God must also love his brothers and sisters.

—1 John 4:21 NIrV

* *Read all three passages again.* **Choose one. Memorize it.**

DAY 131 If Anybody Knew the Real Me

Ann was in one of my classes at school, but I hardly knew her. One morning she came up and said hi. The more we talked over the following weeks, the more she impressed me. Unlike some Christians, she didn't treat me like I was some dumb jock. She always seemed interested in my opinions about God and religion. I came to respect Ann.

One day between classes, Ann handed me a Bible and said, "This is my favorite book, Josh. I think you'll like it too." She then invited me to a Wednesday night dinner and Bible study with some of her friends.

"I'm not into the whole 'God thing,'" I said indifferently. "But is dinner free?"

"Yes, it's free," Ann said with a laugh. "So is the fun."

She was right. The study turned out to be really fun. I kept going. Hanging out with Ann and her friends was amazing for me. It felt like I had a group of good, genuine friends for the first time ever. They actually cared for me.

However, the more I studied the Bible with my church friends, the more I realized how bad I was. While I was trying to be a better person, my life was still one big mess. *If these new friends knew the real me,* I thought, *they wouldn't want me around.*

One day while hanging out with Ann, I broke down. "Ann, you're perfect and so is everyone else at church," I said as I stared downward. "I can't believe you guys like me. I'm so bad. How could God love a messed-up guy like me?"

153

Ann looked at me and said, "Josh, you are guilty of sin. But so am I. We've all messed up. That's why we need Jesus. He's the only one who didn't sin, and he's the only one who can save us from our sin."

"But you don't know all of the bad stuff I've done," I told her.

Ann answered, "What's your point? Jesus still loves you no matter what you've done. He can save you if you believe in him."

I felt tears burning in my eyes. "Ann," I said with my voice shaking, "I want Jesus to save me."

—Josh

Read again

* This time, underline specific actions and expressions of love in the story.

* How did Ann show love to Josh? What practical, real-life ways could you show love like this?

DAY 132 What Love Looks Like

Did you know that many movies have very practical examples of a 1 Corinthians 13 kind of love? Check these out:

Love is humble

Love is patient, love is kind. . . . It does not boast, it is not proud.

—1 Corinthians 13:4

"Farm boy, polish my horse's saddle," Buttercup says to her hired hand, Westley, in *The Princess Bride*. "Farm boy, fetch me that pitcher."

Westley doesn't complain about this treatment, but always looks her in the eye and says, "As you wish."

One day, Buttercup discovers this phrase means "I love you." That's because true love includes deeper things than romance—like humility. In the Bible, humility refers to "strength under control." Think of a sleek, muscular horse who submits all of his power and speed to the will of his rider.

Love wants what's best for others

It is not rude, it is not self-seeking, it is not easily angered.

—1 Corinthians 13:5

In John 15:13, Jesus says, "The greatest way to show love for friends is to die for them" (CEV). This simply means to die to yourself—to put others' needs in front of yours.

In *Enchanted*, Prince Edward knows the only way to save his endangered bride-to-be, Giselle, is with true love's kiss. But Prince Edward realizes that her true love is actually another man, Robert. Without any hesitation, Edward begs Robert to kiss Giselle. He gives up his chance at happiness to save her life.

Love forgives

It keeps no record of wrongs.

—1 Corinthians 13:5

In *Juno*, sixteen-year-old Juno MacGuff admits to her dad and stepmom that she's pregnant. They are clearly disappointed and upset. But her dad tells her: "You know I'll always be there to love you and support you, no matter what kind of pickle you're in."

Keeping no record of wrongs doesn't mean that we erase all memory of a person's mistakes. It means we don't let those mistakes change how we feel about the people we truly love.

Love focuses on what's good

Love does not delight in evil but rejoices with the truth.

—1 Corinthians 13:6

When somebody hurts or betrays us, we can feel like it's our right to give it right back to them.

That's why my favorite scene from *Napoleon Dynamite* is when Deb calls Napoleon to confront him because she thinks he made mean remarks about her figure. She states her beliefs and doesn't back down. But where her loving attitude really shines through is in the things she *doesn't* do. She doesn't get revenge by egging his house or throwing tomatoes during his big dance scene. In other words, Deb doesn't delight in evil.

Love is tough as nails

It always protects, always trusts, always hopes, always perseveres. Love never fails.

—1 Corinthians 13:7–8

Real love isn't about little pink hearts or sweet sonnets. Real love is solid and strong and courageous. Just ask Marlin, the clownfish in *Finding Nemo.*

When Nemo is kidnapped, Marlin charges through hundreds of miles of ocean to save his boy, all the while conquering sharks, mines, a swarm of jellyfish—and a dentist.

That's the kind of strong love that gave Jesus the power to absorb the sin of every human being who ever lived, even while he was dying on the cross. I can't think of a better definition for love than that.

—Sam

Think of your own example

* Below, write a movie scene or real-life experience that shows a trait of love from 1 Corinthians 13:

DAY 133 Hey, That's My Burger!

My friend Hal and I were walking home after grabbing some fast food to go. Up ahead, we saw two men. They were the same guys I'd seen on this street before. One guy stood out on the corner. The other—the guy with only one leg—sat leaning against a building. Both men held cups that they'd push out to anyone who passed.

When Hal started walking toward them I rolled my eyes in disbelief. Just the day before he had given these guys a bunch of change and a sandwich. Now he was offering his dinner to the guys. I was a little annoyed. We'd have to go back to the restaurant now and get him another burger and fries. And if he didn't have enough cash, I'd probably have to pay for it!

My annoyance turned to disbelief when I heard Hal say, "Sorry, I don't have enough for both of you. But my friend here has a cheeseburger and fries."

Three sets of eyes turned to me. I resented the position Hal put me in. I mean, I was hungry! But it felt like I had no choice. I reluctantly handed over my bag of food. After we walked on, I told Hal I did not appreciate him giving away my dinner. He just smiled and offered to buy me another meal.

Bible break

But just as you excel in everything—in faith, in speech, in knowledge, in complete earnestness and in your love for us—see that you also excel in this grace of giving. I am not commanding you, but I want to test the sincerity of your love by comparing it with the earnestness of others.

—2 Corinthians 8:7–8

* Take ninety seconds to think over what this passage has to do with the cheeseburger story.

A love challenge

The Bible says there are lots of ways we can express our faith. We can pray. We can share the gospel. We can attend youth conferences. But it's when we have the opportunity to be generous to others that we put our love for God to the sincerity test. Do we mean it? Do we truly love others?

There's something about giving of yourself, whether it's through food, money, or just a caring heart, that demonstrates your faith is more than just a hobby.

And being generous does more than just show love to others. When we give freely of ourselves, Christians challenge each other to be more loving, more giving. That's what Hal did for me on that city street. He not only gave of himself, he also encouraged me to "excel in this grace of giving." And his encouragement worked.

Since that night, I've found it easier to give to others. And because Hal encouraged me to show the sincerity of my love for God, those guys on the corner weren't the only ones Hal helped that night.

—Nate

DAY 134 An Email from Cupid

Greetings! Allow me to introduce myself: I'm Cupid, that "little flying baby" you see all the time. Yes, *that* guy. I know, you get sick of seeing me—especially if you're single. But here's the thing: the real Cupid J. Valentine isn't some half-naked flying tot trying to make people all lovey-dovey. That's just my marketing people.

Truth is, I'm just a normal guy (well, besides the flying thing) who thinks love is pretty cool. However, the messages I'm trying to put out there have been all twisted. So I'm gonna set the record straight about me and this whole love thing in general:

1. I'm not a baby. I'm just a little vertically challenged.

2. I wear pants. How would you like it if everyone thought you wore only diapers? It's as if I have trouble with my digestive system or something. I don't. Besides, Valentine's Day is in February! If I just wore a diaper all the time, I'd get frostbite.

3. I don't have magic arrows. I think this whole arrow thing started when I took an archery class. However, they were normal arrows—not pink ones with hearts for tips. Just ask my gym teacher: I *did* shoot him in the rear once (accidentally). In fact, you know the myth that my arrows will make you fall in love with the first person you see? Well, maybe the myth should be that my arrows make you give a detention to the first person you see. That's what really happened.

Besides, there's no way "magic love arrows" could possibly work. You can't make anyone fall in love—especially by using sharp objects. In fact, it kinda chaps my hide (which, again, *is in pants*) that love is made out to be just some instant, magical feeling. For instance, most romantic movies make it seem like falling in love is only about a romantic moment when fireworks go off, cartoon birds sing, and everything is happily-ever-after. But real romantic love isn't just about feelings and romance. It's about truly getting to know each other, making the choice to love, working on your relationship, and committing to one another. It can hurt. It can be messy. And it can be tough. It's about work, forgiveness, respect, and making another person a higher priority than yourself.

4. *Love isn't just for couples.* If I had some of those magical love arrows, I'd shoot everyone in the world—not to make them fall in love with one person, but so they'd love everyone. I want people to realize that every moment is a chance to love the way 1 Corinthians 13 describes. Those verses aren't just for couples—they're to help all of us realize what love really is. It is the way we handle ourselves every day. To everyone. Love isn't selfish. It's not jealous or rude. It's kind and patient. It's not judgmental or condemning. It's about giving people a chance and helping when you can. It's supportive, loyal, and trusting. That's real love—the kind of love that God calls us to and that Jesus modeled.

So, I'm sure you'll continue to see pictures of me flying around with arrows. And maybe you will fall in love. But I hope you'll also jump into love—a godly love that changes how you view everyone. Even a baby-faced guy who's accused of wearing diapers in public.

—Cupid J. Valentine

Make it personal

* Read 1 Corinthians 13:4–7, substituting your own name for the words "love" and "it." Then ask yourself: Is that true? How am I doing at demonstrating God's love? How can I do better?

DAY 135 Jesus's Bad Friends

Stupid is as stupid does when it comes to the people we hang around with. Let's say you hang around with a group that smokes dope or plays around sexually. Sooner or later you're probably going to start acting like that. It's just human nature to adopt the values of the group we're with.

So we Christians are smart not to hang around with the "wrong crowd," right? Well, our Lord did this all the time.

Like the Gospel writer tells us in Mark 2:15, Jesus spent a lot of time with "tax collectors." In Jesus's day, these guys had a reputation for being cheats and traitors. They were Jews who turned on their fellow Jews to collect taxes for the Romans. And they earned their pay by charging way more than the Romans asked for—and keeping the extra.

We also know that Jesus spent time with prostitutes. Prostitutes are— well, enough said. They too are not the crowd that respectable religious people should be hanging around with.

In fact, there were so many disreputable people around Jesus that Mark just lumps them together and calls them "sinners." These are people who seemed far from God. They led immoral lives. They were a bad influence. They were people everyone else, especially the religious leaders, looked down on.

So why did Jesus spend time with such people? Simple: he loved them. He loved them more than he loved his reputation (which wasn't so good after he started hanging around them). He loved them even though he faced temptations because of them.

Say what? Yes, Jesus was tempted to sin—just look at passages like Matthew 4:1–11. This temptation in the wilderness wasn't the only time he was tempted. Every time he was with the wrong crowd, you can be sure there was someone trying to break him down.

So if Jesus loved the "wrong crowd," aren't we supposed to love them too? Yes. We're not called to love only the neat, pleasant, good people. We are called to love the hard cases, people who seem to be far from God, people in the wrong crowd.

If Jesus took risks to reach out to this crowd, shouldn't we—his followers—do the same? Yes and no.

No—if we think we can do this all by ourselves. Very few Christians can place themselves in immoral situations and come out clean. Maybe once or twice, but keep it up and eventually we'll find ourselves compromising our values.

But yes—if we are willing to do it alongside other Christians. Please keep in mind that not even Jesus tried to minister to people alone. Mark tells us that many "tax collectors and 'sinners' were eating with him and his disciples." We need the prayers, support, and accountability of fellow believers to minister to those who could easily influence us more than we might influence them.

If two or three Christians agree together to become friends with the "wrong crowd," then they quickly become the absolute "right crowd" with whom to share the love of Jesus.

—Mark

Role model

* How did Jesus demonstrate love? Check out these passages and next to each write characteristics of his love:

Luke 18:15–16

Luke 19:1–10

Luke 23:33–34

John 4:1–29

John 13:1–5

DAY 136 God Is Love—What Are You?

When I first met Jan, I was impressed with her. She was so different. Upbeat. Kind. Giving. One of the most caring and unselfish people I'd ever known. I had met nice people before, but Jan was exceptionally nice.

It wasn't until later that I learned that Jan was suffering from a terminal illness. Jan had every reason to be depressed and think only of herself and her pain. But instead, she found ways to show care and concern for her friends. Most of all, she knew how to love others.

As I got to know her better, I realized it was God working in Jan's life that made her different. In fact, I was discovering something of what that God "looked" like, because I could see his love in Jan, my unselfish friend. Knowing Jan taught me a lot about love and friendship. But most of all, Jan pointed me to a greater love—the love of God. As I grew to better understand God's love, I became a new person.

Now, in my friendships and in the way I treat my family, I want to copy this unselfish love that comes from God. I want my friends to know they can count on me. I want the members of my family to know they are appreciated. And now when I feel impatient, when I'm misunderstood, when I'm tempted to act selfishly, I ask myself: how will God's love within me play out in my life?

—James

Put love into action

* Think of someone in your life who needs your concern, caring, or love. What can you do for them this week?

* Ask your parents or youth leader what sort of project you could get involved in to show your love for others. A few examples include tutoring, visiting a nursing home, or going on a missions trip.

DAY 137 Why Your Parents Are Scared

Ever wonder why your parents seem kind of tough on you sometimes? Or why they tense up when they're around you? Chances are they're just a little bit scared. Here's why:

They are scared because you're becoming more and more independent. When you were born, you were helpless. You needed them, even to eat. They cuddled you, encircled you with their arms, and thought you were such a little darling. They assumed you would always need them.

Now you're shattering their assumptions. Your growing sense of independence tells them what they would rather forget: they chose you, but you never chose them. You may love them (and they hope you do), but you don't belong to them. You need them less and less, and they're afraid they will lose you completely.

They are scared because they know how easy it is to waste your life. They know from experience that there are at least three wrong directions for every right one. They know how easily life slips away through a casual decision to stick with the wrong friends, wrong habits, or wrong thinking.

So they are scared, and they worry about you. All right, you may be stronger than they think. You may be confident, but they're afraid. You may know where you're going, but they're not so sure you're going in the right direction. You don't have to absorb their fear, but can you respect it?

They are scared because they feel powerless. You may sometimes feel your parents control your life. But your parents often feel helpless because they realize how little control they actually have. When you were a child they could command you. Now they have to try to influence you. The shift in your relationship with them makes them uneasy. They see all the dangerous things going on in the world, all the changes that have taken place since they were teenagers, and yet they know they need to gradually give you more and more freedom. They realize they are sending you out into a world full of potential dangers, and they know they can't protect you.

They are scared because they can't talk to you. They love you, and that love forms words that stick to their tongues. They want to share the stories of their lives with you, but their stories seem so out of touch with your life. And you don't laugh at their jokes.

They want to tell you what you mean to them, but they're embarrassed and you're busy doing homework.

They want to give you good advice, but the TV is on and who can talk?

They are scared because they feel insecure as parents. They didn't learn parenting in college or graduate school. No one ever taught your mom and dad how to be good parents. If they were fortunate, they may have learned from their own parents' good example. But times, circumstances, and people change. And what worked a generation ago doesn't always apply today.

At best, parenting is a trial-and-error job. Most parents realize they are going to make a lot of mistakes. They can only hope and pray the mistakes won't be too serious because the stakes, the lives of their children, are so high.

Basically, your parents are scared because they love you. They don't want to fail as parents. But mostly they don't want to fail you. And they're afraid they will.

—Tim

* Did any of these reasons surprise you? Why or why not? How would you benefit from starting a conversation with your parents about why they're scared or worried?

DAY 138 Do Something

Children, always obey your parents, for this pleases the Lord.
—Colossians 3:20 NLT

Children, obey your parents because you belong to the Lord, for this is the right thing to do.
—Ephesians 6:1 NLT

* With these verses in mind, think of ways you can improve in obeying your parents. Is there a pile of laundry in the corner that Mom asked you to wash? Yard work Dad asked you to do two weekends ago? Have you been cheating on the curfew time they give you on Saturday nights? Using the computer for longer than allowed? If you can't think of anything, go ask your mom or dad for ideas of extra things you could do to help them. Be prepared to catch them in case they fall over from shock.

DAY 139 Why Honor Your Parents?

Joel and his mom had a hard time getting along. Ever since his dad left, his mom had been increasingly hard on her son. She yelled. She took out her frustrations on him. Finally he started yelling back. In fact, he acted rebellious just to make her angry.

Maybe Joel's experience is similar to your own. Or maybe you get along really well with your mom and dad. We each live in our own unique situation with our parents—some good, others not so good. God understands this, and yet he still gives us the same instruction in the fifth commandment: "Honor your father and your mother" (Exod. 20:12).

Answer this

* Why honor our parents—especially when it's so hard to do?

. . . the rest of the story

The second half of the commandment holds an answer to the question: "Honor your father and your mother, so that you may live long in the land the LORD your God is giving you" (Exod. 20:12).

Hundreds of years before giving Moses the Ten Commandments, God promised to give Abraham and his descendants a special land of their own (Genesis 12 and 15). A Promised Land.

Christians believe that God's Promised Land for us is actually heaven. We can go to heaven by accepting Jesus as our Lord and Savior (Rom. 10:9–10). But Jesus also made it clear that when he came to earth, he brought a little heaven with him. We don't simply wait until we die to experience heaven. We can live in ways that help us experience a little bit of God's kingdom—God's Promised Land—right here, right now (Matt. 6:10; Luke 17:21).

165

One of those ways is to honor our parents. God promises we will live "in the land" if we honor our parents. In other words, while we live on earth, we'll get to experience bits of heaven. This doesn't necessarily mean our parents will change. They might still do things we don't like or that don't honor God. But by loving and respecting them, and by forgiving them when we need to, we can help bring God's kingdom to earth, and we can experience the joy and peace to be found in that kingdom.

And that's not all. In the midst of struggles with our parents, we can see God transform our attitudes. We can become better people by honoring our parents. And if they see those changes in us, our parents might even make some changes for the better too. This brings me back to Joel.

After fighting with his mom for about a year, he asked his mother for forgiveness and told her he had forgiven her and loved her very much. After that simple act, Joel and his mom argue less, their attitudes toward each other have become far better, and they're even able to laugh together! Joel is experiencing the joy and blessings of living in God's kingdom.

So think for a moment about how you can honor your parents today. Do you need to forgive them? Do you need to thank them? Can you do something thoughtful for them?

Remember that honoring them is not just another commandment to keep. It's an opportunity to bring the transforming power of God's kingdom into our relationships with our moms and dads. And it's an amazing opportunity to see your own life changed for the better.

—Jason

DAY 140 Prayers about Mom and Dad

Skim the prayers below and find one that fits your family situation. Mark this page so you can return to it. For the next several days, pray this prayer or use it as a model for your own prayer.

Hello God,

I love my mom, but sometimes she seems so picky, so demanding, and her nagging really gets to me. She doesn't seem to know I can actually make some of my own decisions. She doesn't seem to understand I'm growing up. Or does she? Maybe that *is* the problem. Is she afraid she's losing me? Is she clinging to a younger me because the older me is growing up too fast for her? Is that it? It seems weird to think she's afraid. But if she is, I probably need to go easier on her. And I probably need to let her know I still need her.

Dear Lord,

I worry so much when my parents fight. I don't know what their fighting means. Are they just mad about something that will soon go away? I really don't know. I guess I should talk to them, shouldn't I? I guess that's the only way I'll know for sure. Help me to know what to do. Most of all, help me to be better at letting them know how I feel.

Lord,

It's not always easy for my dad. There are so many bills, and he seems so tired all the time. Please help Dad realize you love him. Help him, because life seems so hard for him right now.

Heavenly Father,

It seems hard to call you Father, since mine's not around. But maybe that's why I need you so much. I need a father, a real daddy. Help me to know you are my Father. Help me to realize you won't ever leave me, OK?

God,

Thanks for my mom and dad. I really mean it. Even though they're kind of weird, sometimes too strict, and we often just don't get each other, I'm grateful for them.

* *Write your own prayer* about Mom and Dad.

DAY 141 Torn by Divorce

Every Sunday night had been the same since I was five. That's how old I was when my mom, my sister, and I moved two hours away from Dad and I got to see him only on weekends. Even though I'd been driving back to my mom's house with him every Sunday for a long time, saying goodbye to him was never easy.

This time was no different.

As we sat in the driveway, I glanced up at the living room window. I knew Mom would be standing there, watching us. I grabbed my suitcase and went inside.

"So what did you do this weekend?"

"Not much," I mumbled. I tried not to feel guilty for leaving her alone over the weekend or for now missing my dad so much.

The ringing of the phone ended Mom's questions.

"Hello?" I answered.

"You missed it!" my best friend Debby nearly shouted. "It was the best party ever!"

"Sounds fun," I said, trying to hold back my tears.

I listened for another fifteen minutes as Debby talked about her birthday party. It was only October of my freshman year and I'd already missed a dance, a major football game, and now Debby's party.

That night I couldn't sleep. *Dear Jesus,* I prayed, *I have all this pressure on me to choose between friends or family. When will the pain end?*

The next morning, I felt a little better after I saw my friends at school. And I didn't even think about the next weekend until Thursday at lunch. "We're going out for pizza on Saturday night," Debby told me. "Come."

"I'm going to my dad's," I said quietly.

Debby sighed. "It's not the same when you're not around. What about Friday night?" she asked. "Can we plan on hanging out every Friday night?"

Our parents agreed to let us hang out every Friday night for the rest of the year. I still missed some events on Saturdays, but I got the courage to talk to my dad and mom about it. I also took Debby to my dad's house a few times. And when there were really big school events going on, Dad came to Mom's house, had dinner with me, then stayed until my friends picked me up.

It wasn't the same as spending the entire weekend with him, but at least I got to see him for a little while. And honestly, while I had fun with my friends, I missed going to Dad's house.

"You're lucky," Debby told me one Friday night as I packed my suitcase.

"How so?" I asked.

"You have a great family," she said.

"You do remember my parents are divorced, right?" I said as I folded a sweater. "They're hardly ever in the same room together. It's not that great."

"What I mean," she said, "is that you have two different families that you do a lot of cool stuff with. It's like your time together actually counts. My family hardly has time to eat dinner together."

I zipped up my suitcase.

"That's a weird way to look at it," I said. "But I like it."

I flopped down on my bed. "I've been praying for a long time that their divorce wouldn't hurt so much," I admitted. "Maybe I need to look at the good things."

—Amy

Your turn

* Whatever your family situation, how can you change a negative attitude toward your parents into a positive one?

169

DAY 142 Things I Love, Things I Don't

On one side of the chart below, write "Things I Love about My Parents."
On the other side, write "Things I Wish I Could Change about My Parents." Now, fill in the lists.

* Go down the list and thank God for each of the things you love. Either write a note of encouragement or verbally affirm your parents for these things.

* Now go down the list of things you wish you could change. Pray for understanding, clear communication, and peace between you and your parents concerning those issues. And ask for strength and patience to obey your parents when you don't feel like it.

DAY 143 One Question, Five Answers

Q: *I've always gotten along with my parents, but now it seems like I can't do anything right. I even got yelled at for being depressed. I don't know how to talk to my parents about how I feel. Even if I did, I'm not sure things would change. Can anyone help me?*

—Katie

A: *I was in a similar situation with my mom. We even went to counseling. I eventually learned I had to be just totally honest with my mom because she might not know how I was feeling. It worked. It was difficult, but it brought healing and better times for both of us. Try telling your parents how you feel. It could be the start of a better relationship.*

—Alyssa

A: *When you talk to your parents, make sure you're speaking with love. Don't let your emotions take over; let God be in control. Pray that God will give you wisdom and show you the best way to talk about your feelings. God can work anything out when you keep your eyes on him.*

—Manni

A: *If you don't think you can talk to your parents, try writing them a letter. Also, pray for them. There may be things going on in their lives you don't know about.*

—Jennifer

A: *Maybe you've changed in some ways and your parents aren't used to the "new" you. Try spending time with them and helping them learn more about what's going on in your life. You can let them know you think they've been coming down hard on you lately. But be respectful when you talk to them and don't come down hard on them. Treat them the way you want to be treated—with love and respect.*

—Tim

A: *Even if talking with your parents doesn't get you anywhere, treat your parents with respect. That way, no matter what happens, you'll know you're doing God's will.*

—Hilary

Your turn

* What advice would you give Katie?

DAY 144 6 Ways to Get Along Better with Your Parents

1. Seek their advice. No, you don't always want your parents telling you what to do. But you do want to let them know you still value their opinions and their convictions. For example, if you have a problem with a friend, ask Mom and Dad how they would work things out. Seeking your parents' advice will make them feel good. You'll also benefit from their years of wisdom.

2. Let them meet your friends. Your parents really do worry about your friendships. They wonder if you're getting into the "wrong crowd." So invite your friends over and let your parents get to know them. One more thing: if you're afraid to let your parents meet your friends, that might tell you something about the people you're hanging out with. Maybe your parents' concerns aren't so off base.

3. Spend time with them. Sure, you want to be with your friends. And you do have a ton of homework. Then there's your part-time job. . . . OK, you're busy. Even so, your parents need to know how you're doing. Remember, you're changing in ways they may not realize. So spend time with them. Every once in a while, pull out an old board game or join your folks for a movie or a fast-food treat. Whatever you do, just be sure you set aside a little bit of time for them each week.

4. Let them know how you're really feeling. Be honest about your feelings. You don't have to put on a happy face for them. If you're not feeling OK, don't say you are. But if you are feeling great about something, tell them all about it. And don't just give your parents information about yourself ("I had an English test"). Let them in on your feelings ("I just feel horrible/wonderful about my test grade").

5. *Say "Thank you."* Leave a nice note on the kitchen counter. Drop a homemade card in your mom's or dad's briefcase. Just be sure and show them you're truly grateful for all they do for you.

6. *Say "I love you!"* Say it with a card, a hug, a smile, or a little extra work around the house. Be sure to say it out loud too. Yes, they know it. But they still need to hear it again and again.

—Tim

DAY 145 Reaching Out to a Lonely Guy

I was standing in my front yard when I saw Ben walking down the road in front of my house. It struck me as odd because he lives a ways down the road.

I didn't know him very well. He went to the local high school, and I was homeschooled. So our paths hardly ever crossed. But when I saw him that day, I felt like God was pushing me to give him a ride home.

"Hey Ben," I shouted. "Want a ride?" At first, he looked unsure about accepting. But then he said slowly, "Sure, thanks."

As we pulled out of my driveway, he asked, "Why are you being so nice?" I told him I wouldn't want to walk that far and thought he might need a ride. It seemed to satisfy his curiosity. After some small talk about part-time jobs, I got up the courage to invite him to my youth group. He kind of stared at the floor and said, "I guess I'll give it a try. After all, you gave me a ride. I guess I sort of owe ya one." I told him I'd pick him up on Wednesday night.

That's how I got Ben to attend my youth group. But it was something about our conversations in the car that built our friendship and allowed me to share Christ. Not every conversation to and from church was about God. Sometimes we talked about how we both liked dirt bikes or which songs we'd learned to play on the guitar. Stuff about recent movies or music sometimes opened up doors to talk about life and faith. Since neither of us are great conversationalists, talking to Ben wasn't always easy. There were times of awkward silence, when neither of us knew quite what to say. But eventually one of us would break the ice and the conversation would get going again.

Before long, Ben started hanging around my house. He's one of those quiet guys who seems to just observe and take note of what's around him. And I could tell he was carefully watching as I talked to my parents and joked around with my brothers and sister. He also seemed to be paying attention when I was around the other kids at youth group. While I wanted him to know I'm a normal guy, I also wanted him to see Christ in me by the way I acted around others. And I knew he was watching.

Ben hasn't committed his life to Christ yet, but he's been more and more open when we've talked about Jesus. He's also been asking some pretty deep questions about God and the Bible.

As nervous as I was at the time, I'm thankful God led me to give a lonely guy a ride home. I'm also grateful for the friendship I've been able to build with Ben. Maybe someday our conversations in the car will lead him to ask how he could have a personal relationship with Jesus. That would be the best conversation ever.

—Josh

Who's lonely?

* Think about someone at church, youth group, or school who seems very sad and lonely.

* Write that person's first name here: _____.

* Spend one minute praying for this person, asking God to show you how you can offer him or her a glimpse of God's love.

* Write down one small way you can show this person kindness: _____
_____.

* Follow through in the next few days by doing what you wrote down.

DAY 146 What Kindness Won't Tolerate

Kindness is defined, in part, by what it won't tolerate: self-centeredness.

Kindness and self-centeredness just don't enjoy one another's company. They are mutually exclusive. They fight one another. If you invite kindness in the front door of your life, selfishness must leave by the backdoor. Or climb out the window. They don't go together.

We could say, somewhat negatively, selfishness strangles kindness until there is no life left in it. Or we could say, nurture kindness in your life and it will suffocate your self-centeredness.

Want to break out of your selfish ways? (And we all have them.) Look for ways to express kindness. Kindness conquers selfishness.

You might not think of yourself as particularly egotistical, but what do others think? Give your life away in kindness to others and even the unacknowledged, unknown dimensions of your inner selfishness will begin to melt away.

When we lose ourselves in kindness to others, we become new people. Entirely new. Different. More likable. Pleasant to be around.

—James

A great example to follow

Don't be selfish; don't try to impress others. Be humble, thinking of others as better than yourselves. Don't look out only for your own interests, but take an interest in others, too. You must have the same attitude that Christ Jesus had. Though he was God, he did not think of equality with God as something to cling to. Instead, he gave up his divine privileges; he took the humble position of a slave and was born as a human being. When he appeared in human form, he humbled himself in obedience to God and died a criminal's death on a cross.

—Philippians 2:3–8 NLT

DAY 147 Why Was He So Kind?

I didn't deserve the man's kindness. The accident had been my fault.

I was driving alone, trying to make a left turn at an intersection that didn't have a left-turn lane. Across from me, a large truck heading in the opposite direction was making a left turn, and the truck obstructed my view of oncoming traffic. I remember thinking nervously, *Maybe I should go straight. This is too dangerous.* But just then, I thought the way was clear. I turned, and wham! I never saw the red Suburban until my car stopped spinning.

I looked behind me. The back passenger side was bashed in, glass everywhere. Then I looked at the red Suburban. Its right front was bashed in. Shakily I got out of my car and walked up to the driver. "Are you all right?" I asked, fearful of the answer. *What if they're hurt? What if they sue me?* I thought.

"I want to know what she did to my car," complained the woman in the passenger seat. My stomach flip-flopped.

But the driver said, "No, no one's hurt. We need to move the cars out of the middle of the road."

We were each able to drive our cars out of the intersection. I called home. When I got off the phone, a police car parked near my own car. The officer motioned me over. The driver of the SUV and I got into the back of the police car.

"Now," the officer said, "tell me what happened."

I gulped and told him the story. I didn't try to make excuses or get out of anything. I gave him the facts and said I hadn't seen the red car at all because of the truck. "Is that what happened in your opinion?" the officer asked the driver of the SUV.

He said yes. "Do you want me to give her a ticket?" the officer questioned.

I held my breath.

The driver of the SUV looked at me. "Do you have insurance?"

"Oh yes!"

"No," he answered the officer, "you don't need to give her a ticket. As long as she has insurance and you have the report, it's OK."

We exchanged all the needed information and then signed release forms stating we were all OK. Again, relief flooded me. By a miracle, no one was hurt. And the man wasn't planning to exploit the situation by going to the hospital later and claiming injuries.

I stared at this man. He was so calm, so kind.

For weeks after the accident I wondered whether I would have been so generous if I were the one who was hit. The man had a right to be upset, even to angrily chew me out. But he wasn't angry—at least he didn't show it. His attitude seemed to be, "I know you didn't mean to do this. Accidents happen; it's too bad I was a victim of this one. But that's life."

My car is now fixed, almost like new. The trauma has faded. But the sense of relief at the man's kindness lingers. It's like he gave me a gift in exchange for the trouble I caused him. He modeled for me what mercy is all about. It's a gift I hope I will always remember to return to others who wrong me.

I've heard it said that once a car is in an accident it's never the same. Whether or not that's true, I do know that I'm not the same.

But then again, I don't ever want to be the same.

—Diane

Think it through

* When is it hardest for you to be kind? Who is someone you have a difficult time being kind to?

Pray about it

* Ask God to help you to be kind in difficult situations and toward difficult people.

Act on it

* The next time you find it difficult to be kind, take a deep breath, say a prayer, and then try your best to show God's love and patience through kindness.

DAY 148 What Does Kindness Look Like?

We like others to be kind to us, but being kind to them can sometimes be a challenge.

But it's amazing what happens when we rise to that challenge—when we take a bold step to show kindness to others. People appreciate our kindness and are often surprised by it. Sometimes our kindness reminds someone of Jesus.

We all know kindness is a positive trait, and we see the good it brings. So what keeps us from freely expressing it?

Sometimes we hold back because we don't get around to thinking about others. Other times we choose to withhold kindness because someone has been unkind to us: you treat me badly, I'll treat you badly. But isn't it precisely when others have treated us the worst that we have the greatest opportunity for kindness? Isn't this the sort of kindness Jesus expressed even toward those who were unkind to him?

It's not surprising, then, that the Bible links kindness to forgiveness: "Be kind and compassionate to one another, forgiving each other, just as in Christ God forgave you" (Eph. 4:32). Sometimes we have to forgive someone before we can be kind to them.

But it isn't enough merely to feel kindness toward someone. God expects more from us than that. Kindness proves itself by action. Kindness does kind things.

* *What does kindness look like?* Here are a few ideas:

Kindness smiles.

Kindness says encouraging things.

Kindness says "thank you" to a parent.

Kindness shares with a brother or sister.

Kindness cuts the grass or shovels the snow for an elderly person.

Kindness lovingly warns a friend who's heading in the wrong direction.

* What else does kindness do? What can kindness do *through you* today? Make your own list:

* But let's think about kindness in another way. What are things kindness refuses to do? Here are a few ideas:

Kindness won't gossip.

Kindness won't cheat.

Kindness doesn't have time to waste on pouting or jealousy.

* Now it's your turn to list things kindness won't do:

* Of course, lists don't mean much unless we do something with them. So get started now, and show someone what kindness really looks like.

—James

DAY 149 14 Ways to Make Somebody's Day

1. Send "thinking of you" cards to some guys and girls in your youth group who need cheering up.
2. Offer to help an elderly person in your neighborhood with yard work or even by just bringing in the groceries.
3. Call your pastor or youth pastor and volunteer to help out around the church for a few days during a summer, Christmas, or spring break.
4. Surprise a missionary family from your church. Get your youth group friends together, buy some gifts, and assemble a package to send to

the family. (Contact your pastor or youth pastor for ideas on what to send.)

5. Spend a Saturday or a day of your summer break volunteering at your local food bank, soup kitchen, or Salvation Army shelter.
6. Spend a day at the zoo or a park with your little brother or sister.
7. Smile and say hi to someone you don't know.
8. Send thank-you cards to a few of your favorite past teachers—including teachers from your elementary and middle school years. Tell them what you enjoyed most about your time in their classroom.
9. Treat a friend at his or her favorite coffee shop.
10. Buy your mom a single rose.
11. Get together with some church friends and deliver homemade snacks to underclassmen in your youth group.
12. Spend an afternoon visiting residents at a local nursing home.
13. Wash your parents' car without being asked.
14. Don't stop now. Look for little ways to make somebody's day every single day.

* *Go back* and circle three suggestions you're willing to try.

DAY 150 Sin Happens

I wanted to go to a friend's house, but first my mom wanted to know if I'd gotten all my homework done. "Yes," I lied, thinking, *It's not going to affect my grade and it's not a big deal.*

But it was a big deal. Why? Because a little lie about having my homework done is more than it seems. It's rooted in selfishness, pride, and lack of respect for my parents. I want what I want . . . and I don't care what you think!

On the surface I think, *I'm not so bad.* But God looks deep down into my true motives and sees that my heart can be dishonest and deceitful (Jer. 17:9). That's sin.

Let's admit it. We all sin. Sometimes we do it on purpose, and sometimes we just mess up. And sometimes we try to play God. We choose to do life our way instead of choosing God's better way. It's human nature.

It's who we are. As it says in Romans 3:23, "Everyone has sinned. No one measures up to God's glory" (NIrV). Sin happens. And it's destructive.

OK, that's the very bad news. But the great news is this: our loving heavenly Father sees all of this and yet he still loves us. He cares for us like a compassionate doctor cares for a patient who needs a life-threatening tumor removed. But God did more than simply cut out cancer. Through his death on the cross, Jesus took the cancer of sin onto himself.

Bible break

For God made Christ, who never sinned, to be the offering for our sin, so that we could be made right with God through Christ.

—2 Corinthians 5:21 NLT

But God demonstrates his own love for us in this: While we were still sinners, Christ died for us.

—Romans 5:8

. . . the rest of the story

God longs to have an everlasting relationship with us. He wants to forgive our sins so this relationship can happen. We remain far away from God without forgiveness. We remain lost and spiritually dead without forgiveness. But when we accept God's forgiveness, he saves us from condemnation and hell. We will live with him forever in heaven. We can enjoy a day-to-day friendship with God right now.

But God won't do anything we don't want him to do. It's our choice whether or not to receive his forgiveness. He won't force it on us. We have to be humble enough to let go of our selfish pride and tell God we're really sorry for our sins. We have to be willing to let go of our bad habits and ugly attitudes. And this is true for Christians too. While God won't leave those who have a real relationship with him, sin damages that relationship. To keep our relationship healthy and strong, we need to confess our sins and try to live the way God wants us to live.

—Grady

181

Living as God wants

* In the Bible passage below, circle the things God will do. Underline the things we must do.

But if we live in the light, as God does, we share in life with each other. And the blood of his Son Jesus washes all our sins away. If we say that we have not sinned, we are fooling ourselves, and the truth isn't in our hearts. But if we confess our sins to God, he can always be trusted to forgive us and take our sins away.

—1 John 1:7–9 CEV

DAY 151 Nobody's a Lost Cause

One day in middle school, I passed this church on my way to a local park. A bunch of kids were standing on the church's lawn. One of them looked my way and shouted, "Hi, my name's Amanda. What's your name?" I stopped, introduced myself, and started talking to Amanda and her friends.

By the way I looked, and by the people I hung out with, some Christians might have thought I was a lost cause. But Amanda didn't let my tough appearance get in the way. Her friendliness that day made me stop and talk to her. Amanda accepted me and believed that I could come into a relationship with God.

Her caring attitude that day helped me see how important it would be to keep reaching out to my old friends, no matter how far gone they seemed. They needed to come to Christ—and were never, ever too far gone for Christ to reach them.

Not long after I committed my life to Christ, I went up to my friend Steph and just blurted out, "Dude, you should come to youth group with me! It's cool, not boring, and you can learn about Jesus!"

Probably not the best approach. But it worked. Steph said, "Yeah, I'll try it."

And she did. In fact, she eventually made the decision to accept Christ as her Savior. This really made me happy, because Steph had a lot of struggles. She partied quite a bit, and she would also get down and depressed and then cut herself. But Christ has really changed her life and she no longer cuts or parties with her old friends. I'm so glad I told Steph about my youth group and about Jesus. Seeing her life change showed me that God could use me to help my hurting friends.

—Amber

Don't give up

* Have you ever felt someone gave up on you? Write three words to describe how that felt:
    1
    2.
    3.

* Who in your life do you think might feel like a lost cause? List three first names:
    1.
    2.
    3.

* What three small steps can you take this week to make them feel accepted?
    1.
    2.
    3.

DAY 152 Tough Question

Q: *When you ask for forgiveness, I know you're supposed to repent and stop doing that sin. But what if you can't stop? Will God forgive me a second or a twentieth time?*

—*Anonymous*

Your turn

* How would you answer this question?

How IYF's expert answered:

A: Guess what? If people could stop sinning by just deciding to stop, we'd all know a lot of perfect people. But no one stops sinning. No one. I sure don't, despite my best efforts. Even Paul confessed that he continued to do what he didn't want to do. When the Bible tells us to repent, it doesn't mean we're able to stop the sinful behavior by just deciding to (Romans 7).

Instead, repentance means "to turn." We turn our minds back to Christ—confessing where we are and where we long to be. We admit we've sinned and ask Jesus to cleanse us. We can't do that ourselves. It's God who changes us. This process is called sanctification—and it's a result of continued prayer and confession, admitting our dependence on God and seeking his strength.

Through sanctification, sin does lose its power over us and we can become stronger. But we never stop sinning, because we are human. Therefore, all of us have to keep turning back to Jesus time after time. It's only when we stop returning to God and start pretending like our sins are OK that we begin doing very serious damage to our relationship with God.

If we confess our sins, God is faithful to forgive us. Jesus taught the disciples that they needed to forgive people who sinned against them "seventy times seven" (or 490) times. If he expected his impatient and flawed disciples to forgive that many times, we can be sure that God is willing to forgive us as often as we come and humbly confess our shortcomings to him with a desire for him to change our lives.

—Marshall

DAY 153 The Unhappy Prophet

By the third chapter of Jonah, the reluctant prophet had been through a lot: He'd tried to run away from God. He'd been thrown off a boat. He'd spent a three-day weekend inside a fish. He'd been puked up on a beach. He'd also been out telling the wicked people of a large city (Nineveh) that they had forty days to turn from their sins before God destroyed them (the message God had told Jonah to deliver).

Then Jonah waited for the city to get smoked. But nothing happened. Well, nothing except the people of Nineveh turned their hearts to God. "When God saw what they had done and how they had put a stop to their evil ways, he changed his mind and did not carry out the destruction he had threatened" (3:10 NLT).

Destruction diverted! Jonah was happy, right? Wrong.

—Jarrett

Another point of view

To understand Jonah's bizarre reaction to God granting great mercy on Nineveh, Ethan did a fake interview with a for-real Bible character who was on the scene.

Q: How'd you meet Jonah?

A: Well, I was up on a cliff overlooking the city, eating a leaf, when I saw this guy walking to the cliff's edge. He found a nice spot to watch God destroy Nineveh. The funny thing is that God had already told Jonah he'd forgiven Nineveh. But Jonah was too stubborn to accept it. He really wanted destruction. He was furious that God forgave them.

Q: Furious that people didn't die?

A: Yeah. You see, these people were Assyrians—the enemies of Jonah's people. He hated them. He knew they were bad seeds and deserved punishment. When God directed him to go warn Nineveh, Jonah wanted no part in helping them. He knew God was a Lord of mercy and compassion. He didn't want them to be forgiven; he wanted them dead. So he refused to go to Nineveh.

Q: And so that's how he ended up in a fish?

A: Right. After that, he gave in and came to Nineveh. Then God did exactly what Jonah feared. These people were not beyond God's compassion.

Q: What'd Jonah do with his anger?

A: He ranted and pouted for days—even in the hot Nineveh sun. To shade him from the heat, God allowed a vine to grow up over Jonah's

185

head. Jonah loved that vine. But not even a day later, God told me to eat it. I did and the thing died. Jonah freaked out again.

Q: *Why'd God have you eat the vine?*

A: God was showing Jonah that he had no right to be angry. There's more to life than just making Jonah happy. God said, "How is it that you can change your feelings from pleasure to anger overnight about a mere shade tree? And why can't I likewise decide to show mercy instead of wrath toward the 120,000 people of Nineveh?"

God taught Jonah that he is a God of compassion who is pleased when we turn our hearts to him. He encouraged Jonah to get over himself and realize that God's mercy can be extended to all who accept it.

* *Read the real story:* **Who is the real Bible character behind Ethan's fake interview? Find out in Jonah 4.**

Let's talk about you

* **Have you ever been mad that someone didn't get what they deserved?**

* **Have you ever been happy you didn't get what you deserved?**

DAY 154 The Perfect Christian?

In high school, I found Christ and immediately began trying to be the perfect Christian. I would never say no to doing anything for my church. I was busy every night with church stuff. I had a three-page list of people to pray for every day and if I didn't pray for the whole list, I'd feel like I wasn't doing my job as a good Christian.

I was trying to earn God's love. I knew God loved me, but if I ever let him down I could hardly stand myself. I didn't feel worthy of God's love.

Eventually all of this work to be perfect wore me down. I was empty. I was exhausted. I lost my passion for the Lord. I just didn't feel the joy and peace I used to. And that's when God overwhelmed me by revealing through Scripture how much he loves me.

I realized that—unintentionally—my actions were saying that Jesus's death on the cross was not good enough to cover my sins. I thought I had to worry about my sins, make up for them, and feel guilty about them. But Jesus took on the sin and shame of the world when he died on the cross. I don't have to feel shame and guilt if I'm forgiven. While I was trying to earn his love, God loved me regardless. There was nothing I could do to make him love me more or less.

After realizing all this, I had to change my attitude. I needed to give myself some grace. It wasn't easy. In fact, I still remind myself every day that Christ's blood is enough to cover my sins.

—Dawn

All of us have sinned and fallen short of God's glory. But God treats us much better than we deserve, and because of Christ Jesus, he freely accepts us and sets us free from our sins.

—Romans 3:23–24 CEV

DAY 155 Happy News for Sad People

I know this guy named Joe. His life is a mess. Some music on his iPod is morally sketchy. Joe sneaks into R-rated movies and pops onto porn sites now and then. That's just the tip of the iceberg.

Thing is, Joe loves God, and he wants to follow Jesus, but he's not exactly good at following through. He doesn't pray or read his Bible. Some weeks he hardly thinks about God at all.

On top of all that, Joe looks at the world around him and all he sees are war, disease, death, and destruction—and it just makes him feel worse about life. Sometimes he honestly wonders if life is worth living.

And then Joe reads Jesus's words in Matthew 5:3: "Blessed are the poor in spirit, for theirs is the kingdom of heaven." *Really?* I mean, Joe's definitely poor in spirit. But, seriously, he doesn't feel so blessed.

Doesn't make sense, does it? That's because we're often told just the opposite. We're told we should have it together. We're told we should always feel good about ourselves. We should always be upbeat. We should always be happy. Happy, happy, happy!

It's all a lie. Don't believe it. If you do believe it, you're only going to spiral down into worse feelings, because you'll start thinking, *I'm feeling sad, but I should be feeling happy, and it makes me even sadder that I can't be happy like everyone expects!* Get sucked into that type of thinking, and you may never come out of it.

But Jesus says that it's normal to feel really sad sometimes. It's normal to struggle with some messy problems. The world is a messed-up place—there's lots of death, destruction, selfishness, and evil out there. And that doesn't even count what's going on in our personal lives, which sometimes include awful stuff like divorced parents, loneliness, breakups, drug abuse, and sexual abuse.

In fact, something is wrong with us if we don't feel really sad about life sometimes. It means we're not paying attention. That's why Jesus goes further and says it is blessed to feel deep sadness. When you do, it means you really understand that the world is all screwed up, that your life is an utter mess, and that there really is no hope—*outside of Christ.*

And that's the key that prevents us from spiraling out of control into despair. We need Jesus Christ more than we need anything else. And it is only when we are poor in spirit that we can begin to see Jesus clearly. That's the Jesus who died on a cross, who literally feels our pain, who experiences the sadness and destruction of a world gone mad.

In the midst of all the tragedy, Jesus is filling the world with his love and grace.

—Mark

When Christ returns

Through faith you are kept safe by God's power. Your salvation is going to be completed. It is ready to be shown to you in the last days. Because you know this, you have great joy. You have joy even though you may have had to suffer. . . . You may have had to suffer sadness in all kinds of trouble. Your troubles have come in order to prove that your faith is real. . . . Your faith is meant to bring praise, honor and glory to God. That will happen when Jesus Christ returns.

—1 Peter 1:5–7 NIrV

DAY 156 Never Too Dirty to Be Clean

The hurt

Q: My boyfriend and I had sex. I feel really dirty, and I wish I was still a virgin. I pray every night that God will help me and forgive me, but I can't stop feeling dirty. What can I do?

—Anonymous

The hope

A: You aren't dirty. Yes, you feel guilty. Yes, you stepped outside of what God wants for you. But if you've asked God for his forgiveness, know that you are forgiven. If you've recommitted yourself to God's thinking on sex, you have started over. You're a blank sheet ready to maintain Christlike purity.

Whenever I talk to anyone who is struggling with getting over past sin (no matter what it is), I recommend this verse:

> Because of the sacrifice of the Messiah, his blood poured out on the altar of the cross, we're a free people—free of penalties and punishments chalked up by all our misdeeds. And not just barely free, either. Abundantly free!
>
> —Ephesians 1:7 Message

You are free of penalties. Free of guilt. Free of feeling dirty. And not just a little free. Sure, pain and guilt are powerful emotions. But they will never be more powerful than God's grace. God can and does bring good out of bad situations. So look for the ways this experience can draw you closer to God as you work through your feelings and gain the strength to resist the temptation to have sex before you're married.

I would also encourage you to confide in a Christian adult you trust—someone you believe can help explain God's love and grace to you.

—Carla

189

The healing

* What guilt do you feel? What sin or mistakes make you feel unworthy to stand before God?

* By sincerely releasing sins to God, accepting Christ's sacrifice, and turning from sin, you are washed clean (1 John 1:9).

* You are free. Set a goal to memorize Ephesians 1:7 by this time next week.

DAY 157 What's It Mean to Be a Dad?

I've seen it a zillion times. I sit down in front of the TV, flip from channel to channel, and there they are: goofy dads, stupid dads, dads who don't have a clue.

And then I read in the paper or hear about it from friends: a dad does something horrible to his child. Hurts him. Abandons her. Or refuses to pay child support. Deadbeat dads. Mean dads. Just plain bad dads.

Dads all too often get a pretty terrible reputation, don't they?

—Jerry

Describing dad

* Write five adjectives that describe your dad:

    1.
    2.
    3.
    4.
    5.

* Is your dad like the majority of TV sitcom dads? How is he different?

* What things about your dad are you thankful for? What things make you sad? Angry? Proud?

* Write five adjectives that describe the perfect dad:

1.
2.
3.
4.
5.

DAY 158 A Heavenly Father?

A phrase from the Apostles' Creed tells us that God is both personal and relational: "I believe in God the Father Almighty, maker of heaven and earth." That's right, our Creator—the Maker of heaven and earth—is a loving Father.

Even those who have not-so-great dads have a great heavenly Father they can always turn to. He loves us and is interested in every part of our lives: the disappointments and the joys; the stuff that challenges us and the stuff that encourages us; the stuff that confuses and the stuff that's bright and clear. He has never missed showing up for the big moments of our lives, and he has been present for the seemingly unimportant ones as well. Everything about us is important to our loving heavenly Dad.

Of course, Christians believe this truth about God *through faith*. We believe God is a perfect Father who is always there, whether or not we feel like he is there. Even when we don't always see or even experience God's love, our belief—supported by God's Word and the historical experiences of God's people—tells us that God is a loving, caring Father.

—Jerry

No matter what

* Stop a moment and think about what it means to say God is your heavenly Father. He loves you *no matter what*. He is there for you *no matter what*. He knows you and knows all about you, and he wants to guide you, comfort you, and help you learn to live like a true child of God. Spend two minutes praising and thanking God for being your Father.

DAY 159 How's the Father Fit into the Trinity?

The Bible is clear that God is three in one: God the Father, God the Son, and God the Holy Spirit (Matt. 28:18–20). The three parts are separate personalities. And yet together, they form one being: God. For instance, look at an egg and its three separate but equal parts: yolk, white, and shell. Each has its own identity and purpose, and yet all three make up something more.

In a nutshell, God the Father's role is to generate things. Things originate with him and flow from him. God the Father is equal with the Son and the Holy Spirit, but things start with him. The Father sent both the Son (John 3:16–17) and the Holy Spirit (John 14:26) into the world.

This is just a beginning. We can't fully define God the Father—or the rest of the Trinity. He's so awesome, powerful, and inexplicable that we can't wrap our minds around him. Nor would we want to. He just leaves us looking to him with wonder and awe.

If God is three in one, who do you pray to?

God the Father. In Matthew 6:6, Jesus says, "But when you pray, . . . pray to your Father, who is unseen." Then Jesus went on to tell us how to pray, starting out with the words, "Our Father in heaven . . ."

—*Dawson*

But for us there is only one God. He is the Father. All things came from him, and we live for him. And there is only one Lord. He is Jesus Christ. All things came because of him, and we live because of him.

—1 Corinthians 8:6 NIrV

DAY 160 Is God Like My Dad?

When I was a child, my family was poor and my dad was a cocaine addict. He was seldom around. When he was, he'd abuse us physically and emotionally. It was horrible.

One day, Dad was home and set a bag of cookies on the TV set. Not long after, he left the house. He didn't come back for a week. Meanwhile, those cookies sat there. Me and my two brothers were starving. Eventually my oldest brother worked up the nerve to take some cookies. Days later, Dad came home. He demanded to know where his cookies were. None of us would tell on my brother. And so Dad whipped all of us. The beating was so bad, he broke my brother's arm.

These kind of things happened often, and they colored my view of God. I mean, I went to church every Sunday, but I had no concept of a loving God. The idea of his love made no sense to me. I'd hear people call him "God the Father," and I'd think, *If he's anything like my dad, we're all in a world of trouble.*

Intermission

* How could a bad earthly father affect someone's view of their heavenly one?

* What would a God like this guy's dad be like? Why would we all be in trouble?

* Think of a friend who has a rough life with his or her dad. Pray for that person right now. How can you help this friend see that God is a loving heavenly Father?

. . . the rest of the story

When I was twelve, everything changed. My dad was beating my mom one night. It was vicious. My brothers and I jumped in to defend her, but he threw us off. We couldn't take him. Instead, it made us realize that Dad just might kill us. So in the middle of the night, my mom took us all to live with my grandparents. We were finally safe.

Still, I wanted nothing to do with God. Basically I just partied my life away.

One day I asked a friend, "Dude, why don't you party?"

His response was simply, "God doesn't like it."

From that moment on, I couldn't stop thinking about God. It was crazy. I'd ask friends about faith and God. I read the Bible. I was just consumed with finding out what God was about.

Finally I just dropped to my knees and said, "God, do something with me. I am a mess."

After that day, I saw my heavenly Father in a whole new way. I realized that he loved and cared for me.

The strangest thing is that God has slowly changed even my view of my dad. I started praying for him, and over several years I found those once short and angry prayers changing. I used to be mad at him, but now I feel sorry for him. God has put a real love in my heart for my dad. He's also shown me how he can be the Father that an earthly dad never could be.

—Billy

DAY 161 Welcome to the family

You are all children of God by believing in Christ Jesus.
—Galatians 3:26 NIrV

And I will be your Father, and you will be my sons and daughters, says the LORD Almighty.
—2 Corinthians 6:18 NLT

Your Father knows what you need before you ask him.
—Matthew 6:8

Whatever you say or do should be done in the name of the Lord Jesus, as you give thanks to God the Father because of him.
—Colossians 3:17 CEV

Read these verses again

* This time, underline words and phrases that really stand out. What are these verses saying about you? About your heavenly Father? About God's Son?

DAY 162 Always There

And when you go
to cry by yourself
think of me.
I love you
and I care about you.
If someone hurts you,
I'll make it better.
Don't fret, dear child,
I'm there for you.
There is no reason to worry.
Someday it will be OK.
One day it will be better.
When your face is finally dry,
notice,
I'm still here for you,
I won't leave you.
Ever.

—*Evelyn*

Memorize this

God told them, "I've never quit loving you and never will. Expect love, love, and more love!"

—Jeremiah 31:3 Message

DAY 163 A Dad Who Never Leaves

Magda's eyes were red. I could tell my new friend had been crying.

I wasn't sure why she was upset, but I decided to try and comfort her by talking about God's love. I sat down next to her on the couch and said softly, "You know, Magda, in Psalm 139 it says that God knew you before you were even born. He has always loved you, and he wants to be your heavenly Father."

A troubled look came across her face at the mention of "father." After that, I don't remember much of what either of us said. She just seemed to be in so much pain and very troubled by something. A few days later, I found out why.

Magda handed me a long letter that explained so much. She wrote about her parents' divorce and how hurt she felt when her dad left. She said she had a hard time thinking of God as a loving Father because she felt so abandoned and betrayed by her own father.

I know it took a lot of courage for her to write that letter. She was being so honest and open. After that I did everything I could to show her the love of God. And when it seemed right, I tried to explain that God is the kind of loving, caring Father who would never, ever abandon her.

—Jennifer

A letter home

* Write a letter to God your Father. Like Magda, you can explain your struggles and hurts. Or express your thanks or gratitude. Tell him about any fears or doubts. Just release the feelings you have for your heavenly Father. If you have trouble beginning, read Psalm 139 and use your reactions to it as a place to start.

DAY 164 A Father's Love

Derek Redmond, a British runner, was lined up for the 400-meter semi-finals at the Barcelona Olympics. The feeling had to be sweet. After all, four years earlier, Derek had to withdraw from the Olympics because of an injured Achilles tendon—just ninety seconds before the race was to begin.

But five surgeries later, Derek was ready to roll. The starting gun went off.

A hundred meters into the race, Derek crumpled to the track with a torn hamstring.

Paramedics rushed out to help him, but he refused their help, waving them aside. He struggled to his feet and started hopping, sometimes even crawling, determined to finish the race.

And then a big guy came charging out of the stands. He pushed a security guard aside, ran to Derek's side, and embraced him. It was Derek's dad.

With his arm around his son's waist, Derek's dad helped his son limp the rest of the way around the track.

The crowd was on its feet, cheering and weeping. Eventually Derek and his dad crossed the finish line together, arm in arm—long after the other runners had finished the race.

This story is such a vivid picture of the love of God, our Father in heaven. God will carry us all the way to the finish line.

—Mark

His father saw him and was filled with compassion for him; he ran to his son, threw his arms around him and kissed him.

—Luke 15:20

I am he who will sustain you. I have made you and I will carry you.

—Isaiah 46:4

DAY 165 What Was I Afraid Of?

Katie and I met my freshman year when we both played on the girls' basketball team. When we traveled to compete against other schools, we'd sit together on the bus and talk about everything—from our favorite candy to our interest in guys. But our times together never led to talking about what was most important in my life—my relationship with Jesus. I didn't want to risk losing her friendship, so I stayed silent.

* **Have you ever felt like this? How can you overcome this fear?**

. . . more of the story

As sophomores, we both made the tennis team. By this time, I felt the need to ask her about God. I still feared her response, but I cared about her life, especially her eternal life.

One afternoon, after finishing a tennis match at a rival school, we boarded the bus for the long trip home. I said a quick prayer and decided this would be a good time to bring up my faith.

I felt really awkward, but I started anyway. "What do you think about God?" I asked.

Katie looked surprised at my question. "No one has ever asked me that."

"Do you believe in him?" I asked gently.

"I believe he exists, but there are things I don't get," she responded. "I try to read the Bible, but sometimes I don't understand what any of it means."

As we talked, I found out Katie had heard many different opinions about what she should believe, and now she didn't know which was right.

"What do you believe, Ashley?" she asked.

I had asked a couple of friends what they thought about God, but that was usually where the conversation ended. This time, Katie gave me the chance to talk about my beliefs.

* **Look up Ephesians 5:15–16. How does this passage apply to this girl's story? How can it apply to yours?**

. . . the rest of the story

OK, God, here I go, I thought. "I believe God is perfect and he created us for a relationship with him," I began. "But because our sins make us imperfect, we're separated from him. That's why Jesus came. His death on the cross paid for our sins and restored our relationship with God." I noticed Katie was listening intently.

She stayed quiet for a long time. I asked, "Does this make sense? Do you have any questions?"

"Yes, it makes sense, and I don't have any questions right now," she said.

"If you ever have any questions about the Bible," I continued, "I'd like to help you understand."

"You'd really go through the Bible with me?" she asked.

"Absolutely."

Soon after that, the bus came to a stop and we were back at school. As I said goodbye to Katie, I thought to myself, *Why didn't I have this conversation before?*

It's been a year since that bus ride. I wish I could say Katie asked me to study the Bible with her. She hasn't. More than that, I wish I could say she's accepted Jesus. That also hasn't happened. But I'm glad I finally took a risk to share Christ with her. It didn't mess up our friendship. And now she knows what I believe and that I'm willing to answer any questions.

I'm not sure when I'll talk to Katie about my faith again. I do know that when the time seems right for another conversation about God, I won't be afraid to speak up.

—Ashley

DAY 166 4 Steps to Faith Sharing

An organization called Sonlife offers these four practical steps to sharing your faith:

1. I grow in my love for God; he gives me a heart for other people.
2. I build genuine friendships with people and get involved in their lives.
3. I start to involve my friends in my life and relationships that matter to me.
4. I include them in my community of faith and help them experience God.

* **Write down which step you think you're on.**

* **If you're not on step #4, write down three action steps that can help get you there.**

   1.
   2.
   3.

Think about this

Therefore go and make disciples of all nations, baptizing them in the name of the Father and of the Son and of the Holy Spirit.

—Matthew 28:19

DAY 167 I'll Never Give Up on Patrick

One Wednesday night of my sophomore year, my non-Christian friend Patrick sat quietly next to me during our youth group discussion. After my youth pastor introduced the night's topic, he encouraged us to ask questions and share our thoughts. Patrick didn't say anything.

After the meeting, Patrick told me, with an edge to his voice, "Eva, it's just not for me! Don't ever try to get me to come to your church or youth group again."

"But why?" I asked.

"Look, I didn't agree with the discussion, and I didn't feel welcome there. So just drop it."

I wanted to yell back, "You chose not to feel welcomed. It wasn't because you weren't welcomed by the group!"

Instead, I kept quiet. I decided not to bring up God for a while. In fact, I waited until the beginning of my junior year. But rather than talking, I decided to write my thoughts about faith in letters to Patrick. Doing this allowed me to get advice from my youth pastor. And I thought it would give Patrick time alone to think about what I had to say. I felt this approach would keep both of us from getting angry or defensive.

At school, I handed him my first letter and told him about my idea.

"I'll read what you have to say," he said. "But that doesn't mean I'm going to believe it."

Here's what I said to him in my first letter:

Thanks for reading this letter and being open to what I have to say. I care about you and want you to know why Jesus is so important to me.

I know even before I share about Jesus that you have questions about God's existence and how man ended up on earth. Well, imagine you found a perfectly working iPod in the dirt. Would you assume that the screen,

200

computer chip, plastic casing, etc., came together by chance to create this machine that plays your favorite tunes?

As Patrick and I wrote back and forth, he wasn't all that impressed by what I had to say. And he always argued that evolution was just as defendable as Christianity. Even so, his letters didn't seem angry or full of sarcasm.

Patrick and I wrote letters back and forth for about three weeks. When I figured I didn't have much more to say, I stopped writing.

These days Patrick and I spend most of our time together talking about stuff that's on our minds—and on occasion it has to do with God. The most important thing is that through my letters I had a chance to explain what I believe.

I do know one thing: God loves Patrick. I think he's patiently waiting for him to become one of his children, just as it says in 2 Peter 3:9. Verses like this one give me hope that God will continue to use my friendship and prayers to help Patrick come to Jesus.

—Eva

* Think about a friend who may be a lot like Patrick. Is there anything in Eva's story that can help you as you try to share Jesus with this friend? Even when friends are resistant to faith, why is it important not to give up on them?

DAY 168 The Ripple Effect

Fill your kitchen or bathroom sink with water. Drop an object like a rock or a quarter in the center of the sink. Watch the water closely for ripples that move out from the object.

How are those ripples like sharing your faith?

What can you do to make more "ripples" in your circle of friends?

Start the ripple

* 1. Write down the names of one or two friends you'd like to share Christ with. (If you can't think of any, ask God to bring those names to mind.)
* 2. Pray for those people right now. Pray that their hearts would be open to the gospel, that God would give you the right words to speak to them, and that your friendship would demonstrate the love of Christ to them.
* 3. Share these names with a few close Christian friends (like the members of your small group) so they can pray with you and keep you accountable for speaking up.

DAY 169 7 Reasons Not to Share Christ
(and Why We Should Go Ahead and Do It Anyway)

1. "I'm not smart enough." Fact: Jesus's disciples weren't known for their brains or theology degrees. They were pretty ordinary guys. Take the time Peter and John were telling a hostile crowd of religious leaders about Jesus. Acts 4:13 says, "Now when they saw the boldness of Peter and John, and perceived that they were uneducated, common men, they were astonished. And they recognized that they had been with Jesus" (ESV). Knowing Jesus is what matters. You are smart enough to tell others about Jesus because you have a friendship with him.

2. "I don't want to make anybody mad." Maybe you've been around Christians who are annoying. The way they act—all smug and self-righteous—can make non-Christians angry. So we keep quiet. Understandable. But look at Jesus: People crowded around him. People wanted to know and follow him. Why? He cared about hurting and lost people, listened carefully, and responded to their deepest needs. Now, he did occasionally make people mad. He was really good at ticking off religious know-it-alls. But it was the message that ticked off people, not the messenger. Sometimes the truth hurts. So it's OK if people get a little mad sometimes—as long as it's the true message of Jesus that upsets them and not the obnoxious messenger.

202

3. *"My friends will make fun of me."* You'd be surprised at how often people will respect you for your beliefs. They might not understand why you don't drink at parties and avoid dirty jokes, or why you like youth group. And you might hear an occasional "fanatic" or "religious nut." But people often find genuine faith pretty interesting—confusing, but interesting. They might even respect you for your strong convictions.

4. *"None of my Christian friends do it."* Ever talk to your friends about why they don't witness? There could be a ton of reasons. Maybe they're just not sure how to witness. Why not use what you're reading here to get the conversation going?

5. *"I'm not a very good Christian."* You're a believer, but you don't pray or read your Bible as much as you should. And you sin. Every day. So why should you tell other people about Christ? Fortunately, being a believer isn't about getting it right. It's about God's love and forgiveness. Does this mean you can act however you want? No. But you don't have to be perfect to share Christ. Instead, tell your friends, "I'm sure not perfect. That's why I need God's forgiveness." Chances are, your friends will appreciate your honesty.

6. *"All of my friends are Christians."* It's great to have good Christian friends. But we also need to, as Jesus put it, "go and make disciples of all nations" (Matt. 28:19). We can't do that if we don't have any non-Christian friends.

7. *"I don't even know where to start."* Why not start by inviting a non-Christian friend to your youth group? At least invite a non-Christian to take in a movie with you and your Christian friends. When the subject of faith comes up, talk about why you're a Christian and how God helps you live life. Just be honest, be real, and be you—you might be surprised at how much God can use you to reach out to others.

—Chris

> * *Identify* any of the reasons you've used not to share Christ. Write them on a sheet of paper, and put the paper in a place where you'll see it often. Use it as a reminder that those reasons actually *aren't* good reasons not to share Christ.

DAY 170 How Do I Witness to My friend?

Q: *My best friend and I have been friends for five years. I'm a Christian and she's not. I really care about her, and I want her to get to know Jesus. Every time I try to talk to her about Jesus, she gets offended and gives me the cold shoulder. She says my beliefs are offensive to her. How can I talk to her about God's truth when she won't listen?*

—Anonymous

Your turn

* **How would you answer this question?**

How IYF's expert answered:

A: To be honest, the gospel of Jesus Christ is offensive to many non-Christians. After all, Jesus said, "I am the way and the truth and the life. No one comes to the Father except through me" (John 14:6). If you aren't following Jesus, that's not very good news.

My guess is you'll need to communicate your faith through actions and commitment instead of words. The apostle John said it best when he said, "Dear children, let us not love with words or tongue but with actions and in truth" (1 John 3:18). If I were you, I would maintain a strong friendship with this girl and realize that your witness might take place over years of shared experiences.

Even though she may not say it, your friend is watching you and listening to you. She is forming her opinions about Christianity based on what she sees in you and other Christians.

That doesn't mean you have to be perfect. Too often, Christians think they can be good witnesses only if they act like they never struggle or fail. But nothing is further from the truth. Christians stumble all the time. That's why we so desperately need God in our lives every day. If you make a mistake, let your friend see you deal with your failure, ask for forgiveness, and move on with God's help. That honest expression of faith can often say more to a non-Christian than any sermon.

Let me also mention two cautions. As I said, it's natural and perfectly acceptable for you to talk about the things God is doing in your life. But don't try to convince your friend that she needs to accept Christ as her Savior right now. While that's part of the truth she needs to hear someday, it's clear she isn't yet open to the gospel.

My other caution is this: don't go it alone. Make sure you have solid Christian friends surrounding you to keep you strong in your own life. If you're not already, get involved in your church youth group or a Christian club at your school. Talk to your youth leader about your friend and ask him or her to pray with you periodically. And if your parents are Christians, include them in your witness to your friend.

You may never see the fruit of your efforts to share Christ with your friend. But trust that God is using you right now to help her find the way, the truth, and the life.

—Jim

DAY 171 Don't Give Me Jesus . . .

Don't give me Jesus,
if giving me Jesus means
telling me about your beliefs,
then walking away.

Don't give me Jesus,
if giving me Jesus means
judging me by appearance,
but never trying to see who I really am.

Don't give me Jesus,
if giving me Jesus means
you're right no matter what,
and I'm wrong no matter what.

Do give me Jesus,
if giving me Jesus means
walking beside me just like
Jesus walked beside
lepers and losers.

Do give me Jesus,
if giving me Jesus means
listening more than talking.

Do give me Jesus,
if giving me Jesus means
laughing with me when
I need to laugh,
and crying with me when
I need to cry.

Do give me Jesus,
if giving me Jesus means
letting me know when
my actions are harmful
or destructive.

Do give me Jesus,
if giving me Jesus means
being my friend.

If you give me Jesus
wrapped in your friendship,
I may be more ready to listen
to what you have to say.
                                            —*Anonymous*

A friend loves at all times.
                    —Proverbs 17:17

DAY 172 Tighty Whitey Worship

Sometimes during worship I'll be singing my heart out . . . really loud . . .
right after everyone stops singing. *Idiot!* And so I nervously look around
to see who noticed. During the next song I'll sing more quietly. Or not
at all. I'll get so focused on what people might be thinking that I'm no

longer focused on God. That's why I like to read (and reread) a crazy story from the life of David.

The story starts in 2 Samuel 5. In the beginning of his reign as king, David had planned to bring the ark of the covenant back to God's city—Jerusalem. (Remember the thing from the old Indiana Jones movie that melted Nazis' faces off? It's that . . . minus the drippy-faced Nazis.) The ark was Israel's most sacred possession. It was a symbol of God's presence. So in 2 Samuel 6:1–2, David and his men traveled to the house of Abinadab, who had been keeping the ark safe and sound in his basement for thirty years.

David and his men couldn't hold back their excitement. They'd hardly crossed the street with the ark when the celebration kicked in and they were breaking out the piñata and partying.

Throughout the journey back to Jerusalem, David worshiped God with all of his might (2 Sam. 6:14–15). This was full-body, no-holds-barred worship. It's such a beautiful image . . . if you leave out one little part of the story. David was getting his praise on wearing nothing more than a linen ephod, a sleeveless undergarment that came down to about the hip. It was essentially nothing more than his underwear. It's a powerful picture, if not a little bizarre. A world leader, dancing and singing in front of all of his people, in his underwear.

Why does the Bible tell us about David's ephod? Because it shows that David worshiped God with complete abandon, with complete disregard of how he looked or what others thought, including his wife Michal. She was very offended that a king would be seen dancing around in his underwear. But David didn't care how he looked. His primary concern was worshiping God. David told his wife, "I will become even more undignified than this, and I will be humiliated in my own eyes" (2 Sam. 6:22).

I would love to live that way. I long to be so connected to God that everything else seems insignificant. I long to be so free that the only voice I care to hear from is God's. I long to care less about the things of this world and more about the things that are on God's heart.

Intermission

* *Ask* . . . God to help you worship him with complete abandon.

* *Confess* . . . those times you've let what others might think get in the way of all-out worship.

* *Offer praise* . . . for a God who is worthy of total devotion and uninhibited worship.

. . . the rest of the story

When was the last time you broke out in a happy dance for God? When was the last time you sang your guts out in worship of him? Or laughed out loud with joy, or cried your heart out to God, or raised your hands in praise, or sat in silence and stillness? When was the last time you expressed your faith and could care less about what people think? Not that you should bust out the linen ephod. But instead of worrying about how you're dressed, or how you sound, or what others might think, maybe it's time for you to worship like David did—uninhibited, unashamed, and utterly in love with God.

—Jarrett

DAY 173 His Song

Lord, too many times
I feel sorry for myself
and get caught up
by dead-end thoughts.
I believe lies and feel afraid.
Depression,
oppression,
and obsessions
cloud my vision . . .

But then suddenly,
you bring a song to mind,
and I can't help but sing it.
Then another comes—
and another.
You remind me of songs

about your goodness—
songs filled with truth
and hope.
Songs that put my eyes
back on Jesus—instead of
the stresses of my life.

Thank you, Lord,
for the wonder of music
and the joy of singing songs.
—*Elaine*

DAY 174 Soak in the Music

I will sing to the LORD, for he has been good to me.
—Psalm 13:6

Grab your iPod

* Listen to one of your favorite worship songs at least three times. Let the truths in the song sink deep into your thoughts and wash away your worries.

Let worship ring

* Why not download a worship song as your ringtone? That way you'll be reminded of the rich truths in this tune each time your phone rings.

DAY 175 What Worship Isn't

Back before he was writing and singing worship music, Todd Agnew didn't connect with the old hymns he sang in worship services. Then the summer before eighth grade he went to church camp and heard worship music more his style. As he and his friends sang powerful, guitar-driven praise songs, Todd felt something he'd never experienced.

209

"I felt closer to God during those services than I had before," Todd says. "I decided the difference must be the music. I assumed that singing old hymns in church wasn't really worship because it didn't affect me emotionally. I didn't feel anything, so I thought God was only working through new, exciting praise songs."

By the time he was nineteen, Todd felt God calling him into music ministry. He traveled to different churches to play moving, emotional praise songs he wrote to express his feelings about God.

One weekend, he was playing for a church in the middle of nowhere in Oklahoma. He was disappointed when he saw he was at least forty years younger than anybody else. "The bulletin read like the greatest hits of the church: 'Amazing Grace,' 'How Great Thou Art,' and 'Victory in Jesus,'" he says. "I was like, 'Oh, this is going to be so boring. This isn't going to be active worship at all.'"

But Todd was wrong. The congregation worshiped God with passion. "Man, did they express their affection for the Lord through these old hymns," Todd says. "That was eye-opening for me. I had judged the old hymns as boring and ineffective, but God was saying, 'No, what matters is they love me and they're saying that.' I realized worship is never about what kind of music you're singing—it is about an encounter with the almighty God. You can do that with whatever song you're singing. And I learned that those old hymns are very important for Christians because of what they express."

Soon after, Todd happened to read Romans 12:1: "Therefore, I urge you, brothers, in view of God's mercy, to offer your bodies as living sacrifices, holy and pleasing to God—this is your spiritual act of worship."

As he mulled over the truths of the verse, he thought, *Worship doesn't have anything to do with music at all!*

"I realized God is after my heart," says Todd. "And since that is true, not only do the specific songs not matter, but there doesn't need to be any music at all. If worship is about pleasing God with our hearts, then he wants our hearts worshiping him all the time. Worship isn't about singing or feeling good. It is in everything I do. It is pleasing God."

—Quentin

What's God-pleasing worship?

If worship does not change us, it has not been worship. To stand before the Holy One of eternity is to change. Worship begins in holy expectation; it ends in holy obedience.

—Richard Foster, Christian writer and speaker

DAY 176 5 Ways to Connect with God

1. Pray with somebody. Read Mark 14:38—even Jesus realized prayer took some effort. And while we need private prayer times, we also need the prayerful support of others. So, ask a friend to meet with you once a week during lunch or after school. Share issues in your life and pray for one another. It might feel a little awkward at first, but it will get better with time—and you'll get closer to God and to each other.

2. Unplug. Every once in a while, unplug all your tech toys. Video games, TVs, cell phones, iPods, Internet—everything. (The world won't end, I promise.) Use this unplugged time to read the Bible. Or just sit quietly, allowing God to speak to your heart without all the normal distractions.

3. Memorize Bible verses. Why? Because God's Word "exposes our innermost thoughts and desires" (Heb. 4:12). And Psalm 119:9 says we can keep ourselves *pure* by obeying God's Word. When we memorize Scripture, we have it ready when we need it. It's in our heads, helping us make good decisions and helping us reflect on God's promises. Pick a favorite verse and write it on your mirror with a dry-erase marker. Whenever you look in the mirror, repeat the verse in your head. When you've memorized it, put up a new verse. Why not start with Hebrews 4:12 and Psalm 119:9?

4. Do something nice . . . in secret. When we do nice things for others without them knowing, we keep ourselves from becoming arrogant or from needing the approval of others. So why not write an anonymous note of encouragement to someone and put it in his or her locker? Or maybe leave a small gift for a teacher or friend? You can also pray for someone without them knowing it. Whatever you do, do it for God. He's watching and he's pleased with your selfless and secret acts of kindness (Matt. 6:1–6).

5. *Live it up!* Life in Christ is the best thing around, so celebrate it! And there are many ways to celebrate—dance in the sunshine, sing a song to him, take photos of his beautiful creation, write a poem, paint a picture, share a delicious meal with friends, play basketball, laugh! Whatever you do, do it as a way to praise and thank God for the great gift of life.

—Ann

DAY 177 I'm Stressed about Worship

Q: I love the Lord, but when it comes to worshiping by singing in public and raising my hands, I get so nervous. I do want to praise God, but I just feel like everyone is staring. How can I get over that?

Your turn
* How would you answer this question?

How IYF's expert answered:

A: First of all, you can definitely love and praise the Lord without singing in public or raising your hands. God understands we each will worship him differently—he made us that way! The key is to find ways to express your love to God and draw yourself closer to him.

One of the most helpful Scriptures to me is John 14:21: "Whoever has my commands and obeys them, he is the one who loves me. He who loves me will be loved by my Father, and I too will love him and show myself to him." The important part of loving God is being as obedient to him as we possibly can be. That is true worship: showing our love for God and getting to know him better.

If singing in public or raising your hands is uncomfortable for you, don't do it. And don't worry that you're not worshiping "right." God wants you to worship him in your way. Besides, it sounds like doing these things adds stress and distracts you from the reason we worship God in the first place. If you're curious about this style of worship, try it in your private times of prayer or worship. Eventually it may feel natural to raise your hands and sing in public. But if that doesn't happen, God knows you're still worshiping him—not by your hands but by your heart.

—Jim

DAY 178 Another Boring Talk?

I sat near the middle of the room as the worship band hit a guitar chord and asked us to stand. Eventually I got up, stuck my hands in my pockets, and stared blankly toward the front of the room.

When the worship time ended, Sam, the special speaker for our retreat, walked to the front of the room. I braced myself for a long and boring talk. But for some reason, Sam immediately caught my attention. Maybe it was his cool personality. Or maybe it was the great stories he told. Whatever the reason, he was anything but boring.

I don't remember everything Sam said during that first talk. I do know he challenged us to live for God. He also stressed that our day-to-day actions were ways to worship God.

After Sam ended his talk, I found myself singing pretty loudly during the closing worship time. When the session ended, I wasn't ready to go yet. And it was like that for the whole retreat.

Throughout the retreat, Sam kept relating God and worship to our daily lives. Whether we're doing chores around the house or hanging out with friends, he said, we should try to act in a way that would make God happy.

I want my life to make God happy to know me, I thought. *I want to live in a way that will bring a smile to his face.*

During his closing talk, Sam said something like this:

"Don't let what's happened here slip away in a week. Don't go back to your normal life. Live for Christ every single day."

I must admit that it would have been easy to just let the excitement of the retreat die away and go back to my "normal life." So shortly after the retreat, I got into a small group with some other guys who were also serious

213

about living for God. We did devotions together. Our group leader, Nate, showed us how to make the Bible more real in our lives. We supported each other through tough times and just had a lot of fun together.

It's been a couple of years since that retreat and my life hasn't been the same. I don't mean to say that I'm somehow perfect. There are plenty of times I don't live like I should.

But I am different. I don't fight with my older brother nearly as much as I used to. I also find myself wanting to share God's love with others. Awhile back, I was kicking a soccer ball around the church parking lot with some of my friends. I noticed this kid standing all by himself. So I kicked the ball his way and encouraged him to kick it back. He did. It didn't take long for him to join us.

Before attending that retreat where Sam talked, I don't think I would have even noticed a kid standing all by himself. But now it comes kind of naturally.

Worshiping God is really important to me. It keeps me on track. It helps me do the right thing and make better choices. And I really do believe that each act of worship brings a big grin to God's face. What could be better than making God smile?

—Andy

Imagine . . .

* Imagine that God is looking down at you. He has a great big grin on his face. Why would God be smiling at you like that? What are you doing that would make God so happy? Now turn your imagination into action—and put a real smile on God's face.

DAY 179 Let the Eye Have It

So if your eye—even your good eye—causes you to lust, gouge it out and throw it away. It is better for you to lose one part of your body than for your whole body to be thrown into hell.

—Matthew 5:29 NLT

If I had taken Matthew 5:29 literally early in my Christian life, I'd have been blind before I turned fourteen. I admit I have looked at a few girls and haven't had the best of thoughts.

I don't think I'm alone. It's an easy trap to fall into.

Fortunately, I've never taken this verse literally. But there was an early Christian who did. His name was Origen. He didn't want anyone to even suspect that he was lusting after women. So he cut off the part of his body that, well, would guarantee he could never have sex.

Now, Origen was mostly a very wise theologian. But the church has never believed this is what Jesus meant. Instead, the church has always taught that Jesus was simply exaggerating to make a point. You and I use hyperbole all the time.

For instance: "I'll just die if he breaks up with me." Uh, probably not.

But we exaggerate to make a point more entertaining and forceful. Jesus exaggerated for the same reasons.

First, Jesus exaggerated to make sure we're hearing him. It's his way of grabbing our attention. He's saying, "Listen up! Don't mess around with lust! You'll get carried away pretty quickly, and before you know it, you're living a life that's going to send you straight to hell."

Second, Jesus used exaggeration to make it very clear he wasn't joking around. He had to be clear because it's too easy to just ignore reminders to not mess with sin. For instance, another famous early Christian, Augustine, once wrote something like, "Lord, make me sexually pure, but not just yet!" That pretty much describes my attitude toward some of my sins. I know they're wrong, but I'm lazy about doing anything about them.

I have a friend, though, who did something about his temptations. He had such a terrible time staying off Internet porn that he stopped using the Internet. That's pretty radical, and not necessary for everyone. But he realized that, for him, it was necessary; it was his way of plucking out an eye.

Not long ago, I sat at my computer and could feel more and more lustful thoughts battering my brain. I knew I could easily hop online and see things I shouldn't, so I emailed a friend and asked him to be my accountability partner. Through an Internet program I subscribed to,

215

he got to look at every website I visited. Less radical than canceling my Internet service, but it worked.

Whatever your major temptation, Jesus is saying, "Pay attention! Individual sins have a way of turning into habits. Habits turn into mega-habits. And mega-habits can so corrupt the soul that eternal disaster is the consequence."

—Mark

Now what?

* Whatever sin is a struggle for you, think of a practical step you could take today to halt temptation in its tracks. And then do what it takes to "gouge out an eye."

DAY 180 Stop the Actions, Stop the Thoughts

Dear friends, I urge you, as aliens and strangers in the world, to abstain from sinful desires, which war against your soul.

—1 Peter 2:11

Do not lust in your heart after her beauty or let her captivate you with her eyes, for the prostitute reduces you to a loaf of bread, and the adulteress preys upon your very life. Can a man scoop fire into his lap without his clothes being burned? Can a man walk on hot coals without his feet being scorched?

—Proverbs 6:25–28

Put to death, therefore, whatever belongs to your earthly nature: sexual immorality, impurity, lust, evil desires and greed, which is idolatry.

—Colossians 3:5

You have heard that it was said, "Do not commit adultery." But I tell you that anyone who looks at a woman lustfully has already committed adultery with her in his heart.

—Matthew 5:27–28

Reread all four passages . . .

* Underline anything that challenges you. Circle anything you don't understand, and then take your questions to your youth pastor. Choose one of these scriptures to memorize this week.

DAY 181 Everything but All the Way

When Ben and I started dating, we both agreed it was smart to save sex for marriage. But we never really talked about how far we would or wouldn't go.

After one long day of snowmobiling, Ben and I watched a movie alone in his basement. We snuggled close and started to kiss. And then we went further that day than ever before—all the way to oral sex. Afterward I felt gross. I left his house quickly, avoiding his mom's eyes.

We watched a lot of movies in the dark that winter. I often left Ben's house feeling guilty and dirty for what I'd done with him. But being Ben's girlfriend—feeling beautiful, experiencing the rush of physical pleasure, enjoying his attention—outweighed my shame.

It wasn't long before we broke up, but the damage had been done. I felt sad and anything but sexually pure.

One evening during a Bible study, the leader, Betsy, read Song of Songs 2:7: "Daughters of Jerusalem, I charge you . . . do not arouse or awaken love until it so desires."

She said there would be a time to be married—naked and unashamed—but God intends that kind of intimacy and vulnerability for married couples only. She also said that the point was not just staying a virgin but remaining pure. She challenged our standards of sexual purity, urging us not to ask, "How close to the fire can I get without being burned?" Instead, she said we should ask, "How far away from the fire can I stay?"

As Betsy talked, I realized that while I was rightly committed to virginity, I'd gone too close to the fire. I hadn't been following God's instructions on sexual purity. But then, Betsy said exactly what I needed to hear: "It's never too late to be washed clean of our sins, no matter what choices we've made in past relationships."

Over the next few weeks, I often read passages about confessing my sins before God, like these verses from Psalm 51: "Wash me clean from all of my sin and guilt. I know about my sins, and I cannot forget my terrible guilt. . . . Create pure thoughts in me and make me faithful again" (vv. 2–3, 10 CEV). I would read these passages and cry for a very long time, wondering if God could really forgive me.

In time, I cried out of joy because I knew God had forgiven me—even though I didn't deserve it.

—Katie

Wash me clean

* Take a minute to pray. Confess your missteps with lust, sex, and physical temptation. Pray the words of Psalm 51. Accept Christ's forgiveness. Thank God that you are now clean, new, and guiltless.

Faithful again

* After Katie confessed her sins and accepted forgiveness, she had to start over. She allowed God to help her change her thoughts, and she guarded herself in relationships by dating Christian guys with a similar commitment to purity and by drawing careful boundaries. As she says, "We drew the line pretty far away from the fire."

* If you have made sexual mistakes in your past, what do you have to do to walk in faithfulness again? What boundaries do you need to set? What temptations do you need to remove from your life?

DAY 182 My Daily Battle

Josh Schwartz, bassist for the band Seventh Day Slumber, always wanted to remain a virgin until marriage because the Bible calls for purity. But as a young teen, he realized that remaining pure physically was only part of the battle. God calls followers to be mentally and spiritually pure as well.

"You have to watch not only what you do, but also what you look at and what you think about," Josh says. "There's so much out there that can put thoughts in your mind."

He learned this difficult lesson while checking email one day. An Internet window for a porn site popped on-screen. "From that young age, I had a problem with pornography," Josh says. "I wanted to be pure before God, but everybody has weakness. This is something I have to be very careful about."

Porn in the Bible?

* Did you know that in the Old Testament, God tells Ezekiel about a woman whose lust is inflamed by pornography? It's true. It's in a section where God tells his people about two sisters (who represent Samaria and Jerusalem) with major sexual sin.

What God told Ezekiel

Oholibah [one of the sisters] saw images of Babylonian men carved into walls and painted red. . . . As soon as she looked at them, she wanted to have sex with them. And so, she sent messengers to bring them to her. Men from Babylonia came and had sex with her so many times that she got disgusted with them. She let everyone see her naked body and didn't care if they knew she was a prostitute. That's why I turned my back on her.

—Ezekiel 23:14–17 CEV

Weapons for the fight

In this Ezekiel passage, it's clear that what we see can lead to sexual sin. And for Josh, that temptation to find images online was so great that he asked Christ-following friends to keep him accountable and he limited his online time. He now has four "weapons" that help him win his battle against lust:

1. *Josh tries to spend time each day with God.* "The more you're in the Word and in prayer, the closer you get to God," he says. "There will always be temptations and trials. But if God is first in your life, he gives strength."

219

2. *Josh watches what's in his mind.* He says, "When things come into my mind that shouldn't be there, the only way I can stop them is to imagine God's hand grabbing the thought, pulling it out of my head, and throwing it away. You're gonna see things that tempt you. The trick is not letting yourself dwell on them."

3. *Josh tries to keep God first in his dating relationships.* "When you want to please God and do his will together, it's a lot easier to keep boundaries," he says. "It's important to talk about it. Sit down with the person you're dating and say, 'I want to live a lifestyle that's pure before God.'"

4. *Josh won't let guilt get him down.* "You're never going to be perfect or completely pure," he says. "You'll make mistakes, but God loves you no matter what. You can start over. I have. Again and again. It's only been through God's grace that I'm able to keep going."

—Todd

Now what?

* Which of these weapons would most benefit you?

* Why would using this weapon help you?

* What do you need to do today to start applying this weapon?

DAY 183 No Longer Alone

For months I felt God urging me to tell someone about the ugly stuff I privately wrestled with. In fact, everywhere I turned, I read or heard Christians talking about accountability partners. The problem: I had no idea what that really meant. Would it mean I'd have to tell someone that fantasies and masturbation had trapped me into sins like pornography, envy, lust, and selfishness?

Then one day—out of the blue—my friend Travis said, "So, my accountability partner is moving and I need someone to help me with stuff. I have a real problem with lust."

I exhaled with relief. "Really? You?" I said. "Me too. I feel like lust is controlling my life."

Travis nodded. "Well, I guess neither of us should be surprised," he said. "I need someone to ask me questions, push me, and keep me accountable to the life I want."

"So, that's what accountability partners do?"

"Yup," he said. "They're just devoted friends who talk about personal stuff. No one can follow Christ alone. So they team up to live out their faith and fight off temptation."

"Man, I've never had that," I said. "I used to think I didn't need anyone else—as if I could take care of my life myself."

Travis looked at me and said, "You can't. And you don't have to anymore."

Bible break

And let us consider how we may spur one another on toward love and good deeds. Let us not give up meeting together, as some are in the habit of doing, but let us encourage one another—and all the more as you see the Day approaching.

—Hebrews 10:24–25

Two are better than one, because they have a good return for their work: If one falls down, his friend can help him up. But pity the man who falls and has no one to help him up!

—Ecclesiastes 4:9–10

. . . the rest of the story

Travis and I agreed to meet once a week to talk about what was going on in our lives. I learned from Travis that accountability wasn't some complicated theological concept. Instead, it was merely about giving a trusted Christ-follower complete access to my life. I gave Travis full permission to get personal with me at any time in order to see how I was living—publicly and privately. He did the same. Back and forth, we'd challenge, support, and check up with one another.

I'd love to say Travis and I completely overcame lust. Didn't happen. Won't ever happen. Instead, Travis and I will always need a relationship like this. I love that I have Travis to help me remember my commitments to God. And I also love that God is using me in Travis's life.

And that's the bottom line: we're no longer alone. I used to feel like a single, thin thread that could be easily snapped by temptation. But now I like to think my thread is interweaved with those of Travis and God. That makes a pretty strong rope. As Ecclesiastes 4:12 says, "Though one may be overpowered, two can defend themselves. A cord of three strands is not quickly broken."

—Scott

DAY 184 I Want to Be Like Joseph

My problems with lust really started one night when I hit a couple of numbers randomly on my remote and was suddenly staring at slightly blurred images of naked bodies having sex. In that short period of time, I'd placed powerful images in my mind that would play over and over like a continuous instant replay.

I tried to stop dwelling on these memories. But then I'd go to that secret channel again. Or just be set off by a model in a commercial. Or maybe I would stare longer than I should have at a girl at school in a midriff-baring top or low-cut shirt. I'd find myself daydreaming about what I'd seen. Sometimes those images I tucked into my brain led me to masturbate. But whether or not I masturbated, I knew I'd let myself fall into sinful lust.

I agonized. I pleaded with God, "God, forgive me!"

During this time, I came to the incredible Bible story near the end of Genesis. In it, a young man named Joseph was sexually harassed by a powerful and probably very beautiful woman. She wouldn't leave him alone, yet he consistently ignored her advances. One time she approached him, grabbed him by his coat, and insisted, "Have sex with me!" He didn't try to reason with her. He didn't pause to think about whether he should or shouldn't hang around. His first impulse was to get out of there—and quickly. So he ran away without his coat.

To make sure I hadn't missed anything important, I reread the story. Then I prayed, "God, help me to be more like Joseph."

Still, I kept finding myself hounded by impure thoughts and wrapped up in guilt every time I strayed from what I knew was God's thinking on purity. Around this time, I heard an adult leader from the church speak. He said, "You need to ask God for forgiveness and then forget about it. After all, God forgets about it! There will always be sin in our lives, so don't dwell on it. Confess it, then move on and focus on prevention. But don't focus so much on what you shouldn't do. Instead, get rooted in God. Don't just run away from lust. Run toward God."

Everything became a bit more clear for me. I had to flee temptation like Joseph and run straight to Christ. By drawing closer to Christ, it was easier to distance myself from lustful thinking and actions. I came to realize that Jesus died not only for our sins but also for our guilt and shame. Up to that point, guilt and shame were like an enormous weight I dragged around wherever I went. But Jesus's death meant I didn't have to drag around that weight. What an amazing truth!

I must be honest and say that I haven't gained total control over lust. I don't believe that will happen until I get to heaven. But I'm doing much better than I was a few years ago. I'm becoming more like Joseph. God is answering that prayer.

Most importantly, God is changing my heart. And it really is about turning to God. When I fill my mind and my heart with thoughts of him and with the things he loves and desires, there really isn't room for much of anything else.

—Mark

Your thoughts

Whatever is true, whatever is noble, whatever is right, whatever is pure, whatever is lovely, whatever is admirable—if anything is excellent or praiseworthy—think about such things.

—Philippians 4:8

DAY 185 Thought Stoppers

Quote #1

I can't stop the birds from flying over my head, but I don't have to let them build nests in my hair.

—Martin Luther

Say what?

* How do you think this applies to lust and sexual temptation?

* How could you apply this quote to your life?

Quote #2

I made a solemn pact with myself never to undress a girl with my eyes.

—Job 31:1 Message

Say what?

* Why would it matter whether you undress someone in your mind—or have any kind of sexual thoughts—if you don't actually act on your fantasies?

* How do sexual thoughts devalue the person you're thinking about?

* How do those thoughts affect your relationship with God?

* What lustful or unhelpful thoughts or actions are hurting your attempts at godly, pure living?

Your pact

* I make a solemn pact with myself to never _____.

Next steps

* What can you do today to help yourself keep that pact? Who could help you?

DAY 186 Am I the Only One?

I crossed the room to my dimly lit closet and rummaged though my secret stash of paperbacks until I found the cover that showed a wild-eyed, barely dressed couple clinging to each other.

I turned to a graphic sex scene. Sexually excited by what I read, I locked my door. Then I masturbated for the first time.

I wasn't planning to have sex anytime soon. I had grown up in church and knew premarital sex was wrong. Still, I found myself drawn to thoughts about sex. After this first experiment, it became habit. I couldn't stop, and my thoughts got to the point where I no longer needed romance novels. There were plenty of sexual images and thoughts already stored there.

For a while, I wondered if I might be the only seventeen-year-old girl to do this and if maybe there was something wrong with me. Could my brain be wired funny, so that I thought more like a guy than a girl? As far as I knew, Christian girls didn't masturbate.

Looking in the Bible, I couldn't find the word "masturbation" anywhere. A good "you may" or "thou shalt not" from God would have been really helpful.

I looked at Christian books. They said masturbation wasn't good for me because of how it could trap me into sins like lust, porn, or coveting. This act could consume me with selfish thoughts that were not pure and healthy. What these books didn't say was how I could clean up my mind. I eventually found three things that helped:

1. *My friend Carrie asked to be my accountability partner.* Finally, I could talk freely with someone and learn that I wasn't alone. It's normal for girls to lust too. As we met weekly, Carrie asked me specific questions about whether or not I'd let my sexual thoughts run wild and control me.

2. *I took a second look at the Bible.* While it didn't say not to masturbate, many verses stress the importance of purity. Purity, I learned, was both the choice to be pure and the action of remaining pure. In the New Testament, the apostle Paul offered solid advice about how to choose purity: "Flee from sexual immorality" (1 Cor. 6:18). For me, "fleeing" meant tossing those romance novels.

3. I let go and let God. One Sunday morning, my pastor said, "God doesn't expect you to focus on your failures. Don't feel guilty. Don't feel dirty. God wants you to ask for forgiveness and then look to him for help."

While I was trying to be a good Christian, I overlooked the fact that being a Christian means focusing on Christ. I can't fix myself. But when I spend time with God—feeling his love for me—I see lust and masturbation for the empty imitations of love that they are.

These days I continue to stay away from romance novels, because they are just too much of a temptation for me. Even though I still deal with lustful thoughts and the desire to masturbate, I don't feel trapped anymore. God has set me free.

—Renee

True freedom

Jesus said, "If you hold to my teaching, you are really my disciples. Then you will know the truth, and the truth will set you free."

—John 8:31–33

* What does this passage say will set you free? Free of what?

* How can you apply this passage to your own struggles with lust?

DAY 187 Far from God

When I was thirteen, I was at my friend Tyler's house playing computer games. We clicked on what we thought was a game download, and our lives changed. It wasn't a game, but a video of a naked woman. We laughed nervously as if to say, "That's so stupid. Turn it off." But we didn't turn it off. We watched it. The next day, we did the same.

I bounced between feeling guilty and wanting to see more. Some days I was strong. Other days I was like a lustful porn addict looking for a fix. It's embarrassing to say, but when I looked at porn, these nude women made me feel loved. My eyes would feast on their skin and it made me feel like a man. For just one moment, I felt wanted. I felt pleasure.

But that moment of fulfillment would pass. Always. And in its wake I fought pounding waves of regret and guilt. I felt a million miles from good, a billion light-years from God. But I knew this wasn't true. I knew I was a Christian. And I knew God saw me as just as lovable as he saw his very own Son. I knew all this. Grace. Love. Forgiveness.

But I didn't feel it. And I grew more and more depressed and frustrated with myself. I'd promise myself over and over that I wouldn't mess up again, and I'd end up in the same exact place.

Eventually, I got involved in a group of believing friends who would talk honestly about our struggles with lust. I learned two huge lessons.

Lesson 1: Run away. One guy always said, "Alcoholics shouldn't live across the street from a liquor store." To me, that means I have to put space between me and porn. I can't walk alone into the magazine section of a store. Or use a computer alone without Internet filters. I can't have certain catalogs in my house.

Apply

* How could you apply this lesson to your life?

Lesson 2: I must increase my desire for God and decrease my desire for lust. Someone once told me that there are two dogs in my heart's backyard. One dog always craves pleasure, sin, and selfishness. The other dog craves justice, mercy, and obedience to God. Every day I choose which dog gets fed. The one I feed grows until the other dog can't even be seen.

I need to feed the right dog. I do that by having honest relationships with Christian guys and by reading the Bible and studying it with other people.

Apply

* How could you apply this lesson to your life?

On most days, the good dog outweighs the bad one. But the bad one surprises me every once in a while. He's the loudest when I'm not careful about avoiding temptation. So I flee. I get up and leave. And I pray: "God, help me do what's right today. Save me from pornography and make me closer to perfect. Make me love you more than myself and surround me with people who remind me that you love us even when we mess up. Surround me with friends and a church that feed the holy side of me and teach me how to starve the bad dog. Feed the good one. Amen."

—Shaun

Make it your own

* Write Shaun's prayer in your journal or on a sheet of paper to keep close at hand. If porn is not your struggle, replace that word with something that is. When you feel like your bad dog is winning, say this prayer.

DAY 188 Movie Heroes

* List five of your favorite bigger-than-life movie heroes—men and women who save the day.

1.
2.
3.
4.
5.

* Go back and add after each hero what traits and characteristics make them heroes.

Real heroes

* List five real-life heroes. They could be people you hear about or your own personal heroes.

1.
2.
3.

4.

5.

* Go back and add the traits and characteristics that make them heroes.

Compare

* What characteristics do your movie and real-life heroes share?

* How are they different?

* What makes someone a hero?

DAY 189 Portrait of an Everyday Hero

Recently, I realized that my definition of a hero can be a bit narrow. A hero doesn't have to run into a burning building or capture bad guys. No, everyday heroes possess many of the same traits as bigger-than-life movie heroes—but in more realistic ways. Here are five:

Trait #1: Bravery

Courage and bravery are all about boldly confronting fears and dangers without turning back. And, seriously, we're faced with dangers and fears every day: The danger of someone making fun of our weight or our acne. The fear of not being accepted.

Maybe bravery for you is refusing to believe what bullies say about you, and choosing to like the way God created you. Maybe boldness is sitting next to the kid everyone seems to hate. Maybe courage is living proudly and publicly for Christ. After all, Philippians 1:27–28 offers this challenge: "Whatever happens, conduct yourselves in a manner worthy of the gospel of Christ . . . without being frightened in any way by those who oppose you."

Trait #2: Sense of Justice

It is very easy to think that we surely cannot help solve the world's problems. They are just so big. But everyday heroes can make a difference.

After all, a twelve-year-old founded Loose Change to Loosen Chains (myspace.com/lc2lc) to fight modern-day slavery. Imagine what you can do. Maybe it's volunteering in your community. Maybe it's deciding not to spread rumors in your school. Whatever it is, it starts with praying for God to reveal injustice to you—and asking him how you can help bring about change.

Trait #3: Persistence

Persistence for an everyday hero means not surrendering—no matter the odds. It might mean not calling yourself a failure when you don't do well on a test or praising God even when he feels far away. Luckily, our strength to persist comes from God. "We don't give up. Our bodies are becoming weaker and weaker. But our spirits are being renewed day by day" (2 Cor. 4:16 NIrV).

Trait #4: Integrity

It's easy to lie to save our own skins or cheat here and there to get by. But integrity means doing the right thing no matter what. For Christians, that means trying to consistently live out the Bible. That may mean going against friends, feeling like the only one who's still a virgin, or being dubbed a "goodie-goodie" for not peeking at the test key on the teacher's desk.

Colossians 3:5–10 sets the bar for believers: "Put to death, therefore, whatever belongs to your earthly nature: sexual immorality, impurity, lust, evil desires, and greed, which is idolatry. . . . Rid yourselves of all such things as these: anger, rage, malice, slander, and filthy language from your lips. Do not lie to each other, since you have taken off your old self with its practices and have put on the new self, which is being renewed in knowledge in the image of its Creator."

Trait #5: Selflessness

Each of us will be called to give up something to follow God's amazing plan. As John 3:30 says, "Jesus must become more important, while I become less important" (CEV).

Recognizing what temptations, selfish desires, or dreams we have to give up—and actually doing it—is a heroic act. And it's something we have a great model for.

Philippians 2:5–7 says, "Think the same way that Christ Jesus thought: Christ was truly God. But he did not try to remain equal with God. Instead he gave up everything and became a slave, when he became like one of us" (CEV).

—Todd

DAY 190 Fearless Heroes?

In Acts 5, the apostles are beaten and forbidden from spreading the gospel. Here's how the story goes:

> They called the apostles in and had them whipped. The leaders ordered them not to speak in Jesus' name. Then they let the apostles go. The apostles were full of joy as they left the Sanhedrin. They considered it an honor to suffer shame for the name of Jesus. Day after day, they kept teaching in the temple courtyards and from house to house. They never stopped telling the good news that Jesus is the Christ.
>
> —Acts 5:40–42 NIrV

Read it again

* This time underline anything that really challenges you—any phrases that describe actions of the apostles that you don't feel you could do.

Prayer time

* Set an alarm to go off in three minutes. Go to prayer. Pray for faith, courage, and confidence—traits demonstrated by the apostles. Pray

about anything you underlined. Finish with thanking God for making his strength and fearlessness available to the apostles—and you.

DAY 191 Talking to the Shy Kid

"What're you guys doing over Christmas break?" my buddy Justin asked as a few of us walked from the food line toward our usual cafeteria table.

"Sleeping!" I replied. "And maybe a little skiing when I'm awake."

"Sounds like a plan!" my friend Tyler said.

Just as we were about to sit down, I noticed a guy who was sitting all alone in the far-off corner of the cafeteria, his head hung low like a scolded puppy. A part of me wanted to just enjoy my burger and ignore the fact that I spotted this lonely-looking kid. But for some reason I felt this pull, like God wanted me to reach out to this guy.

"I'll catch up with you guys later," I told my friends.

"Where you going?" Tyler asked.

"I've gotta take care of something," I answered. "See ya in class."

Tyler and Justin looked confused. Honestly, I felt a little perplexed myself. But I heard a distinct voice in my head telling me, "Nick, go sit with this guy."

I didn't really know what to say, but I figured God would provide the right words. So I set my tray down next to the kid and introduced myself. He looked at me funny, like he was trying to figure out what I was up to. I tried making small talk. Nothing. I cracked a couple of jokes but couldn't even get a half smile out of him. This kid wanted nothing to do with me.

What a waste of time, I thought. I was so sure God had a plan for me to help this guy out, but I guess I was wrong.

The next day as my friends and I headed to the cafeteria, they gave me a hard time for ditching them the day before.

"You gonna join us today?" Justin asked. "Or would you rather sit with your mute pal?"

I glanced over and saw the same guy sitting alone, his head still hung low.

Tyler could tell by the look on my face that it bugged me that I couldn't get through to the kid.

"Hey man, you tried," Tyler said. "What else can you do?"

Clearly my friends wanted me to let it go. But as I sat down at our table, I couldn't stop thinking about the kid in the corner. I still felt like God wanted me to reach out to him. So I stood up.

"You're kidding, right?" Justin asked, sensing where I was going. "Hey, if you wanna be on Nerd Patrol, go for it."

This time when I sat down at the table in the corner, I was met with a little less skepticism. The guy even told me his name: Austin. And then something amazing happened. Austin started talking! He told me how he'd just transferred from a school out in California. He said he really missed surfing. By the time the bell rang, I actually felt like I knew Austin a little bit. I also felt like I had helped make someone feel less alone. And I knew that pleased God.

—Nick

* List some heroic traits Nick showed in this story:

1.
2.
3.

* In what specific ways could you serve God confidently like Nick this week?

DAY 192 The Hero behind the Hero
(Todd's fake interview with a for-real Bible character)

A war hero—that's who I was told I'd be interviewing. But when I met this "hero," he didn't look like a mighty heroic warrior.

Q: *So, I hear you're a great war hero.*
A: Well, I'm no hero. I just did my part.
Q: *Your part? Kill dozens of men?*

A: No. I held a guy's arm in the air.

Q: What? That's it?

A: Well, you know, his arm got heavy.

Q: OK. I think we need to back up to the beginning.

A: Sure. After Moses led us out of Egypt, we were camping out in Rephidim. God was teaching us about trusting him. Honestly, not all of us trusted that God knew what he was doing. But Moses did. He had a lot of faith in God and tried to obey him, even when God's instructions seemed crazy.

Q: Let's get to the war. What happened?

A: Well, we were minding our own business, camping out and eating bread off the ground. And then the Amalekites attacked us. Moses sent this guy Joshua to lead our men in fighting. But not all of us went to fight. Instead, Moses told Joshua, "I will stand on top of a hill with the staff of God in my hands."

Q: What good did you think that would do?

A: I wasn't sure. But I knew Moses did some big stuff with that crazy walking stick of his. When we needed to cross the Red Sea, God told Moses, "Raise your staff and stretch out your hand over the sea to divide the water." Moses trusted God and did it. So I knew that God worked through Moses's faithfulness. So when Moses, his brother Aaron, and I went up on that hill, all I could do was just trust God had a plan.

Q: So what happened?

A: Well, like he promised, Moses stood on the hill with his arms up holding the staff. But then we noticed something weird about the battle. First we were winning. Then we were losing. And then we were winning again. It kept changing. Aaron and I realized that it all depended on where Moses's arms were. We were like, "Moses, quit moving!" Moses put his arms up, and once again the battle was going our way!

Q: So when did you save the day?

A: Oh, I didn't save the day. I just helped out. Moses had faith that God would protect his people in this war and held his arms up as part of

234

that faith. But have you ever held your arms up for an entire battle? It's not easy. Moses got tired, so Aaron and I each supported one of his arms. We kept his arms up until the sun went down, and God allowed us to win that battle.

Q: Your big moment in the Bible is that you held up an arm?

A: It's not about me. I just did what had to be done. It's hard to have big faith when it matters, and Moses did—but he couldn't do it alone. He needed someone to support him. And that's what Aaron and I did—helped a friend do what God called him to do. Behind every Moses, there is a faithful follower doing what needs to be done to help them follow God's will.

> *Read the real story:* Who is the real Bible character behind Todd's fake interview? Find out in Exodus 17:8–13.

Your turn

* In what ways are you Moses?

* In what ways are you the guy holding Moses's arm?

* How could you be a supportive hero to a friend this week?

DAY 193 Sidekicks Are Heroes Too

Supporting characters often bring comedic relief or heart to movies, but they are also literally supporting characters: they encourage, challenge, and love their main-character friends. The lead characters would be far less without their supporting friends beside them.

It's no different in real life. The Bible puts it this way: "Don't push your way to the front; don't sweet-talk your way to the top. Put yourself aside, and help others get ahead. Don't be obsessed with getting your own advantage. Forget yourselves long enough to lend a helping hand" (Phil. 2:3–4 Message).

If I had an award show for living out this verse, I'd definitely give out three big honors:

Best Encourager

This role is so simple and yet so often overlooked. In *The Lord of the Rings*, Sam Gamgee never allowed Frodo to be overcome by the weight of the ring. And when Frodo did get brought down by his burdens, Sam not only helped his friend carry those burdens, but he literally carried Frodo! That's what this kind of supporting role is all about.

When I was in high school, my girlfriend was in a terrible car accident eight hours away. My best friend was at my house within three minutes to pray with me and share Scripture about trusting God.

Of course, not all encouraging opportunities are that intense. Sometimes it comes down to simple things like reminding our friends they're OK the way they are. Hebrews 3:13 tells us to "encourage one another daily, as long as it is called Today, so that none of you may be hardened by sin's deceitfulness."

Best Truth-Teller

In the Batman movies, the Dark Knight is a great hero. But so is Alfred. Think about it: Alfred is a great mentor to Bruce by lovingly—but firmly—giving advice and pointing out Bruce's bad decisions. Like Bruce, we need truth-telling friends in our lives.

If I gave an award for Best Truth-Teller in the Bible, it'd go to Nathan. In 2 Samuel 12, God prompted Nathan to confront his friend King David about his secret sin. When David got the whole picture, he confessed and his entire life turned around, all because a friend was willing to speak the truth to him.

Are there people you know who are making seriously destructive choices while everyone around them remains quiet?

Best Display of Loyal Love

First John 3:18 says, "My dear children, let's not just talk about love; let's practice real love" (Message). What does this look like? It's a way of living that looks for opportunities to put others first and love them no matter what. We've seen characters do this a lot in the movies. But the biggest award winner for loyal love in the movies is none other than . . . Chewbacca from *Star Wars*. Really! He loyally stayed beside Han Solo, had his back in any situation, and gave him big furry hugs—just because he loved him.

How do you show your love to someone every day? You can begin right now by stopping and praying for three people in your life.

Seriously. Do it. Write down the names of three people and pray for them:

1.
2.
3.

Now, ask God to show you new ways to show his love to these friends. And then do whatever God says. It's a crazy idea, I know, but I think you might be blown away by how much God will support you as you play a supporting role in others' lives.

—Jarrett

DAY 194 What Is Faith?

Now faith is being sure of what we hope for and certain of what we do not see. This is what the ancients were commended for.

—Hebrews 11:1–2

Theologians define faith—as discussed in Hebrews 11—as "confident action in response to what God has made known." When viewed in this way, our genuine faith and trust in Christ become great heroic acts. In fact, Hebrews 11 lists several heroes of the Bible. Before recounting each hero's deeds, the writer clearly states that his or her accomplishments were by faith. For instance, Hebrews 11:11 reads, "It was by faith that even Sarah was able to have a child, though she was barren" (NLT).

Your turn

* What does it mean to live out a life of faith? How is that heroic?

* In what ways do you find faith difficult?

* How could you be more courageous in your faith?

DAY 195 What Am I Going to Be?

The other day, my English teacher announced to the class, "Today we're going to be talking about careers. And not just careers in general, but the career you would someday like to have. In fact, this will be the topic of your upcoming term paper. . . ."

For as long as I've attended school, I can remember teachers and other adults wanting to know what I wanted to do with my life. It seems like someone's always asking, "Rachel, what do you want to be when you grow up?"

"I want to be a bus driver!" "I want to be a nurse!" "I want to be a teacher!" "I want to be a pro basketball player!" My answer to the question changed a lot when I was younger. And that was OK, because being a grown-up was still a long way off. But now that I'm older, I need to think more seriously about the kind of career I want.

The problem is, I don't know what I want to be! It's frustrating. The adults in my life have expectations for me. They expect me to "make something of myself." You know, "become a productive citizen." Of course, I think that's important too. And as a Christian, I really hope my life will make some kind of a lasting difference.

But right now, as I think about my English assignment, my thoughts about the future are cloudy.

Can you relate to Rachel's confusion and frustration?

* Why or why not?

* What advice would you give her, or what Scripture would you point her to?

. . . the rest of the story

I do know one thing for certain: God really does have an ultimate plan and purpose for my life. As it says in Ephesians 1:11–12, "It's in Christ that we find out who we are and what we are living for. Long before we first heard of Christ and got our hopes up, he had his eye on us, had designs on us for glorious living, part of the overall purpose he is working out in everything and everyone" (Message).

As I think about those two verses, I realize a future career isn't nearly as important as living my life for Christ. So rather than worrying about what I'm going to be, God wants me to concentrate on who I really am and what my true values are.

Yes, I have to get busy and write that paper. But more importantly, I need to make sure I'm living out my faith one day at a time. If I'm doing that, I believe my future will work out just fine.

—Rachel

DAY 196 The Forgetful Felon (Todd's fake interview with a for-real Bible character)

I was supposed to meet my interview subject at noon for lunch. At about four, he finally showed up. He said he forgot. I was surprised he was so careless since he once had an important job for the ruler of Egypt.

Q: So you had a prestigious job?

A: I was Pharaoh's right-hand man.

Q: Really? What did you do?

A: Well, I drank stuff for him. But don't laugh. That's a big deal. He trusted me to drink everything that would cross his lips in order to check for poison. I was his closest adviser.

Q: But didn't he send you to prison?

A: Um, I don't remember that. Oh wait, yes. That was a big misunderstanding. He got angry with the baker and me and tossed us in the slammer.

Q: Didn't you meet someone interesting in jail?

A: Hmmm, I don't think so. Did I mention the baker was in there?

Q: Yes, you did. But you also met Joseph there, right?

A: Joseph? Not ringing a bell.

239

Q: *There wasn't a guy in there who interpreted dreams?*

A: Oh, Joe! Yeah, good guy. God gave him the ability to interpret this dream I had. In return, he asked me to tell Pharaoh he didn't deserve to be behind bars.

Q: *Did you?*

A: Ooh boy, I knew you were gonna ask that. Yeah, I helped Joe get out of jail, you know, eventually.

Q: *Eventually?*

A: Yeah, eventually. But, you know, I . . . well, I kind of forgot to do it for a little while.

Q: *A little while?*

A: Two years, OK? I said I forgot. Cut me some slack. When Pharaoh was no longer mad at me, he brought me back to work and, well, I forgot all about Joe. Two years later, Pharaoh had a weird dream and nobody could interpret it. I instantly remembered Joe.

Q: *What did you tell Pharaoh?*

A: I told him all about Joe. Pharaoh let Joe out of prison so he could tell him about his dream. Joe explained that God was revealing to Pharaoh what he was about to do in Egypt. It was amazing. He had such a great gift from God. And to think, my bad memory made Joe stay in the slammer for two extra years!

Q: *But obviously it turned out OK.*

A: That's true. I can see God's big plan now—allowing me to see Joe's gift and relay it to Pharaoh. After all, this plan allowed Pharaoh to prepare Egypt for the future and led Joe to become Pharaoh's second-in-command! God knew what he was doing. My flaws and mistakes didn't stop God from working out his will. In fact, I think God even used my flaws in his big plan for Joe. No one has to be perfect or do things "right." God's plans succeed because of his strength—not ours.

* *Read the real story:* **Who is the real Bible character behind Todd's fake interview? Find out in Genesis 40 and 41.**

DAY 197 If God Wills It . . .

If you could ask God three questions about his will for your life, what would they be? Would you want to know where you'll go to college? What kind of job you'll get? How much money you'll make? Would you ask him who you'll marry—or if you'll get married at all?

We wonder about God's will. But our questions sound like the kinds of things someone might ask a fortune-teller. Do we really want to know God's will? Or are we just curious about the future?

James has some harsh words for people who look toward tomorrow without thinking of God first. He writes, "Now listen, you who say, 'Today or tomorrow we will go to this or that city, spend a year there, carry on business and make money.' Why, you do not even know what will happen tomorrow. . . . Instead, you ought to say, 'If it is the Lord's will, we will live and do this or that'" (James 4:13–15).

That phrase, "If it is the Lord's will," really does make a huge difference. If I leave it out, I'm basically saying, "You just sit tight, God. I've got my life under control." But if I remember to include those words, I'm reminding myself and others, "Nothing is more important to me than the desires of God."

God cares about our tomorrows, of course. But he also cares a lot about how we live today. And to recognize where God wants to lead us tomorrow, we must work on our spiritual vision today. We can start with questions like: What is God's will for my temper? For my choices about sex? For my relationships? For my attitude toward church?

When we really think about the answers to these questions, we'll notice some areas in our lives that need to change. It might seem like those changes are too hard, or that God's will is just a big bunch of rules designed to take the fun out of life.

In truth, God's will isn't like that at all. Ultimately, God's will is that we love him. And because of who he is, loving him should be as natural as breathing.

So what is God's will for you tomorrow? It's the same as his will for you today: to follow him, to serve him, to love him. If you do that, the future becomes a lot clearer.

—James

241

Fill-in-the-blanks prayer

* God, I have so many plans for my life. Right now, I want to
_____ and _____ and _____. After
high school, I'd like to _____. And then I hope to
_____. I'd like to be successful in _____ and serve
you by _____. My real dream is to _____ and
to _____. I know you might have other plans for me; I give
you these hopes for my life, and ask you to help me follow your plan
for my life. Help me to remember that, whatever I end up doing, the
most important thing is that I'm seeking you first and loving you with
all my heart, soul, mind, and strength. Amen.

DAY 198 My Worries Drove Me Crazy

"This shouldn't be so difficult," I complained to my mom. "I don't know
why it's so hard to make this decision!" It was the fall of my senior year,
and I still didn't know which college I wanted to attend.

I'd visited three colleges that were a few hours from my home. I was
certain one of the schools would just "feel" like the right place for me.
It didn't happen. Even worse, I let my worries drive me crazy. I felt like
this one decision was setting the path for my whole life! The pressure
was just too much. Each time my parents even mentioned college I would
burst into tears.

Halfway through my senior year, I was still working through the pros
and cons of the three schools. I needed to make a decision soon, and I
was feeling really scared. My mom encouraged me to keep praying.

So I continued to pray that God would make the right choice clear to
me. I wanted so badly to do what was in his will for me. In spite of my
uncertainty and anxiety, I often found comfort and encouragement in
Philippians 4:6–7: "Do not be anxious about anything, but in everything,
by prayer and petition, with thanksgiving, present your requests to God.
And the peace of God, which transcends all understanding, will guard
your hearts and your minds in Christ Jesus."

As decision time inched closer and closer, I decided to revisit my top three schools. As we prepared to make one last college tour, my dad asked me to consider these schools from a new perspective. "Amanda, this time I challenge you to try to see each place through the eyes of someone who might live there," he said.

That change of perspective helped me get a better sense of where I would fit in—where I would feel most at home during my college experience. When I revisited one particular school, I felt like the community was a place in which I could thrive. I felt like I could relate to the students I met. I felt good about learning from the professors. After all those prayers, a lot of anxiety, and this second visit, I finally felt confident making my final decision. I believed that God was allowing me to feel peaceful about this place.

I had second thoughts when I went to freshman orientation the summer after graduation. I had some awkward moments because I didn't know anyone yet. But I just kept reminding myself that I believed God had led me to this school. I decided to focus on that instead of my feelings of discomfort and fear, and eventually I got past my shakiness.

Now I'm in my second year here, and I feel satisfied in my choice. I feel God's peace. As I look back to those anxious days of senior year, I think part of the reason I was so afraid was that I wasn't really focused on seeing God's plan for the future. But he guided me. I learned that I don't have to know the whole future to trust God. When I seek his will and trust that he'll listen to my prayers, I can rest knowing that he will give me the wisdom and courage to make wise choices.

—Amanda

Wise words from a wise guy

Your imagination makes things harder on you than God ever could . . . sometimes you become overwhelmed by events that have not yet happened. All moments are in God's hands. Walk humbly with God.

—François Fénelon

* *Write your own* wise saying about worrying about your future:

DAY 199 What's God's Plan for Me?

Q: I'm confused and unhappy with my life right now. I know God has a plan for everyone, but I don't know what that means for me. If I don't know what God wants me to do, how can I follow him faithfully?

—Anonymous

Your turn

* How would you answer this question?

How IYF's expert answered:

A: You're not alone. Many Christians struggle with trying to figure out God's will. However, the Bible is quite clear that we can learn much of his will from his Word. The Bible can show you the type of person you should marry; it will teach you about money, relationships, parents, friendships. . . . The list could go on and on. I would suggest you saturate yourself in the Word. Start reading the Bible and attending Bible studies to find out how to faithfully follow God.

Wise Christian friends can also help you learn what God wants you to do and who he wants you to be. Hang out with people who will challenge you to walk with God. That's how I learn the most, through those friends who help me stay close to God.

Jesus said in the Sermon on the Mount, "But seek first his kingdom and his righteousness, and all these things will be given to you as well" (Matt. 6:33). I think if you seek him with all of your heart, a lot of your confusion and unhappiness will go away. God doesn't always take away all our pain or confusion, but he does promise to walk with us throughout our lives.

—Jim

DAY 200 What God Says

Want to know God's will? Look to his Word. The Bible tells us it's God's will for us to:

meditate on his Word (Josh. 1:8)
do what he requires (Mic. 6:8)
seek him first (Matt. 6:33–34)
remain in him (John 15:4–5)
give him everything (Rom. 12:1–2)
care about others (Phil. 2:3–4)
focus on Christ (Col. 3:1–3)
be joyful always (1 Thess. 5:16–18)
submit to authority (1 Peter 2:13–15)

* *Look back* over this list. Identify any way you might not be acting in accordance with God's will right now. Write down ways you can improve in those areas:

* Now *ask God* to give you the strength to put those ideas into action.

DAY 201 Worried about My Future

I slowly flipped the page in my photo scrapbook, hoping to somehow freeze time.

There was Katie, her hair tangled with cookie dough after a baking party gone bad. Erik, with dreadlocks, holding his electric guitar. Laura, crumpled on the ground in laughter.

Looking through my memory book had become almost a nightly habit. The closer graduation got, the more I realized how much I'd miss all my school friends. I also feared all the change that would come after I walked down the aisle to receive my diploma . . . and headed to a new world filled with so many scary unknowns. Fear soon turned into feelings of sadness and loneliness.

As tears welled up in my eyes, I decided not to simply stare at the ceiling until I drifted off into a restless sleep. I decided to call Laura—my friend whose upbeat attitude and fun-loving spirit always cheered me up.

"Laura!" I blurted out as soon as she answered the phone. "What if I don't make any friends next year? What if I choose the wrong major and have to start over again? What if I fail?"

"First of all," Laura said, "you are not going to fail! And of course you're going to make friends! I know next year is kind of scary, starting over from scratch and not having your parents around to always help you out. But don't think of starting a new chapter in your life as a burden. Try to think of it as an adventure!"

"But am I going to make it? Am I going to succeed at anything?"

Laura was silent for a moment, as if she was making sure she said the right thing. Knowing my friend, she was probably praying for God's help. Finally she spoke.

"Don't try to figure out the rest of your life right now. Take one day at a time. Yeah, you might have to change majors in a few years, maybe it will take you awhile to make friends, but a little challenge will be good for you."

"Why are you so sure?"

Then Laura quoted Colossians 3:23, a verse she'd heard me quote to her many times: "Whatever you do, work at it with all your heart, as working for the Lord, not for men."

"So?" I asked, failing to see how the verse connected to my current situation.

"Nothing else matters, as long as what you're doing is for God. Even if you don't have your new friends already lined up outside your door, and even if you don't know what your major will be, you do know one thing. Whatever you do, you'll be doing it to glorify God."

"Thanks, Laura," I said, wishing I could give my caring friend a big hug. Feeling a lightness I hadn't felt all evening, I smiled to myself and continued. "Oh, one more thing, Laura. If I don't make any friends, I'm going to call you every night to complain about it."

"Right, if you don't make friends," she said. "It's a deal."

—Allison

* *Go back* to the story and reread Colossians 3:23. What is the "whatever you do" in your life? Make a list of as many things as you can think of—general things like school, job, relationships, youth group, sports, clubs, rest; and specific things like riding your skateboard backward, spending money on clothes, drinking chai tea in the morning, and teasing your younger brother.

* *Ask God* to help you glorify him in those things.

DAY 202 A Famous, Faithful Follower . . . and You

If we want to ponder the will of God, it's good to think about Abraham, because he played such a pivotal role in what God wanted to do in the world. And we learn quite a bit about Abraham in Genesis. We know he struggled and doubted, just as we do. But we also know he was a person of great faith, just as we can be.

Skim chapters 12 through 25 of Genesis. Stop and read more carefully when something about Abraham's experience catches your attention. Now, having the whole story of his life in front of you, what do you think was God's will for Abraham's life? (Hebrews 11:8–19 will give you some clues.)

Think again about Abraham's experience. What were his challenges? What might have caused him to doubt or to feel confusion about God's will? What did God want most from Abraham?

Now ask yourself the same questions. What are your challenges? What makes you doubt? What does God want most from you right now?

247

DAY 203 | I Believed All the Put-downs

"Hey chubby," Dan said as he strutted by my desk.

Not again, I thought. Every day of seventh grade was the same. It was impossible to escape Dan's put-downs. Others teased me, but Dan's comments were the worst. They were constant reminders of something I didn't like about myself: I was overweight. I was also awkward and often the last one picked during gym. Although I wasn't religious, I prayed God would change the way I looked. But God didn't seem to be listening.

Can you relate to this story?

* When it comes to how you look or feel about yourself, what are your personal struggles?

. . . the rest of the story

One day, a guy named Tim came up to me. Although he went to the church my family attended, I didn't really know him.

"Do you want to come to youth group?" he asked. "We're hoping more guys from your grade will join. It'll be fun."

I was hesitant, but I gave it a try. As I walked into the youth room one night, the youth pastor greeted me with, "Hey, I'm Jason! I'm really glad you're here." Everybody was nice and friendly. After that night, I attended every Sunday.

One week I was talking to Jason about school and sports. During the conversation I blurted out, "I wish I could play basketball."

Jason said, "Being on the basketball team won't make you happier. It has to be about God, not the way you look or what sport you play." I couldn't stop thinking about Jason's comment. I wondered, *Could I find real happiness with God?*

I got my answer during an all-guy sleepover at Jason's house. He and I talked until two o'clock in the morning. Before the sun came up, I'd asked Christ to forgive my sins and change my life.

My life did change. While Dan didn't stop saying mean things, his words didn't hurt quite as much. And the more I grew in my relationship with Jesus, the more my self-confidence grew. I'll never be athletic. I'm

OK with that. God has given me other gifts and abilities, like playing the guitar. I'm now on our youth group's worship team.

Sometimes I'll look in the mirror and find things I don't like about myself. But then God gently reminds me he really loves me for who I am.

—Scott

> * Think about Scott's relationship with God and Scott's self-image. How can one affect the other?

DAY 204 In God's Eyes . . .

On one side of the list below are declarations of who you are in God's eyes. The other side lists where that truth is found in Scripture. Read the listed verses and then draw a line to the declaration that sums up what it says.

I am God's child.	Philippians 3:20
I am Jesus's friend.	1 John 1:9
I am a whole new person with a whole new life.	Ephesians 2:5
I am a place where God's Spirit lives.	Galatians 3:26
I am God's incredible work of art.	Matthew 5:13
I am totally and completely forgiven.	John 15:15
I am created in God's likeness.	Ephesians 4:24
I am spiritually alive.	Matthew 5:14
I am a citizen of heaven.	Ephesians 2:10
I am God's messenger to the world.	Romans 5:8
I am God's disciple-maker.	Acts 1:8
I am the salt of the earth.	1 Corinthians 6:19
I am the light of the world.	2 Corinthians 5:17
I am greatly loved.	Matthew 28:19

DAY 205 I Felt Like a Nobody

During her sophomore year of high school, Tricia Brock switched to a new school where it seemed as if every girl was beautiful. *How'd they grow up so quick?* she wondered. Tricia, now the lead singer for Superchick, worried that something was wrong with her.

Even worse, her school was full of cliques. She felt like a nobody. All she could do, she says, was say a simple prayer each day: "God, I need you to make me beautiful on the inside because I don't feel like I measure up to these girls."

As time went by, Tricia began to realize something about the girls she envied. Although they seemed to have it all together, many of them actually hated themselves. Some slept around to gain self-worth. Tricia no longer envied these girls and their troubled lives. In fact, she wanted to help them. But how?

Eventually, she just started reaching out to anyone she could. "I would be friends with the wild kids, the kids who got picked on, everyone," she says. "God brought people into my life who said they didn't have any friends. I still have a letter saying, 'I really wanted to kill myself that year, but you came to our school and became my friend. I didn't even think I was worth being anyone's friend.'"

By just being a friend, Tricia found a way to talk with others about their troubles. Now, as part of a Christian band, she still has many opportunities to talk to people who are hurting—and every day she takes time to ask God to help her make the best use of her opportunities.

—Todd

Your turn

* Do one of the following:

 Write a letter, email, or Facebook message to someone who's encouraged you or been your friend when you were hurting. Thank them for being there or for speaking kind words to you.

 Write a letter, email, or Facebook message to someone who needs encouragement and needs a friend. Let them know they're valued and loved by God.

DAY 206 Ugly Me

From junior high through high school, I can't remember ever looking in the mirror and being happy with what I saw.

I compared myself to other girls—girls who were thinner, prettier, smarter. I had curly hair; everyone else had straight hair. I played tennis and the cello; the "popular" girls played basketball and the clarinet. I was a good friend, a decent student, and a fun person, but those things weren't enough to boost my sagging self-esteem.

What really clinched my whole self-image problem was the nonexistence of romantic attention from guys. I had great guy friends who didn't want to date me. I was smart and funny and could attract all the friends I could ever want. But I didn't get dates because, I thought, I didn't look quite right.

I felt horrible on the inside but acted like it didn't bother me to be the "dateless wonder." I filled my life with theater and choir and the pom-pom team. Sometimes those activities contributed to my feelings that I was fat and ugly. While I ended up with leading roles in school plays, I was never the pretty girl who ends up with the guy. Instead, I played the roles that got lots of laughs.

So I hated myself. I hid my feelings behind an outgoing personality and a sense of humor. No one knew how I felt, and I was determined that no one ever would.

But during the spring of my senior year, something happened that changed all that self-loathing. One night, when I was in one of my usual I-hate-me funks, I walked outside. It was a clear spring night with no clouds, a full moon, and a sky bursting with stars. I thought about God's amazing creation. And it hit me. In God's eyes, I am more precious, more valuable, more beautiful than the sky, the mountains, the oceans, and the stars.

At that moment, I thought about myself from God's perspective. I imagined God crafting me by hand—choosing just the right shade of brown for my eyes, the right shape for my hands, the perfect amount of curl for my hair. Then I imagined him watching me day after day as I looked in the mirror and criticized how he had made me.

251

Later that night, I flipped to Psalm 104, which celebrates God's incredible creation. I thought, *Look at how much care God took in making this world. And he's sharing it with you, Carla.*

As I fell asleep that night, I felt something I hadn't felt in a very long time: peace and contentment with myself. I knew I was one of God's most amazing creations and that to doubt it was an insult to God.

I still don't look like a model, and I know I never will. But that's just surface stuff. The truth is, God made me, and I'm fine just the way I am.

—Carla

* *Reread* the last sentence of the story. Now, write down three reasons why this is also true about you:
   1.
   2.
   3.

DAY 207 8 Ways to Feel Good about Yourself

1. Picture it. Flip to your favorite memories in an old photo album. As you reminisce about fun times in your life and the people you really care about, you'll see how many truly fabulous gifts God's given you.

2. Focus on the positive. If you're in the habit of keeping nice notes, cards, and letters from others, dig 'em out. Or you can just listen extra hard for encouraging words. Sometimes other people are better than you are at identifying your great God-given traits.

3. Make a change. Identify the behaviors and situations that undermine your self-confidence, then try your hardest to change them. Stop hanging out with people who make you feel crummy. Instead of criticizing your reflection in the mirror, give yourself a compliment.

4. Come clean. Unresolved issues with other people or with God can weigh you down and trick you into thinking no one would love you if they knew the truth. Plus, confession leads to forgiveness—often from other people and always from God.

5. *Challenge yourself.* Read a classic novel. Start an exercise plan. Try a new sport or pick up a musical instrument. Memorize a book of the Bible. In the process of accomplishment, you just might discover a talent you never knew you had.

6. *Excel where it counts.* You'll probably never be the most athletic, attractive, intelligent, popular person you know. But you can make it your goal to be something even better. You could strive to be the most caring, the best listener, the most patient, or the kindest. These things won't win you trophies, but they'll lead to the best kind of success: becoming more like Jesus.

7. *Lend a hand.* Try to focus on others. Volunteer—whether that means helping a neighbor or helping coach a soccer team of five-year-olds—and you'll be amazed at the results. Making a difference in others' lives has a boomerang way of making a huge difference in your own.

8. *Remember who loves you.* The ultimate reason to feel good about yourself has to do with how God feels about you. Read 1 John and think of it as God's love letter to you. Here's a little sneak preview (1 John 3:1): "How great is the love the Father has lavished on us, that we should be called children of God! And that is what we are!"

—Carla

* *Pick your favorite* from this list. Make a commitment to putting it into practice sometime this week. Write it on a note card and put it on your mirror as a reminder.

DAY 208 I Felt Like a Loser

Fans know Mark Hall as the talented lead singer for worship band Casting Crowns. But he wasn't always the confident performer you see on stage. In fact, Mark spent years feeling like one of life's big losers. He traces those feelings way back to third grade, when school specialists learned that Mark had attention deficit disorder and dyslexia (a learning disorder that affects reading ability). His parents placed him in classes for students with learning disabilities.

"As I got older, I saw I was in the classes that everybody made fun of, so I never told anyone I was in them," Mark says.

Every day Mark hid and waited until the halls were clear before going to his special classes so no one would see what room he entered. Although he was in separate classes almost all day, even his best friend didn't know Mark's secret.

"That's when Satan started whispering to me that I was weak," Mark says. "Anytime I felt God was leading me to do something, it was as if this little voice said, 'Look, if you try this, they're all going to find out.' I was an adult before I admitted having dyslexia."

When he was twenty-one, Mark went to a conference where a speaker told his testimony about being dyslexic. Mark couldn't believe it. *Why is he telling these people this?* he thought. *No one is going to listen to him now!* But suddenly he felt God telling him that people were listening to the speaker because of his struggles. Mark realized that he didn't need to be perfect—just willing to let God use him.

"He doesn't choose people who are 'good enough' to do his work," Mark says, "but those who will listen. The little inadequacies that scare me don't bother God. I'm often reminded of 2 Corinthians 12:9. God's strength is made perfect in our weakness."

—Todd

* *What is your weakness?* How can God's strength be "made perfect" in that weakness?

254

DAY 209 Better than I Know Myself
(a prayer based on Psalm 139:1–7 NRSV)

O LORD, you have searched me and known me.

You know everything about me; you know who I really am on the inside. I can hide myself from the kids at school and hope that my mom can't read my mind, but I can't hide anything from you.

You know when I sit down and when I rise up; you discern my thoughts from far away.

You know when I'm putting off my homework to watch TV, and you know when I actually get up to do it. You know what I'm going to do even before I do. You know my good intentions, and you know when I fall short. And when I'm really down on myself, you know there's goodness in me.

You search out my path and my lying down, and are acquainted with all my ways.

You know what is going on in my day, and you know how I'm going to react. You know my habits and values. You knew I was going to panic on that pop quiz even before I did. You also knew I would ace it!

Even before a word is on my tongue, O LORD, you know it completely.

You know what I am going to say even when the words are just thoughts and even before the thoughts come into my head. You know when I want to say something—but bite my tongue. Every thought, Lord—good or bad—you know them all.

You hem me in, behind and before, and lay your hand upon me.

You watched me take my first breath, and you've watched me grow up. You know what the future holds for me. You know the choices I have to make and the things I have to resist. I know that you will guide me through everything—through tests, through learning to drive, through troubles with friends, through leaving home, through it all.

Such knowledge is too wonderful for me; it is so high that I cannot attain it.

I know that you know me better than my best friend or even my family does. I know that you stand beside me and behind me, that you are above me and below me, that you are to my left and to my right. I know that if only I let your Word echo in my life and listen to you in prayer, you will guide each step of my future. This knowledge is almost too much for me. It is so amazing that I can barely conceive it.

Where can I go from your Spirit? Or where can I flee from your presence?

Why would I want to live my life without you? Why would I even want to try?

—Emily

DAY 210 Journal It

Spend some time journaling a prayer to God. Thank him for the talents, gifts, appearance, personality, and quirks he gave you. Praise God for creating you "fearfully and wonderfully." Rest in the fact that you have value simply because you're God's child!

DAY 211 Read in the Dark

Take today's devo into a dark room and read with your cell phone or a flashlight.

Those in hell will be without God

Our Lord Jesus will punish anyone who doesn't know God and won't obey his message. Their punishment will be eternal destruction, and they will be kept far from the presence of our Lord and his glorious strength.

—2 Thessalonians 1:8–9 CEV

Those in heaven will be with God

We should be cheerful, because we would rather leave these bodies and be at home with the Lord.

—2 Corinthians 5:8 CEV

There will no longer be any curse. The throne of God and of the Lamb will be in the city. God's servants will serve him. They will see his face. His name will be on their foreheads. There will be no more night. They will not need the light of a lamp or the light of the sun. The Lord God will give them light. They will rule for ever and ever.

—Revelation 22:3–5 NIrV

That's the bottom line

If Christ is our Lord and Savior, we live in God's presence. But if we die without Christ, then we're shut off from his presence—and all the love and happiness that come from him. I like to think of it as the difference between living with the sun or without the sun. With the sun, life grows and everything is bright. Without the sun, living things wither and die.

—Todd

* ***Leave the dark*** **and sit in the sun or the light while thanking God for allowing you to be in his warm, life-giving presence.**

DAY 212 Our Real Country

For God so loved the world that he gave his one and only Son, that whoever believes in him shall not perish but have eternal life.

—John 3:16

We've all heard John 3:16 a zillion times. But look at that verse again, especially the last two words: eternal life.

Wow. Believe in Jesus. Live forever. In heaven.

But what will it be like? Christians have wondered that and imagined what it's like for generations. I especially like the way C. S. Lewis

257

describes heaven in *The Last Battle*, the final book in the Chronicles of Narnia. He writes:

> The new Narnia . . . was a deeper country: every rock and flower and blade of grass looked as if it meant more. . . . It was the Unicorn who summed up what everyone was feeling. He stamped his right fore-hoof on the ground and neighed and then cried: "I have come home at last! This is my real country! I belong here. This is the land I have been looking for all my life, though I never knew it till now. The reason why we loved the old Narnia is that it sometimes looked a little like this!"

When I read this description I think about my dad, who died after a horrendous battle with cancer. In the face of those awful memories, I smile because I know where Dad is now—in God's presence, for all eternity, with a brand-new body.

When we get to heaven, God will "wipe every tear from [our] eyes. There will be no more death or mourning or crying or pain, for the old order of things has passed away. He who was seated on the throne said, 'I am making everything new!'" (Rev. 21:4–5).

Everything—including my dad—is made new, and I cannot wait to shout, "I have come home at last! I belong here!"

—Mark

DAY 213 Signs of Heaven

Happy endings are everywhere in movies and TV. Romantic comedies end with couples realizing they were meant for each other and sharing a big kiss. Sitcoms end when misunderstandings are figured out. Action movies end with the bad guy finally being punished.

So why do we crave happy endings? Well, obviously because we wish real life was like that. But I also think it's because happy endings point to the perfect ending of living forever with God in heaven. Here are two signs of God in Hollywood's happy endings.

Sign #1: Hope

It's easy for us to watch *Episode III: Revenge of the Sith* in the Star Wars saga and see the hope of better days. We know what babies Luke and Leia end up doing. But try telling poor, brokenhearted Padmé it will be OK. From her point of view, everything is dark.

When you can't see the full picture, it's easy to miss the hope. All we see is the really bad news of the right now.

But as Christians, we believe in a far bigger picture. We know God is watching over us with "plans to prosper you and not to harm you, plans to give you hope and a future" (Jer. 29:11). So, as hard as it is, we can trust him to turn around the bad times and give us "beauty instead of ashes" and "gladness instead of mourning" (Isa. 61:3).

Sign #2: Justice

There is a reason why we cheer when the bad guy is captured. We are hardwired to see the unjust get taken down. The Bible tells us God is just (Isa. 30:18), which means that he will make everything right. Seeing this justice on-screen taps into a huge longing in our hearts, because let's face it: real life is not just. Bad guys go free. Innocent kids die of hunger. We live in a big world full of evil, homelessness, and sadness. We wonder, *Where is justice?*

Jesus established a whole new kingdom of justice on earth. In Matthew 6:10, Jesus prays, "May your Kingdom come soon. May your will be done here on earth, as it is in heaven" (NLT). He was asking for God's justice to be worked out on earth every day. Jesus calls us, as members of this kingdom, to right wrongs wherever possible and to help the world's poor and oppressed. We are to live and act justly so that others may be drawn into God's wonderful kingdom right now.

—Todd

Top 5

* List your five favorite movies with happy endings.

1.

2.

3.

4.

5.

* For each movie ask yourself, "Why do I like this one?"

* Then think about how each one could show signs of heaven.

DAY 214 Fast Facts about Heaven

We all long for heaven. (Phil. 3:20)

We must believe in Jesus to get there. (John 3:16)

We each have a "heavenly home" waiting for us, prepared by Jesus himself. (John 14:2)

We will get new bodies when we go to heaven. (2 Cor. 5:1–4)

We will see God face-to-face in heaven. (1 John 3:2)

We will not sin in heaven. (Rev. 21:27)

We will experience no more death, no more pain, no more sadness, no more tears. (Rev. 21:4)

Read all about it

* Make time today to read three of the Bible passages mentioned above.

DAY 215 Why Hell?

In Luke 16:26, Jesus tells a story of two men: Lazarus, and the rich man who refused to help him. When the men die, Lazarus ends up in heaven, the rich man in hell. And the rich man is obviously miserable. He begs for help. But Abraham, who is standing with Lazarus in heaven, says that the rich man's real suffering is his eternal separation from God.

Separated from God—forever. That's hell: to live apart from the loving, saving God who created us. And don't think for a minute this separation is what God wants. It hurts him even more than it hurts us.

God created us because he wants nothing more than to be in a relationship with us.

So if hell is eternal separation from God, and if God loves us so much, why is hell even an option? The truth is, no one really knows why. Theologians have debated for centuries and have come up with only a few explanations. One view is that there has to be a flip side to salvation. We can't understand God's mercy unless we understand his wrath. We need to realize there's an alternative to heaven.

Another explanation is that God is so holy he cannot be in the presence of unholiness; it just can't happen. It's like darkness existing where there is light; completely impossible. So there has to be a place for people who don't accept God's gift of salvation. That place is hell.

Even though we may never really understand why there's a hell, one thing's for sure: God loves us enough to give us a way to stay far away from an eternity in hell. When we accept Christ as our Savior, we choose a life that allows us to be best friends with our awesome Creator—a Creator who wants us to spend eternity at his side. We choose heaven.

—Carla

DAY 216 The Happiest Ending

The Spirit of God whets our appetite by giving us a taste of what's ahead. He puts a little of heaven in our hearts so that we'll never settle for less. That's why we live with such good cheer. You won't see us drooping our heads or dragging our feet! Cramped conditions here don't get us down. They only remind us of the spacious living conditions ahead. . . . Do you suppose a few ruts in the road or rocks in the path are going to stop us? When the time comes, we'll be plenty ready to exchange exile for homecoming.

—2 Corinthians 5:5–8 Message

God's home is now with his people. He will live with them, and they will be his own. Yes, God will make his home among his people. He will wipe all tears from their eyes, and there will be no more death, suffering, crying, or pain. These things of the past are gone forever.

–Revelation 21:3–4 CEV

I've read the last page of the Bible. It's all going to turn out all right.

–Billy Graham

DAY 217 Your Invisible Friend

When I was a kid, I thought the Holy Spirit—or Holy Ghost, as he's sometimes called—was the strangest part of my Christian faith. (And let's be honest—there are some pretty strange things in the Bible.) I assumed he was some strange dude under a sheet that God sent to whisper in my ears. It's like a really bad episode of *Scooby Doo*, except I'm not supposed to try to unmask the fake spirit under the sheet. I'm supposed to go to him for help in life. Is that weird or what?

* **Have some fun drawing a cartoon of the kind of "Holy Spirit" described above.**

. . . the rest of the story

Well, the Holy Spirit is not so weird if you can forget about the sheet for a moment. Let's look at what Jesus said about the Holy Spirit. Before he returned to heaven, he made a promise to his disciples. He told them he wouldn't leave them like orphans, all alone in the world. He'd send "another Friend": the Holy Spirit (John 14:15–20 Message).

Jesus said this friend would give them strength and be the very presence of God with them. That's the kind of friend the Holy Spirit is to every believer.

—Grady

List three characteristics of the perfect friend

1.
2.
3.

* Is it hard to think of the Holy Spirit as the Perfect Friend? Why or why not?

DAY 218 With Us, In Us

Jesus gave us the Holy Spirit so we wouldn't be on our own as we struggle to follow him. In every trial, every joy, every temptation, every sadness, every celebration—in every single moment, the Spirit of Christ dwells in us. The Bible calls him such names as the Comforter, the Counselor, the Spirit of truth, the Spirit of wisdom, the Spirit of holiness, and the Spirit of life. The Holy Spirit lives in our hearts, reminding us of our salvation and helping us to live and love just like Jesus did when he walked the planet. What about you? What does all this mean to you personally? Well, find out by grabbing a pencil and circling a few answers . . .

Have you ever experienced guilt for hurting someone's feelings and sensed that you should apologize? Yes No

Have you ever felt moved to worship because you had just experienced a beautiful sunset or star-filled sky? Yes No

Have you ever felt a strange sense of spiritual strength in a moment of weakness? Yes No

Have you ever suddenly found the power to overcome a temptation?
Yes No

Have you ever felt moved to tell a friend about Jesus? Yes No

If you've answered yes to a few of these questions, you can be pretty sure God's Spirit is at work in you.

—Grady and Jerry

Yes!

* Thank God for each "yes" you checked. Tell him you're grateful for the ways he is present and working in your life.

No!

* Think about each "no" you checked. Ask God to help you look for ways he is working in your life that you might be missing. Ask him to help you become more sensitive to the Holy Spirit's guidance. If you simply don't sense that the Spirit is working in your life, talk to your pastor, youth pastor, or small group leader about what it means to be led by the Holy Spirit.

DAY 219 How Does the Spirit Work?

Q: The Bible talks about being led by the Holy Spirit. Can you tell me how the Holy Spirit works in my life?

—*Anonymous*

A: I'm glad you're interested in the Holy Spirit, because it's impossible to follow God unless we are led by the Spirit. And the only way to be led by the Spirit is to follow God's command to be filled by the Spirit. Interestingly, God contrasts being filled with the Spirit with being drunk. Somebody who is drunk with wine or alcohol is controlled by and consumed by alcohol. But somebody who is "drunk in the Spirit" is controlled and consumed by the Spirit, who helps us live holy lives (Eph. 5:18 Message).

How are we filled with the Spirit? The Holy Spirit entered you when you decided to give your life to Christ, to become a Christian. But we need to continually ask the Holy Spirit to lead us, to guide us, to help us do the things God wants us to do. When we're growing as Christians, we should allow the Spirit to take control over more and more areas of our lives.

Now, the Holy Spirit can't do all the work for us. We're still responsible to do our part—especially to consistently read our Bibles and pray, asking the Spirit to show us the truth and teach us how to live.

It's important to remember that the Spirit will not lead us to do anything that goes against Scripture. People sometimes justify their actions by saying, "My conscience told me . . ." We need to make sure we're listening to the voice of the Holy Spirit, not the voice of our own desires. And we know which is which by checking this voice against the truth of God's Word.

How can you tell if you're being led by the Spirit? By the "fruit" of your life—your attitudes and actions. Galatians 5:22–23 says, "The fruit of the Spirit is love, joy, peace, patience, kindness, goodness, faithfulness, gentleness and self-control."

—Dawson

DAY 220 Do This

Grab a glass and a bottle of food coloring and follow these steps:

1. Fill the glass with water.
2. Imagine that this filled glass represents your life.
3. Squeeze one drop of food coloring into the water.
4. Read Galatians 5:22–23 (in Dawson's answer from yesterday).
5. Put another drop of food coloring into the water.
6. Put in another drop.
7. Reread Galatians 5:22–23.
8. Add another drop.
9. Add one more drop.
10. Imagine that this glass represents your life—now filled with God's Spirit.

DAY 221 What the Spirit Does

In the left column are Scriptures that reveal something the Spirit does. The right column contains brief descriptions of the Spirit's activities. Read each Scripture and then draw a line to the activity that's the best match.

Romans 8:6	teaches
1 Corinthians 12:4–7	helps with prayer
John 16:8	gives life to dead bodies
Romans 8:11	reveals the truth about people's sin
Romans 8:26–27	gives inner strength
1 Corinthians 2:7–11	reveals God's secrets to believers
John 3:1–8	gives spiritual gifts
Luke 12:11–12	brings spiritual birth
Ephesians 3:16	gives life and peace

DAY 222 Who Is He Anyway?

Read each passage, looking for "hints" into the true identity of the Holy Spirit:

> Then Peter said, "Ananias, why did you let Satan fill your heart? He made you lie to the Holy Spirit. . . .You haven't lied to just anyone. You've lied to God."
>
> —Acts 5:3–4 NIrV

> Jesus came to them and said: "I have been given all authority in heaven and on earth! Go to the people of all nations and make them my disciples. Baptize them in the name of the Father, the Son, and the Holy Spirit."
>
> —Matthew 28:18–19 CEV

> But Christ offered himself to God without any flaw. He did this through the power of the eternal Holy Spirit.
>
> —Hebrews 9:14 NIrV

Our LORD, by your wisdom you made so many things. . . . You created all of them by your Spirit, and you give new life to the earth.

—Psalm 104:24–30 CEV

I can never escape from your Spirit! I can never get away from your presence!

—Psalm 139:7 NLT

The Spirit alone gives eternal life. Human effort accomplishes nothing.

—John 6:63 NLT

Stretch your brain muscles

* Go back and read each passage again—*slowly*. OK, read each passage a third time and underline the words and phrases about the Holy Spirit that jump out at you, and circle the ones that make no sense at all. Now try to answer these questions: What do these passages tell me about the Holy Spirit? What words and phrases help me see that the Holy Spirit is God? Take your own questions—and your circled words and phrases—to your pastor, youth pastor, or small group leader.

DAY 223 Reflect on This

Unlike us, the Holy Spirit thinks perfect thoughts, feels without sinning, decides with flawless wisdom. The Holy Spirit is a person, capable of knowing and being known, but he is also God as much as the Father is. He is not a junior-varsity God or a second-string deity. He must be honored as God.

—James

DAY 224 The Spirit's Home

Don't you realize that your body is the temple of the Holy Spirit, who lives in you and was given to you by God? You do not belong to yourself, for God bought you with a high price. So you must honor God with your body.

—1 Corinthians 6:19–20 NLT

267

Think about this

* Your body is like a house—a very beautiful house—where the Spirit resides. What's inside the house that makes it messy? What secrets are hidden in the closets that you don't want anybody to know about? What needs to be cleaned out of your house so that the Holy Spirit enjoys living there?

Cleaning house

Don't make God's Spirit sad. . . . Stop being bitter and angry and mad at others. Don't yell at one another or curse each other or ever be rude. Instead, be kind and merciful, and forgive others, just as God forgave you because of Christ.

—Ephesians 4:30–32 CEV

So put to death the sinful, earthly things lurking within you. Have nothing to do with sexual immorality, impurity, lust, and evil desires. Don't be greedy, for a greedy person is an idolater, worshiping the things of this world. Because of these sins, the anger of God is coming. You used to do these things when your life was still part of this world. But now is the time to get rid of anger, rage, malicious behavior, slander, and dirty language.

—Colossians 3:5–8 NLT

DAY 225 Turn the Key

Not long ago, I had the chance to drive a new red Mustang cross-country. It wasn't my car, just mine to drive for the trip.

I climbed into the driver's seat, stuck the key in the ignition, and brought that beautiful red car to life. I headed down the expressway with the windows rolled down and my music turned up. I felt so free!

But even the freedom of driving a Mustang doesn't compare to the freedom I have in Christ. And that freedom starts with God's gift of the Holy Spirit, who lives inside me. What an incredible gift!

Paul talks about this gift in his second letter to the Corinthians. This was a new time in the life of the first Christians. Before Christ's death on the cross, people had to make animal sacrifices to pay for sin and go through a priest to connect with God. Even the temple had a veil separating the priests from the place God's presence resided.

But now they had constant and direct access to God through the Spirit, and their sins were forgiven because of Christ's ultimate sacrifice.

> For the Lord is the Spirit, and wherever the Spirit of the Lord is, there is freedom. So all of us who have had that veil removed can see and reflect the glory of the Lord. And the Lord—who is the Spirit—makes us more and more like him as we are changed into his glorious image.
>
> —2 Corinthians 3:17–18 NLT

As a Christian, I have this same freedom; I can go directly to God. I have access to him through the "key" of the Holy Spirit. Just think of the power, strength, and wisdom that this key can unlock! I can talk to God about life and ask him to forgive and forget when I've messed up—and he will! And better yet, he's molding and shaping me to look more like Christ every day.

I have the Holy Spirit, so why wouldn't I want to put him to use? To not do so would be like saying no to the opportunity of driving a shiny, red Mustang—absolutely crazy!

—Krishana

DAY 226 What the Spirit Gives

> But what happens when we live God's way? He brings gifts into our lives, much the same way that fruit appears in an orchard—things like affection for others, exuberance about life, serenity. We develop a willingness to stick with things, a sense of compassion in the heart, and a conviction that a basic holiness permeates things and people. We find ourselves involved in loyal commitments, not needing to force our way in life, able to marshal and direct our energies wisely.
>
> —Galatians 5:22–23 Message

* This version of Galatians 5:22–23 is different from many other versions of the Bible. Go back to Day 219 and reread these two verses as they appear at the end of Dawson's answer. Compare the two versions. How does the version from the Message help explain or define each fruit of the Spirit?

DAY 227 Wake Up to Yourself

Just once—tomorrow morning, maybe—when you wake up, your mouth tasting like wool and the day outside your window gray and unformed, think about this:

Before you start remembering homework you didn't get done, worrying whether to wear that blue shirt or the yellow one, or wishing you had all the good looks you'll never have—before all that, think . . .

Aren't there good reasons to be glad I'm waking up as "me"?

Maybe you have acne or feel you're too short or your nose is too big. Ignore the little flaws; see the big picture.

Squeeze your pillow with both hands, hold tightly for a moment, and then let go. Stretch your toes to the foot of the bed.

Your body works! It works like a marvel, a dream—faster than thought it does what you want. No buttons, no steering wheel; you think and it responds.

A ball sails high in the air, and in a split second your brain solves a half-hour-long calculus problem. You think, *Got it!* and your body is already on its way to catch the ball. Without calculation, a huge muscle called your heart accelerates to bathe every cell (billions of them) with blood, and your lungs scoop the air for oxygen and harvest your blood for carbon dioxide. It doesn't happen just catching a ball. It happens walking down the hall or springing from bed in the morning.

Take a moment now. Count to yourself all the people you'll talk to today—teachers, friends, parents, brothers, sisters.

Have you ever gone twenty-four hours without talking to someone? Each person on the earth (billions of them) is as much a marvel as you. Yet each person needs others.

We work together: I don't have to reinvent arithmetic to count my socks, or plant wheat seeds in order to eat bread next September. Someone else has already done those things. Is there a radio near your bed? Turn it to the weather report and listen to another amazing creature telling you the day's forecast. He or she got it from another wonderful creature who got it from instruments invented and manufactured by other wonderful creatures.

How well off would you be if this morning you had to do everything alone—make your own food, house, socks, car? Where would you be without all those unseen people? Isn't it incredible how we share?

Before you get out of bed, think about one more thing. . . .

Giraffes move gracefully. Bees share the invention of honey. An antelope leaps quicker than you can think. But no other animal, so far as I know, ever lies awake in the gray morning, eyes wide open in amazement, thinking how wonderful it is to wake up as "me."

—Tim

DAY 228 Faith Like a Child

A half dozen wide-eyed elementary kids bombarded me with questions during my first day in my high school's peer counseling program. I was to meet with these kids every Thursday for six weeks to discuss topics like decision making, peer pressure, and substance abuse.

I hadn't even finished introducing myself when the questions started pouring my way. But questions soon turned to chaos. They chattered with each other. They chattered all at once. It seemed like six voices turned into a hundred. Finally I raised my own voice and shouted in exaspera-

271

tion, "OK! If you guys behave, we'll spend the last five minutes discussing whatever you want to talk about!"

They got quiet. I was amazed.

Taking advantage of the moment, I launched into the topic of the day. To my surprise, they paid attention and were even eager to join in the discussion. As promised, I spent the last five minutes discussing whatever they wanted to talk about.

Over the next five weeks, the kids performed skits, filled out worksheets, and played games to reinforce my lessons. They definitely put themselves into our time together. They laughed. They joked. They even listened! And they continued to get their reward—five minutes at the end to talk about whatever.

Along with their endless stream of questions, they told me about their lives. Anna said she loved her new baby brother. Steven was excited because his dad was coaching his baseball team. And Julie, with an enormous smile creasing her face, talked about the picnic her family had planned.

My peer counseling experience is now months behind me. I just hope some of what they learned will stick with them. I also hope I will never forget what they taught me.

They taught me that questions should be asked for the sake of finding out something new—and not just to get a better grade on a test. They also helped me see that I often take life too seriously. They taught me to laugh more and smile often.

Jesus said the kingdom of God belongs to little children (Luke 18:16). After my experience with those kids, I think I understand this truth a little better. As I grow up, I hope I'll see life through childlike eyes. If I do, I'll never stop being surprised over even the little lessons God brings my way.

—Rachel

Look for little lessons from God while . . .

going to school

walking down the hallway

waiting for class to begin

doing exercises in gym glass

staring out a window

coming home from school

DAY 229 Two Minutes of Silence

Sit in silence for two minutes. No distractions. No iPod. No radio. Not a sound. Clear your mind—of homework, of your Facebook page, of plans and schedules, of all distractions. Take several deep, long breaths. Relax your shoulders. Smile. Yes, smile.

Now, reflect

* Think about the first time you . . .

rode a bike

smelled a flower

marveled at ice-covered trees

rolled down a grassy hill

stared into a blue sky filled with puffy clouds

skipped rope

tasted ice cream

_____(fill in your own)

Journal

* Pick one of the "firsts" above and write a poem, prayer, or reflective story about that experience.

273

Repeat

* Don't let the joy you felt as a young child pass you by. It's still there. Take time to stop and enjoy—and be surprised by—life's daily surprises.

DAY 230 Mysteries and Miracles

With a deep breath I hurtle myself—weighted down with diving gear—backward over the side of the boat and into the arms of the waiting ocean. There is a moment of confusion as I tumble through the water, but soon the sea gently rights me, the bubbles clear before my mask, and I can see for the first time the alien landscape of the tropical coral reef.

At first the only thing my stunned mind can register is color. An explosion of gold and pink and white and green and blue bursts on my unsuspecting eyes. Hues and intensities I've never seen before, incarnated in unearthly shapes and forms my land-worn mind can't comprehend. I float limply as my brain tries to piece together some coherent images from the flood of new information pouring into my head.

A few strong kicks of my fins and I begin to glide slowly over the surface of the reef, hungrily devouring each new detail.

All reef life lives on or around the huge, twisted, labyrinthine mass of rock-like dead coral. The living coral grows upon it in intricate branches of flower-like bouquets. Feathery arms extend out to feed, looking like snowflakes on the smooth stony surface of their fantastic house.

The amount and variety of life living on this one hunk of reef is overwhelming. Crazily shaped Christmas tree worms and brightly colored sea slugs make their homes in the cracks and crevices. There are soft, bulbous sponges and ghostlike, pulsating jellyfish. There are tiny, stinging noctiluca that illuminate the water at night with an eerie glow. And mysterious manta rays glide along the bottom like devil-shaped clouds.

I am nearly overwhelmed by the strange unearthly beauty all around me. It's like nothing I've ever seen. I feel as if I am relearning what childhood was like, when everything was fresh and new and miraculous.

Miraculous. I am in the midst of a miracle. I see once again, as I must have sometime long ago, before the first time I ever felt bored, the fingerprints. God's fingerprints. His mind.

I emerge from the water as from a baptism, my senses reborn. The very air tastes stronger on my tongue. I look at the other people around me on the boat, familiar faces, and I wonder why I never realized how beautiful they were before. When we step back on land, I notice I am looking at the grass in amazement.

I have regained wonder.

Creation had been shouting God's glory, but I had become too accustomed to the sound to hear it.

—Elizabeth

Cartoon it

* In the empty frames below, re-create Elizabeth's experience in your own creative cartoon.

275

DAY 231 A New Day

Beep . . .
Beep . . .
Beep . . .
The alarm clock rings
As I roll over
Sleepily I rise
And open my blinds
The sunshine streams in
Making me squint
Rubbing away sleep
While I stretch and yawn
Birds chirp
The blue sky beckons
For a brief minute
I gaze up
Remembering Him
Endless opportunities
Calling my name
. . . This is the day

—Amy

Think it through

* What opportunities await you today? Think real hard. Ask yourself, *In what ways can I look expectantly for God's little miracles and everyday surprises?*

Make a list

* Write down three opportunities you feel might be awaiting you today:

    1.
    2.
    3.

Pray about it

* Write a one-sentence prayer about each opportunity you listed.

1.
2.
3.

Look around you

* Keep your eyes wide open, looking for ways God might be answering each of your prayers.

DAY 232 When I Feel Lonely

Loneliness. Now that's a scary word. And it's something I've been struggling with lately. It's kind of ironic that I feel this way. I have a big family and can hardly get a minute to myself sometimes. I have parents who love me and show it all the time. My best friend is with me all the time, and we have a great time together.

There's almost always someone around I can talk to and do stuff with. But it feels like there's always something missing, like a space I just can't fill.

Sometimes I think if I just buy something new, I'll be all happy inside. But whatever I buy gets old or breaks—or I simply get tired of it. Then there are times I think if I could find success or popularity, I'd feel fulfilled. And it's tempting to try to fill my emptiness with a guy, but I know that even the best relationship would never completely fill this emptiness I feel.

As I try to find a way to deal with my emptiness and loneliness, I'm finally beginning to understand the solution comes down to my relationship with God. In fact, maybe God wants to use my loneliness to show me more about who he is and how much I really need him—more than anybody, more than anything.

The truth is, God created me and loves me so much more than I can ever understand. During the times I feel lonely, only God knows what I need. And I can trust him to use my lonely times to help me grow into the person he wants me to be.

I think of it this way: I guess God has left an open space in my life so he can enter it and fill it up. That means I need to keep my mind and my heart open to him and to his plans for me. Then when I feel the loneliest, I need to reach out and hang on tightly to him. I know he'll be there. And I know he'll never, ever leave me alone.

—Jaci

Three questions

* What might you be doing to fill the emptiness only God can fill?

* What do you think God is trying to teach you or has taught you through lonely times?

* How can you keep your mind open to him—what does that mean to you?

DAY 233 Jesus Understands Rejection . . .

He was despised and rejected by men, a man of sorrows, and familiar with suffering. Like one from whom men hide their faces he was despised, and we esteemed him not.

—Isaiah 53:3

. . . and will never abandon you . . .

Even if my father and mother should desert me, you will take care of me.

—Psalm 27:10 CEV

. . . because nothing could keep him away.

For I am convinced that neither death nor life, neither angels nor demons, neither the present nor the future, nor any powers, neither height nor depth, nor anything else in all creation, will be able to separate us from the love of God that is in Christ Jesus our Lord.

—Romans 8:38–39

Think about it

* If these verses are true, what do they say about you? What do they say about God? What do they mean about the times when you feel alone and deserted?

Pray about it

* Take a few minutes to write these three verses into a prayer. Start it like this:

* Lord, it is so amazing that you . . .

DAY 234 All Alone?

"I'm gonna throw up," I told my friend Laura. It was getting close to my time to run the 800-meter race, but I wondered if I'd even make it onto the track.

"You've been like this before every meet," Laura said. "Why did you join the track team anyway?"

I knew exactly why I'd joined. I was seeking acceptance and praise from my parents. But it was hard to get their attention. I wanted to prove to my family—and to myself—that I was worth something.

"Are you gonna be able to run?" Laura asked.

A tear trickled down my cheek.

Laura put her hand on my shoulder. "What's wrong, Christy?"

"I just feel so alone," I admitted softly, my voice cracking.

279

"Why?" Laura asked. "I'm here. And your parents are up in the stands. . . ."

"No," I interrupted. "I don't mean like that. I mean I don't feel like I have a thing—nothing that I'm good at or can be proud of or whatever. I'm not talented or popular or anything. I'm just alone."

Laura gently squeezed my hand. "I promise you, Christy—you're not alone," she said. "Remember what we talked about in youth group a few weeks ago? God is with you always."

Bible break

I've commanded you to be strong and brave. Don't ever be afraid or discouraged! I am the LORD your God, and I will be there to help you wherever you go.

—Joshua 1:9 CEV

. . . the rest of the story

I wasn't feeling much better when the announcer called my race.

As I stepped onto the track, my upset stomach gurgled in nervous anticipation. My mind raced with tons of anxious thoughts—so many, in fact, that I didn't hear the starting gun.

Suddenly everyone darted off in front of me.

What's going on? I wondered. Instinctively I started after them. My legs felt like they were full of lead. My body weakened, my breathing quickened, my pace slowed, and my hope sank.

As girl after girl passed me, I started to panic: *I'm gonna come in dead last! Just please, Lord, whatever happens, don't let me get lapped. I would die of embarrassment!*

I tried to calm my fears by thinking of comforting Scripture verses like Hebrews 13:6: "The Lord is my helper; I will not be afraid."

Rounding a corner, I heard Laura cheering like a maniac. "Way to go, Christy! Woo hoo!"

I suddenly recalled what Laura said about God. Recently our youth pastor said, "The Holy Spirit is sometimes called a 'Paraclete,' meaning one who runs beside. He strengthens us, keeps us faithful, and comforts us every day."

It was comforting to think that I was never alone. The Holy Spirit was running beside me not just this day, but every day—even when I felt alone and even if things were going poorly.

All of a sudden I felt a change within myself. I was filled with over-whelming peace. I no longer felt alone or afraid. Instead, I felt confident. No, I didn't win. But I breathlessly crossed the finish line in fourth place, and Mom, Dad, and Laura immediately rushed to my side.

"Thanks for supporting me!" I told my parents.

"Are you kidding?" Mom said. "We wouldn't dare let you run all alone."

I guess Mom didn't know. I wasn't alone.

—Christy

DAY 235 God's Plan

In the very beginning God said, "It is not good for the man to be alone" (Gen. 2:18), even though man was in the garden with God himself. And ever since, we've had a deep need to be known, understood, and accepted by people. We need others. We are created to be part of a community, especially as Christians: "You are the body of Christ, and each one of you is a part of it" (1 Cor. 12:27). That means we need each other if the body of Christ is to function as God intended.

And based on what we know from Jesus's example on earth, I think God understands that while he is chief in our lives, we are to love other people too. After all, he said the second most important commandment was to love others.

At the same time, there is the example of Job. He lost everything, including his family. All he knew fell apart. Still, he knew God was in control. As the apostle Peter said, "We must obey God rather than men" (Acts 5:29).

So enjoy the people God has placed in your life, and thank God for them. But in those times when it seems like you are alone, know that God does care. He knows your pain and will never leave you (Rom. 8:37–39).

—Marshall

DAY 236 Isn't God Enough?

Q: Every day it seems like I'm learning to love God more and more. But I still feel very lonely. I'm not very close to my family. My friends don't really know me. Even though I try to find refuge in God, I still feel so alone. I don't know what to do. Why isn't God enough?

—*Anonymous*

Your turn

* How would you answer this question?

How IYF's expert answered:

A: Loneliness is difficult. Even with your knowledge that God is in your life, you will still feel the need for deepened relationships with family and friends.

Your letter reminds me of a girl in my youth group named Cristy. One day she said, "All my friendships are superficial. I can't talk to anyone. Most nights I sit home alone."

After that, Cristy made three smart decisions. First, she joined a small group of girls who got together to pray and talk once a week. She didn't wait for them to invite her; she just asked if she could join them, and they were happy to have her. Second, she decided to find times to talk with her parents and grow closer. They had assumed she was happy with life and content with their relationships. And third, she began to accept the fact that loneliness is a part of many of our lives, but that we can use those times to grow closer to God.

As her youth pastor, I periodically talked with Cristy about her loneliness. We talked about how many people cover up their empty feelings of loneliness with drugs and alcohol or sexual promiscuity. I then recommended she take a close look at the book of Psalms. David, who wrote many of the psalms, was sorting through all kinds of emotions as he wrote, including loneliness. I want to encourage you to read those Scriptures. They won't always make your feelings of loneliness disappear, but many of the psalms will remind you of God's presence in your life.

—Jim

DAY 237 Didn't God Care?

"I have some bad news," Andrea said softly. "My dad's getting transferred."

"You're moving?" I asked, stunned. "Where?"

Tears fell down Andrea's cheeks. "About a thousand miles away," she sobbed.

I went home that night and couldn't stop crying. My best friend was moving, and I felt like God was totally letting me down.

I'd always considered Andrea's friendship an answer to prayer. Before I knew her, I honestly didn't have one friend at school. I was the kid no one wanted to eat lunch with. For some reason kids always made fun of me. I felt so alone.

I prayed every day that God would bring me one friend. I often wondered why he didn't answer my prayers.

I'd almost given up hope when I met Andrea. We clicked instantly. Finally I had someone to talk to at school and hang out with on the weekends. She was a strong Christian and we often went to her youth group together.

Now that Andrea was moving, I felt like God was taking back his answer to my prayer. I was sure I'd once again be the friendless girl who was lonely and depressed.

A few weeks after Andrea moved, I started my junior year feeling more empty and alone than ever. One day I ran into some of the kids from Andrea's youth group. I was surprised when they invited me to eat lunch with them. I mean, I'd hung out with them a few times before, but I figured they only talked to me because I was Andrea's friend. They encouraged me to come to their youth group even without Andrea. I figured it couldn't hurt anything.

Eventually I told the group's youth pastor that I didn't understand why God hadn't answered my prayers for Andrea to stay. He explained that God answers all of my prayers, but sometimes the answer is no. He told me that with faith, I could have peace about God's answer.

That was hard for me to swallow. "All I wanted was a friend," I complained. "I don't understand why God would say no to something that's so important to me."

283

The youth pastor then said something like this: "Why don't you pray that God would use this experience to deepen your faith? And pray that he would bring new friends into your life." I did what he suggested.

One night several months later, something suddenly hit me: God had been listening to me. He had answered my prayers—and this time with a yes. Even though my best friend was no longer around, God had given me an awesome youth group. I had many people who supported me and loved me.

A lot of time has passed since Andrea moved. I've grown really close to the kids from youth group. It didn't happen overnight, but I slowly started to open up to them. I've even gained enough confidence to reach out and meet other people at school.

As hard as it was when Andrea moved, I can see God's hand in it all. If Andrea hadn't moved, I don't think I would have ever seen the need to make more friends in youth group. If Andrea was still going to my school, I probably wouldn't have gained the boldness and confidence I needed to reach out to others.

When I look back, I know God answered my prayers. I also know he had my best interests at heart.

—Gabby

DAY 238 How It Can Feel

My God, my God, why have you forsaken me? Why are you so far from saving me, so far from the words of my groaning?

—Psalm 22:1

How it really is

The LORD doesn't hate or despise the helpless in all of their troubles. When I cried out, he listened and did not turn away.

—Psalm 22:24 CEV

DAY 239 Caught between Two Worlds

My gym shoes squeaked on the wood floor as I moved in tight on the guy I was guarding. With my hands raised in front of his face, I pressed as close as I could without drawing a foul. Then I started the trash talk, saying whatever I could to put him down.

The coach had warned us against trash talk. "It's wrong!" he'd lectured us sternly. "It's just poor sportsmanship! Don't let me catch you doing it!"

As a Christian, I knew deep down inside he was right. Even so, I felt I had to do whatever it took to win. I couldn't let my team down.

I hadn't always had this win-at-all-costs attitude. As a matter of fact, when I'd joined the team my freshman year, I'd wanted to live out the Christian beliefs I'd committed myself to in seventh grade.

I did OK for a while. I read my Bible, I prayed, and I attended church and youth group. By my sophomore year, I was a student leader in my youth group.

But then I'd get together with the guys on the team, and I'd find myself slipping into their bad habits. Along with talking trash and acting pretty full of myself, I also let them influence the way I thought about sex. They'd pull out a *Playboy* magazine, and I'd end up looking over their shoulders. They'd tell a dirty joke and I'd find myself listening and laughing.

Their way of thinking about girls and sex began to influence my own dating relationships. Although I wouldn't have sex, I'd often do things with girls I knew were wrong. For the longest time I felt awfully guilty about my actions and attitudes. I knew I was being a big hypocrite. But it was so difficult to change. I felt like I was caught between two worlds.

After basketball season ended, I knew I needed to make some serious changes. First off, I knew I needed to spend less time with my basketball friends and more time with my Christian friends.

As I reconnected with Christian friends, I soon realized something: you really do become like the people you spend your time with. Now this doesn't mean I've completely cut my old friends out of my life. But it does mean I need to make sure they aren't my only group of friends. I've also become bolder when I'm around them, letting them know what I believe in and what I stand for.

I know I'm not perfect. Far from it. But I know that when I mess up, God is always there to forgive me and help me do better the next time. In spite of my shortcomings, he is working in my life and helping me become more like the person he wants me to be.

—Kyle

Your turn

* What changes might you need to make so that you're not "caught between two worlds"?

DAY 240 My Two Worlds

CHURCH WORLD

SCHOOL WORLD

Do this

* Somewhere close to the "Church World" circle, list at least five actions or behaviors that typify you while you're at church or with your youth group. Somewhere close to the "School World" circle, list at least five actions or behaviors that typify you while you're with school friends.

Think it through

* Compare the two lists. How are they alike? How are they different?

* Would it make you uncomfortable if your youth pastor or pastor saw your School World list? Why or why not?

* Would it make you uncomfortable if your school friends saw your Church World list? Why or why not?

* What about God? How do you think he feels about each list?

DAY 241 Free the Puppet

Sometimes I feel like a puppet
pulled over somebody's hand.
The words I speak are not my own,
and I cannot move
without feeling like I'm being
scooted across a puppet stage.

I long to be a fully liberated puppet
with true freedom to live my life,
but something keeps holding me back
and pulling me down.
How can I break free
from this sock-puppet world?

—*Marie*

How not to be a puppet

Put off your old self, which belongs to your former manner of life . . . and put on the new self, created after the likeness of God in true righteousness and holiness.

—Ephesians 4:22–24 ESV

Therefore, if anyone is in Christ, he is a new creation; the old has gone, the new has come!

—2 Corinthians 5:17

You have given up your old way of life with its habits. Each of you is now a new person. You are becoming more and more like your Creator, and you will understand him better.

—Colossians 3:9–10 CEV

DAY 242 I'm Not Who People Think I Am

Q: I put up a happy and perfect front to hide my hurt and sin. And honestly, I think a lot of my youth group friends are the same way. How do I start being honest? How do I get over my fear of showing my true self?

—Anonymous

A: You're not alone in your struggles. In fact, great heroes of faith have felt the same way you feel. The apostle Paul wrote, "I do not understand what I do. For what I want to do, I do not do, but what I hate I do. . . . I know that nothing good lives in me. . . . For I have the desire to do what is good, but I cannot carry it out. For what I do is not the good I want to do" (Rom. 7:15–19). Basically, Paul is admitting that he's no good without God. And he's right. The Bible is clear that "all have sinned and fall short of the glory of God" (Rom. 3:23). We all hurt. We all sin. And like Paul, we hate some of the things we do and we don't understand our actions.

So what's the easiest way to deal with these faults? We hide them. We cover them up. We dress up and go to church and smile. People ask how we are and we politely say "fine"—even though we're definitely not fine. Why do we do this? Because we don't want to admit we're not perfect. We don't want to spill our messiness on others. If we do, we think people will judge us and reject us.

But church is the one place we should be able to be real and messy. We all know we're flawed. We all know we're carrying burdens and secret sins. So let's admit them and help each other. Now, I'm not saying you should stand up in church and announce your sin. Instead I've found that meeting weekly with a small group of guys helps keep me on the right path. We are very open and honest with each other. These men hold me accountable to walk closer with God. They cheer me on to do good and

288

call me on the carpet when I mess up. I know I'm a stronger Christian and a better man because of my relationship with these four guys.

It's not easy, though. It's hard to be open and real. When my group started meeting, we talked mainly about surface stuff. One day, one guy had a family crisis. As he opened up, it gave each of us the freedom to open up. We realized we wouldn't be rejected for being real. Now we have a very honest, blunt, and unashamedly Christian group.

So my advice to you is to find at least one other person you can be real with and who will accept you for who you are (a sinner saved by grace). In doing so, I believe you'll begin to overcome your fears about being yourself. Most importantly, you'll be following the scriptural advice of Galatians 6:2: "By helping each other with your troubles, you truly obey the law of Christ" (NCV).

—Jim

Follow Jim's advice

* Think about two or three Christians you trust—who accept you even when you don't quite measure up, who have offered you good advice and guidance in the past, who have encouraged you to develop your gifts and talents. Talk to one of them this week about being your spiritual mentor or accountability friend.

DAY 243 I Lived a Lie

My cheek pressed hard against the toilet seat, and I clung desperately to the bowl with both arms. My body was going numb from alcohol poisoning, but I couldn't let myself pass out. There was too much alcohol in my system. I had to keep throwing up or I wasn't going to walk out of there.

The pounding beat of techno music echoed from inside the dance club. The noises around me faded, and through the darkness, events from my life zoomed through my mind. I remembered junior high when I'd go to five church services a week. I'd thought I was more committed to God than anyone around.

289

A light tap on the stall door snapped me back to the present. "Are you OK?" a female voice asked from the other side. Two feet in strappy, magenta-colored platforms were all I could see.

"Yeah, I'm OK," I replied weakly. I was too ashamed to admit I was in trouble.

"Drink this." She stooped to push a cup of water under the stall door. I grabbed the cup and sipped until I started vomiting again.

My sluggish memories turned to high school. While still claiming to be a strong Christian, I excused sips of beer at parties by convincing myself it was OK because I didn't get drunk.

College life offered freedom—and choices. I partied and drank more and more because, I kept telling myself, "It's what everyone does in college." Worst of all, I kept telling people how great it was to be a Christian when I didn't live or even feel like one.

There was no way I could change my past. But there was one thing I could do.

"Forgive me, Father," I prayed. "Forgive me for all the mistakes I made. It probably doesn't mean much now, Lord, but I really want you to be in control of my life."

I let go of the toilet bowl and slunk down to the floor. I closed my eyes and began to lose consciousness.

Loud voices suddenly flooded the bathroom. "She's in here." It was the girl in the magenta shoes.

A dark figure was scrambling over the side of the locked stall. He picked me up. I could make out the letters E-M-T on his shirt. I closed my eyes and said a prayer of thanks.

Only God could lift me out of my own mess, clean me up, and give me another day. I'm keeping my promise to let him take control of my life. It's been a long process to let faith in and push my own pride out. I can feel the difference: I have stopped living the lie.

—Holly

Looking back

* **What about Holly's past showed she was headed for future trouble?**

Getting personal

* What do you do that has the potential of causing problems in your walk with Christ?

Living the truth

* What does it mean to live the truth? How can you protect yourself from living a lie—now or in the future? Write your answer in the space below.

DAY 244 Sometimes People Fool You

Sometimes people fool you. They're not what they appear.

Shannon, for instance.

When she's with her school friends, she parties. When she's at church, she speaks God-talk. If you only knew her from church, you'd think she was a Christian. If you only knew her from school, you'd think she'd never heard of God. If you knew her from school and church, you'd be confused.

Sometimes people fool you.

Like Shannon.

Or, truthfully, like me. And just as truthfully, like you.

On the other hand, some things are hard to fake. True faith is like that. You can talk like a Christian, but that doesn't mean much.

The real test is how you live.

What you are on the inside will be expressed outwardly.

Jesus explains it like this: "Do people pick grapes from thornbushes, or figs from thistles? Likewise every good tree bears good fruit, but a bad tree bears bad fruit. A good tree cannot bear bad fruit, and a bad tree cannot bear good fruit" (Matt. 7:16–18). Jesus is saying there is something different inside when a person knows God. The changes may not come immediately, but they do come.

When you look more closely, you begin to notice if there are changes. There are clues. Is the person struggling to be new and different? Or is he or she just a fake, content to be a fake? We can't judge for certain; that's not our job. But you begin to wonder when you only see thorns and thistles, if you know what I mean.

I wonder about Shannon, for instance. Which is the real one? The Shannon who drinks and parties? Or the Shannon who acts religious once or twice a week?

What happens, I wonder, when there are only God-words and crummy living?

It's frightening to think about.

Jesus tells us why: "Not everyone who says to me, 'Lord, Lord,' will enter the kingdom of heaven, but only he who does the will of my Father who is in heaven" (Matt. 7:21).

Sometimes people are not what they seem.

But the clues to the truth are all here, waiting to be discovered in the way we live.

—James

The clues

* What are the clues that God is at work in your own life?

The inconsistencies

* What areas of your life seem out of sync with who God made you to be?

The prayer

* Thank you, Lord, for the way you have worked in my life. Forgive me for my inconsistencies. Help me to be the same person at school that I am at church. Help me to be real. Keep working in my life. Turn me more and more into the person you want me to be. Amen.

DAY 245 Trash Talker

After buying our drinks and chips from the vending machine, my friends and I sat down at our usual corner table in the cafeteria. Then we started our daily routine—twenty straight minutes of putting down our classmates.

"There goes Amy," Britney said.

Brooke rolled her eyes.

"Why does that girl walk so funny?" she asked as she popped open her Diet Coke. "It looks like she's got a ten-pound weight strapped to her foot!"

"Forget her walk," I added. "The real mystery is why she wears that hideous green visor every day."

"Hey, at least it shields that huge nose of hers!" Jessica said with a mean laugh.

Ripping people apart was something my friends and I were really good at. We commented on everything from their ugly clothes to their funky post-P.E. smell.

Pause and think

* Have you been on the receiving end of these kinds of put-downs? The giving end? Both? With this in mind, write down your initial reaction to this scenario.

. . . the rest of the story

Summer came and I went on a three-week missions trip to Thailand with my youth group. I worked on a fish farm washing nets and flattening out the land around ponds to prevent erosion. As I worked side-by-side with kids from my youth group, I realized they were a lot different from my lunch crowd. They cared for each other. And their friendships weren't built on trashing anybody.

My stomach churned as I thought about how disappointed in me God must be. Making fun of people and putting them down—whether it was to their face or behind their back—was not right. The more I hung out

293

with my youth group friends, the more I realized how pointless and unkind gossiping was. During that summer I promised myself I'd quit.

When I returned to school in the fall, I told Brit, Brooke, and Jess that I wanted to stop gossiping. They gave me a hard time about my decision. And no matter how much I tried not to join in when they gossiped, I discovered I really couldn't stop. It soon became clear I had to stop spending so much time with them. So I started hanging out more with Abby, a Christian girl who transferred into my history class. At first it was hard to pass Brooke, Brit, and Jess in the halls. They'd whisper to one another as they shot me dirty looks. Although their mean stares hurt, it reminded me of why I'd pulled away from them in the first place.

With time, it's gotten easier to avoid talking about other people. Sometimes I still slip up. When I do, Abby is great about gently stopping me before I get carried away. And her kindness is definitely rubbing off on me. Instead of constantly finding fault with others, I now look for—and more easily see—the good in people.

—Joy

DAY 246 Two Bubbles

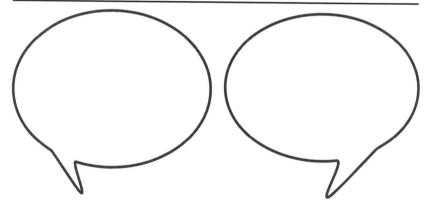

In one bubble, write some of the damaging or hurtful things you've said about or to someone. Confess those to God; ask for forgiveness. Now cross out those nasty words.

In the other bubble, write some of the encouraging and uplifting things you've said about or to others. Thank God for placing those words on your lips; ask God to continue to fill your thoughts with kindness and encouragement that would flow into your speech.

Now memorize the verse below. After you've memorized it, you can turn it into a prayer when you're tempted to gossip, use filthy language, or put someone down.

May the words of my mouth and the meditation of my heart be pleasing in your sight, O LORD, my Rock and my Redeemer.

—Psalm 19:14

DAY 247 Foolish Words

My friend Nathan and I were hanging at his house when his kid sister Gretchen walked in the room. "Hey squirt!" Nathan gave her a good-natured poke in her side.

"Stop it," Gretchen protested, but the smile behind her pout made it clear she enjoyed her older brother's attention.

"Hey Gretchen," I said. "I haven't seen you since you got out of the hospital—how's it going?" I hadn't meant to embarrass her, but she ducked her head and mumbled a quick "OK," letting me know she didn't want to say more about it. But Nathan did.

"She's doing great now," Nathan said. "She ought to after all the time and money it took to fix her up." Nathan went on to tell me more about Gretchen's rare disease, but he seemed really preoccupied with how much his sister's treatment and hospitalization had cost. "Dad figures the total is close to twenty thousand dollars!" Nathan exclaimed. "I mean, just think of what we could do with that much money!"

What Nathan didn't notice was the effect his report was having on his sister. Gretchen's eyes were hardly visible as she hid her face in her hands. Her frail frame looked even smaller as she slumped further into her chair.

Bible break

The tongue of the wise commends knowledge, but the mouth of the fool gushes folly. . . . The tongue that brings healing is a tree of life, but a deceitful tongue crushes the spirit.

—Proverbs 15:2, 4

. . . the rest of the story

I knew Nathan wasn't trying to hurt his sister's feelings. In fact, I could see how much he loved her and feared losing her during her illness. But his words were unintentionally foolish. He hadn't taken the time to think about his words before they tumbled out of his mouth.

Because I wasn't the one spouting the words, I was able to notice their impact on Gretchen. I found myself searching quickly for some way to turn Nathan's crushing words into healing words of life.

"So you're saying this little girl cost twenty thousand dollars?" I said, giving Nathan a chance to shut up and listen to what his words implied.

"Uh, well sort of . . ." Nathan's hedging reply showed me he would love to have some of those words back.

"And," I said, "she's worth every penny, right?" Gretchen lifted her face quickly and looked to Nathan for his reply.

"You better believe it," he said. "Worth every penny and a whole lot more."

As I left Nathan's house, I wondered how many times I'd foolishly let words fall out of my mouth without realizing the effect they could have on someone else.

—Nate

DAY 248 Do This

Think about a time in your past when your words have come out wrong. What could you have said instead? Before you joke around or tease someone, take half a second to think about how your words will come across.

Ask yourself, "Is there a chance my words will be taken the wrong way? Could I hurt someone's feelings?"

DAY 249 It Seems Like Everyone Swears

Q: I've decided not to watch movies or shows that have offensive language in them, but the place I hear the most swear words is school. What do I do about that? While I can't stop going to school, the stuff I hear there is affecting my thoughts. What can I do?

—Anonymous

Your turn

* **How would you answer this question?**

How IYF's expert answered:

A: First of all, congratulations for taking steps to keep offensive language out of your mind. The Bible is clear when it says, "Whatever is true, whatever is noble, whatever is right, whatever is pure, whatever is lovely, whatever is admirable—if anything is excellent or praiseworthy—think about such things" (Phil. 4:8). You are truly taking steps to make that true in your life. Good for you.

Stay away from swearing whenever you can, but when you do hear it, don't dwell on it. Today I sat near three guys in the airport who probably used the F-word in every other sentence they said. I prayed for them, then got up and moved.

It won't always be that easy. If your friends (or parents or teachers) use bad language, it's going be harder to get away from it. What can you do? Try to let it go in one ear and out the other. You may want to tell them—as politely as you can—you'd appreciate it if they tried to use cleaner language around you. Be careful not to come off as judging them or saying they are bad people. Just explain that it makes you feel uncomfortable.

Of course, some people aren't going to respect your wishes. In fact, it could get worse. And you're not going to be able to stop or get away from

297

all the swearing in the world. So try praying that God will help protect you from harmful influences. Pray that you won't hear it or that you'll have the ability to just let it go. It's amazing what God can do when we admit we can't handle a difficult situation on our own.

—Jim

DAY 250 My Words Hurt Her

"Come here," Kristen ordered. "You too," she said, motioning to our friend Lisa. "I've gotta tell you guys something!" We'd made it to history class a little early, so we had time to chat.

Kristen lowered her voice a bit. "Did you hear about how Melissa blew it during the relay at the track meet yesterday? On the third leg, she dropped the baton before passing it to her teammate, and it cost them the race."

"No way!" Lisa said, sounding a little too excited. "I mean, how hard is it to hold on to a tube and run?"

Before I even thought about what I was saying, I added my own juicy bit of gossip.

"Oh, do you know who else I heard messed up?"

Both Kristen and Lisa leaned in, obviously wanting to hear more.

"Apparently Grace was running hurdles when her foot somehow got caught," I said a little too loudly. "She stumbled and fell flat on her face!" I then snickered as I imagined her tumbling like a cartoon character. Kristen and Lisa erupted in laughter.

"She fell in gym class last week too!" Kristen said. "How klutzy can you get?"

"We should start calling her Graceless!" Lisa joked.

That's when I noticed that Grace was sitting a few desks over. I watched as her eyes filled with tears. I wanted to melt into the floor.

My mind raced as I tried to think how I could smooth this over. As my heart pounded against my chest, I slumped low as if I could hide from what I'd done. But I couldn't hide from the guilt I felt. My guilt only increased as I remembered a Bible passage we'd studied a few weeks earlier

298

in youth group: "Don't use foul or abusive language. Let everything you say be good and helpful, so that your words will be an encouragement to those who hear them" (Eph. 4:29 NLT).

Talking and laughing about how Grace had fallen certainly isn't good or helpful, I thought. *And who am I to rip on someone else for falling anyway? Like I've never tripped or made a fool of myself?*

I knew what I had to do. "I'm going over to Grace to apologize," I said softly.

"No, no! Just pretend it didn't happen," Lisa whispered.

That would have been the easy way out, but it wouldn't have been the right thing to do. I needed—and wanted—to apologize for saying something so hurtful and mean.

Lisa and Kristen looked at me like I'd lost my mind. Maybe they'd start a buzz around school about how I'd been crazy enough to go to Grace to apologize.

Let 'em talk, I thought as I sat down beside Grace. *I'm sure that's the kind of gossip God would like to see catch on.*

—Meryl

* *Look up* Proverbs 18:21 and Proverbs 21:23. **Write down what these verses say about the words you speak.**

DAY 251 When Words Are Weapons

Ever say something in an unguarded moment and then feel like an idiot? I know I have, and I'd hate to think I was the only one.

As careful as I try to be with my words, I know I've blurted out some pretty stupid stuff. I've heard words come out of my mouth and wondered, *Where did that come from?*

I've also been on the receiving end of angry words. Hateful words. Taunting words. I know how they can burn.

Take a moment to think of words that have hurt you—or words you have used to hurt others. It probably isn't difficult to remember those harsh words. It's one of the mysteries of speech: once spoken, words hang around to haunt us.

The Bible says, "We all stumble in many ways. If anyone is never at fault in what he says, he is a perfect man, able to keep his whole body in check" (James 3:2).

It sure would be great to have that kind of control over my words. Even though words can last forever, they leap past my lips in an instant—sometimes even quicker than my brain can consider them. Because of this, just thinking about changing my speech isn't good enough. I need to go deeper than my brain, all the way to the source of my words: my heart.

The Bible offers these insights: "Out of the same mouth come praise and cursing. My brothers, this should not be. Can both fresh water and salt water flow from the same spring?" (James 3:10–11).

Where good water flows, there's a sparkling spring at its source. In the same way, where good words flow, purity, compassion, and love are somewhere behind them.

When true faith enters my life, it sets a process in motion. It begins purifying the spring of my words right there at the source—my soul. As I fill my mind with Scripture, the purifying process accelerates. Before I know it, I am tasting good words instead of bitter regret.

If we want to know what's in our hearts, all we have to do is listen to our words.

—James

DAY 252 Do This

Make a list of people around you. Who on the list needs a word of praise or appreciation?

Circle two or three names that come quickly to mind. This week be sure to encourage or say something kind to the people you've circled.

DAY 253 Watchin' Your Words

"Retard!" my friend Vicki said teasingly to her friend Amanda. The near-empty hallway fell silent and all heads turned toward me. I said nothing.

"What? What did I say?" asked Vicki, confused and glancing around at our group of friends. "I don't understand," she stammered. A couple of people were looking nervously at me and then back at her.

"Vicki," Amanda explained, "Margaret has a sister who is mentally handicapped. Don't say the word *retard* like that. It's just not cool."

"Oh, I'm sorry. I didn't know. I didn't mean anything by it."

"Don't worry about it," I said softly as everyone moved on to the next subject. I was grateful for Vicki's willingness to change the direction of the conversation.

Throughout high school, I refused to participate in any kind of name-calling. I never liked it when people made fun of me or someone like my sister, so I didn't want to make fun of anyone else. Pretty soon word got out about the way I felt, and everyone stopped that kind of teasing around me.

I didn't have to get preachy about why I felt that way. I just gave my reasons once or twice, and that's all it took. After that my silence was usually enough to move the conversation in another direction.

Last week I was with another group of friends when one of the guys began gossiping about a person we all knew.

"Did you hear about . . ."

I started to feel uncomfortable. And by the silence in the room, I could tell others were also bothered by what was being said. Finally Sarah spoke up: "Hey guys, let's talk about something else."

That's all it took.

It's amazing how a simple, nonthreatening phrase, or even silence, can turn a conversation around. It can also do something else: each time I make the decision not to participate in put-downs and gossip, I show respect for another person. Even in silence I am saying, "You are important."

—Margaret

DAY 254 Pray This

Father, I'm thankful that you've created me with the ability to speak. Help me to use my words to build up rather than tear down, to spread peace and truth rather than discord and lies. Like the people in yesterday's story, help me to stand up for what's right and to guide conversations toward topics and speech that would honor you. In Jesus's name, amen.

DAY 255 Out of My Mind

A thought crawled out of my mind
the other day.
It didn't seem all that bad,
so I opened my mouth
and let it out.
The small thought
suddenly grew long and large and slithered
up to my little brother,
striking with venomous delight.
Throughout the day
other thoughts slipped
from my lips.
One bit my mother,
another hissed and spat at a teacher,
yet another cornered a friend
and struck deep.

A thought crawled out of my mind
the other day.
This time I pressed my lips together
and refused to let it out.
It struggled, it fought,
but my lips remained locked.
To my amazement, the small thought
soon withered and died
without a whimper.

302

Thought after thought
leapt out of my mind
the other day,
and I gladly let them take flight:
They soared and swooped with joy.
Wherever they landed,
they brought peace, praise,
and smiles.

—*Marie*

The words of a good person give life, like a fountain of water, but the words of the wicked contain nothing but violence.

—Proverbs 10:11 NCV

DAY 256 Joy in a Chicken Sandwich

In high school, worship musician David Crowder attended church on Sunday mornings and youth group on Wednesday nights. He scheduled quiet time with God every day. These were the specific times David shared his life with Christ.

"I had put God in little time blocks where I'd experience him," David says. "One day, God showed up in the middle of the day where I didn't expect him to poke his head up. In that moment, my view of God expanded."

Believe it or not, this big moment happened in a mall food court. "When you think spirituality or experiences of God, you're thinking church and praise hymns," David says. "But it was over a fast-food sandwich. I took one bite and was like, 'This is the best chicken sandwich ever.' I was feeling down, and this sandwich was like the rediscovery of joy. So here I am sitting in a mall food court with tears coming to my eyes."

Right then, David realized that everything good in life comes from the giver of good, God. And he can pop up anytime—not just Sundays and quiet times. He's everywhere. "God's at work in places that we wouldn't suspect him to be at work," David said.

"That's when I realized that every second is an opportunity for us to experience God. There's not a second he's not there and available to us."

—Todd

DAY 257 Reflect on This

Think of a time you had a really joyful or happy experience. Did you think about God during that time? Why or why not?

How can you bring God into those times you're laughing or just enjoying life?

DAY 258 14 Ways to Make People Laugh

1. At your next pep rally, gargle (or belch) your school song.
2. The next time a sporting event gets boring, draw a tiny face on your little finger and let Mr. Pinky give a play-by-play description of the game—in a high-pitched voice, of course.
3. During a conversation with your friends, say "chirpledeekirpledeedum" in the middle of each sentence.
4. Get some friends together and stuff as many grapes as possible behind your upper lip. Now try to carry on a conversation.
5. Stop someone on the street, pull out a map of Greece, and ask for directions to the Parthenon. (Caution: this won't work if you're actually in Greece.)
6. The next time you look through a microscope, announce to your lab partner: "Hey, look in here. It looks just like my uncle Stu!"
7. !sdneirf ruoy ot drawkcab klaT
8. Blow soap bubbles and say to each one, "Good Witch Glenda, oh Good Witch Glenda, are you in there? It's me, Dorothy."
9. Paint smiley faces on an old pair of shoes and wear them to school.
10. Put a cute little dress on your pooch and take her (or him) for a walk in a crowded park.
11. The next time you're at the zoo, do your best imitations of the animals that are drawing the biggest crowds.
12. Hit yourself in the face with a whipped cream pie.
13. Wear socks on your hands. When people ask about it, say matter-of-factly, "My toes are protesting."
14. Just laugh—it's contagious, ya know.

—Chris

DAY 259 Celebrate!

Psalm 126:2 says, "We celebrated with laughter" (CEV). Whether you're at an amusement park, forest preserve, city park, miniature golf course, or the beach, listen for joyous laughter. Each time you hear someone laugh, take a moment to silently thank God for the gift of laughter. And be sure to celebrate by laughing often.

DAY 260 God's Best Jokes

Have you ever thought about how funny some of the stories from the Bible are?

Like the time God told ninety-nine-year-old Abraham and his ninety-year-old wife, Sarah, they would have their first child. At first Abraham laughed *at* God, but after the birth of Isaac he learned to laugh *with* God. In fact, it was God's idea to name the kid Isaac (which means laughter).

Or the time in 2 Samuel 6:14 when we see King David so caught up in worship that he dances in his underwear! Add that to the list of things you can't do in church.

Or in 1 Kings 18:25–29 when Elijah challenges the prophets of Baal. In the first recorded instance of trash-talking, Elijah suggests Baal isn't answering because he is probably on the toilet.

What about Acts 20:9–10? It's the story of the time Paul preached for so long that a young guy named Eutychus fell asleep and fell three stories out of the window he was leaning against (funny) and died (not funny) but was miraculously brought back to life by Paul (OK, funny again!).

Then there's Jesus. Don't think that he didn't know how to have fun. His first miracle was at a wedding party where he turned water into wine so the party could keep rolling. Jesus did other wacky things. On more than one occasion, Jesus used spit in healing miracles (thankfully not something he did when he turned that water into wine).

Jesus also said some stuff that would have been pretty funny to those around. In Matthew 23:24 he tells the Pharisees, "You blind leaders! You strain out a small fly but swallow a camel" (CEV). While this is a funny mental picture, it's also an example of Jesus having fun with words. In Aramaic, the word for gnat (*galma*) sounds a lot like the word for camel (*gamla*).

In Matthew 23:27 Jesus told a group of Pharisees that they were nothing more than sparkling tombs, nice and clean on the outside, but filled with rotting corpses on the inside (to which I'd like to imagine Peter quickly replying, "Oh snap! Thou hath burnt him, Jesus!").

This is all fun, but God's love for laughter goes much deeper than funny or playful Bible verses. It's most revealed in the life, sacrifice, and hope of Jesus. In his final dark hours before death, Jesus kept talking about joy. He told his disciples that while there is sin, pain, and chaos in this world, they would have joy—we would have joy—by trusting and following him. In John 15:11, Jesus told them, "I have told you these things so that you will be filled with my joy. Yes, your joy will overflow!" (NLT).

The joy Jesus talks about is a joy bigger than what's going on in your life right now. It is a joy that can dance in the face of death. It is the joy of God that flowed from his heart into the everyday life of Jesus, and through his death was made available to you and me. It is the joy of Jesus that gives us every reason to laugh, to dance, to sing, and to know the heart of the Father.

—Jarrett

* Is "funny" a word you have ever used to describe God? Why or why not?

* How does looking at these passages of Scripture change or reinforce the way you view God?

DAY 261 Make a List

Think about some of your funny, fun, and joyful experiences. Maybe laughing with your friends so hard that your stomach hurt. Maybe a fun vacation with your family. List some of those memories below:

1.
2.

3.

4.

5.

Now thank God for those blessings. If the mood strikes, laugh about your fun times during your prayer. Really.

> Every good and perfect gift is from above, coming down from the Father of the heavenly lights, who does not change like shifting shadows.
>
> —James 1:17

DAY 262 Break Time!

My eyes were glued to the television as the words across the bottom of the screen listed school after school. "Where's my school?" I whined as I shut off the TV and continued working through my mound of homework.

It was nearly midnight, and the snow and ice fell rapidly. As I stared out my window before I went to sleep, the streets and yards looked like a sea of marshmallows. I couldn't believe I'd have to gather up my books in the morning and trudge to the bus stop.

When my radio alarm went off, I listened as the DJ read the list of schools that were closed. This time my school made the list!

I fell back on my pillow, smiling as I drifted back to sleep. Around noon I dragged myself out of bed. I got on the phone and started calling friends to find out how everybody else was spending the day off. Somebody suggested we pull out our sleds and meet on the hill over by my old elementary school. After bundling up, I headed for the schoolyard.

As I prepared for another ride down the slippery hill, a snowball smacked me on the back of my head. I turned to see Katie standing several feet from me, grinning and reaching for more snow. I grabbed my own handful of snow, pressed it into a solid white ball, and tossed it, hitting her on the side of her arm. I shouted, "Gotcha back!" Before long, all my friends had joined the fight.

We spent that whole afternoon sledding, and making snowmen and snow angels. Sometime during the day, something besides a snowball hit me. I realized I was actually having fun. Fun? Boy, that was a word I hadn't thought of for a real long time. I'd been so busy with papers, tests, and worrying over grade point averages that I'd forgotten how to have a good time.

As we continued to play in the snow, I was amazed at how young I felt—and acted. With thoughts of homework, tests, and papers on hold, I felt so carefree. It was almost as if I was five years old again!

I believe God used that big snowfall to wake me up to an important truth: no matter how "grown up" I think I am, no matter how busy my schedule gets, I have to take time to play and laugh. After all, decent grades aren't worth much if I'm too burned out to enjoy them.

—Rachel

* Are you stressed out? yes no

* Have you taken a break lately? yes no

* If the answer was yes to the first question and no to the second, take a cue from Rachel. Do something fun. Soon.

DAY 263 Commit to Have Fun

Stuck in a no-fun rut? Here are some commitments worth making:

1. I will spend an afternoon in the children's department of my local library reading books I loved as a kid.
2. I will watch a cartoon show that used to be my absolute favorite.
3. I will show up at youth group with a gallon of ice cream, whipped cream, chocolate syrup, and sprinkles, and announce, "Sundaes for everybody!"
4. I will jump rope with my younger sibs (or with a little kid from my neighborhood).
5. I will spend one Saturday morning playing at my old elementary school playground.
6. I will spend an afternoon with a friend making snow angels (or sand angels).

7. I will go to McDonald's with my friends and talk everybody into ordering Happy Meals.
8. I will wear socks that don't match.
9. I will do somersaults down the biggest hill I can find.
10. I will smile for no reason at all—except that it makes me feel good.
11. I will _____(fill in the blank with your own idea).

DAY 264 Think about It

Studies show that laughter has a role in fighting viruses, bacteria, cancer, and heart disease. It's also known to release chemicals that fight stress and help you relax. God knew what he was doing when he put laughter in our DNA.

Try this

* Discover what really makes you laugh and keep doing it. Hang out more with that crazy, fun-loving friend. Regularly watch movies that leave you rolling on the floor. Just be sure to take time to give yourself a much-needed laugh.

Memorize Proverbs 15:13 (Message)

A cheerful heart brings a smile to your face; a sad heart makes it hard to get through the day.

DAY 265 Forgive My Friends?

"So what's the big news?" I asked my best friend Ben over the phone. I was working as a lifeguard at a Christian camp, and I'd just hung up with a girl from back home. Cassie and I liked each other and planned to discuss dating after I got back from camp. As we were saying goodbye, she mentioned Ben had something to tell me. So I called him right away.

"Well, I broke up with my girlfriend this week," Ben replied slowly. "And I have a new one."

My stomach dropped. I didn't want to ask, but I had to. "Who?"

He said *her* name. I could barely breathe. I finally managed to say "bye" and hung up. I was filled with anger and hurt. Betrayed.

Think about it

* What would you do in this situation?

* How has a friend betrayed you?

* Were you able to forgive that friend?

. . . the rest of the story

Later that night at a campfire, the chaplain encouraged campers to share testimonies. Slowly I stood. "Life stinks sometimes," I began. "But when the bad times come along, just remember God is there for you. Always. Remember his promise that all things work together for the good of those who love him."

When I sat down, I felt a wave of peace wash through my entire body. The storm of thoughts that had raged through my mind vanished, and a passage came to mind: "Do not be anxious about anything. . . . Present your requests to God. . . . The peace of God, which transcends all understanding, will guard your hearts and your minds in Christ Jesus" (Phil. 4:6–7).

God knew I needed to be reminded of his promise. But still, how would I react when I saw my friends at church? I didn't know, but I wasn't worried or angry anymore. I knew no matter what happened with Ben and Cassie, God would help me through it.

You know what? He did. Not that it was easy. It'll take awhile for my friends to earn back my trust. But I could honestly tell them that I forgave them.

—John

Keep thinking

* Why was John able to forgive?

DAY 266 When I Don't Forgive, I Feel . . .

When I don't forgive, I feel . . .

Judgmental ("You're a jerk!")

Hateful ("I despise you!")

Guilty ("I feel bad about how I reacted.")

Unforgiven ("If I cannot forgive, do I deserve God's forgiveness?")

When I forgive, I feel . . .

Nonjudgmental

Merciful

Guilt-free

Forgiven

* *What about you?* How do you feel when you forgive? How do you feel when you don't?

DAY 267 Why Forgive?

Sometimes forgiveness seems impossible. God never said it was easy. Do you think it was easy for Jesus to forgive the people who hung him on a cross? But whether it is easy or not, forgiveness is the right thing to do. And it is right not just because it brings us nice, warm feelings of freedom and joy—but because God wants us to do it.

And that's reason enough.

—Mark

* Is there anyone God wants you to forgive?

DAY 268 Letting Go of Bitterness

On the fifth season of *American Idol*, Mandisa Hundley got national attention for her response to Simon Cowell's rude comments about her weight. Mandisa first heard the judge's comments—like everyone else—when the episode aired.

"I was watching the show with Christian friends," Mandisa said. "Three of them immediately prayed over me that God would give me peace. And then one friend prayed that the Lord would help me forgive Simon."

Right then, Mandisa realized her hurt and pain were not as important as forgiveness. "I've said worse things about others than what Simon said about me—and God keeps forgiving me," she says. "Besides, I learned forgiving has more to do with the person forgiving than the person being forgiven. I found peace. I let go of the bitterness."

When she next saw Simon, she said, "You hurt me, I cried, and it was painful, but I want you to know that I've forgiven you. I figure that if Jesus could die so that all of my wrongs could be forgiven, I can certainly extend that same grace to you."

—Todd

Memorize this

Put up with each other, and forgive anyone who does you wrong, just as Christ has forgiven you.

—Colossians 3:13 CEV

DAY 269 Tough Question

Q: I know I'm supposed to love others, but what do I do about people who are just mean or who seem to hate me? I find myself wanting to react in an ungodly manner. What can I do?

—Anonymous

A: Loving everyone no matter what isn't easy, is it? Dealing with jerks starts with trying to ignore them. Sure, their words and actions hurt, but don't give them any satisfaction by reacting to what they say and do. Find some trusted friends or a teacher or counselor to share your hurts with and try your best to stay away from them.

If these mean people are deeply affecting how you view yourself or are causing you physical harm, you need to talk to someone at school. Get yourself out of that situation. But whatever you do, try to show respect for both yourself and them. That's right: respect them. Keep treating them how you wish they'd treat you.

Bible break

Treat others as you want them to treat you. This is what the Law and the Prophets are all about.

—Matthew 7:12 CEV

As hard as it may sound, you should also pray for those unlovable people who mistreat you.

When my daughter Heidi was in eighth grade, three of her best friends turned on her. It hurt her badly, but she treated them with kindness and we often prayed for them. That didn't mean the girls stopped their bullying, though. They kept going, even though Heidi never treated them the same way.

Heidi is now a senior, and just last week two of the mean girls apologized. Heidi forgave them, and she was also very honest with them about the hurt they'd caused. These girls will never be Heidi's good friends again, but the moral of this story is this: even when you feel like it, do not stoop to the level of mean kids. Don't let their hate make you hateful too.

—Jim

DAY 270 God's Miracle Cure

I hated her. And who could blame me? My onetime friend was spreading rumors that I'd lied to her. I became obsessed with the damage this girl was doing to my reputation.

313

Forgiveness was out of the question. She deserved judgment, and I daydreamed about payback. She deserved it and I wanted my revenge.

But then God got in the way.

A friend of mine told me that he was praying for me—and the girl who hurt me. I was shocked. "You're praying for *her*? Why?"

"Because that's what God wants us to do," he replied. "And I think you should pray for her too."

I wanted nothing to do with that, but deep down I knew my friend was right. God had shown me the kind of love he expected me to show to my ex-friend. Like my friend suggested, I started praying for this girl. At first the prayers were very short and completely guilt-driven. But after a few weeks, something incredible happened. I grew tired of my grudge. Forgiveness seemed to be the only way to break the hold that anger and hatred had on me. So I told her I forgave her. And I meant it.

I wish I could say my act of forgiveness went over well with the girl who'd hurt me. It didn't. But it did some amazing things for me.

First, by offering this girl forgiveness, I gave up my right to get even.

Second, by forgiving her, I changed the way I thought of her. Now she was no longer the girl who hurt me. She was someone who needed my prayers.

Third, by being forgiving, my feelings of anger and hatred were changing to feelings of compassion and eventually kindness.

Forgiveness may not have been the magic formula to repairing our friendship, but it was repairing me. Miraculously.

—Harold

Be like Harold

* Who should you pray for right now?

* Whom do you need to tell, "I forgive you"?

DAY 271 An Idiot Finds Forgiveness
(Sam's fake interview with a for-real Bible character)

My editor assigned me to learn about King David, so I talked to a guy who witnessed one of the worst days of David's life.

Q: What happened the first time you met King David?

A: Well, I didn't really "meet" him. He was actually just passing through my little town with those in his army who still supported him.

Q: What happened to David's other supporters?

A: Well, David's son Absalom had gathered a large following in a conspiracy to kill his father and take over the throne. So David and the soldiers who remained loyal to him were fleeing for their lives through my hometown.

Q: So you went out to support your good king?

A: I . . . well, I called him a scoundrel and a "man of blood." I was glad that he had been kicked out of the kingdom. I wanted to make him as miserable as possible. You have to understand that I'm a relative of Saul's, the guy who was king before David. If the crown had stayed in the family, I could have been an earl or a duke or something.

Q: So you thought some name-calling would bother the king? You know what they say: "Sticks and stones will break my bones, but words will never hurt me."

A: Well, I *did* throw stones. I climbed up a hill and chucked rocks at David and his men as they marched by. When I ran out of rocks, I kicked a bunch of dirt down on their heads.

Q: Did you not notice David's army?

A: Not really my smartest decision. I'm an idiot. Luckily David told his men not to hurt me. He just kept moving.

Q: So how'd you feel when Absalom was defeated and David returned to power?

A: I knew I was in big, big trouble. So I went to see David on his first day back. I admitted what I had done was wrong, apologized, and asked him to forgive me. And he did. He gave me an oath that he wouldn't let any of his commanders harm me.

315

Q: *Just like that?*

A: Just like that. I'd never understood what the people meant when they talked about David as "a man after God's own heart." But when he forgave my mistake without even thinking about it, I realized he did have a loving and forgiving heart—just like God.

* **Who is the real Bible character behind Sam's fake interview? Find out in 2 Samuel 16:5–14.**

DAY 272 They Didn't Deserve Forgiveness

Rap artist KJ-52 had this to say about his decision to forgive his parents:

I had a lot of held-in anger after my parents' divorce. If someone said the wrong things, I'd go off. It was easy to play the victim and to use my parents' divorce as an excuse. It was easy to think, *I can act this way because of what happened.* Of course, it's OK to feel, to mourn, and to be angry. But eventually I had to reach a point of saying, "I'm not going to dwell on anger or bitterness. I'm going to move forward because I trust God is going to give me the strength to do that." I realized that if God could forgive me for all the things I'd done, then surely he could give me the strength to forgive my parents. That really pulled me through.

Even when you have the right to be angry, it's not always right to exercise that anger. It's so much better to walk in love with somebody than to walk in hate or anger. It got to the point where I had to choose to say, "God, I'm going to do what you tell me to do, because that's what you want—even when it's hard."

—KJ-52

DAY 273 The Unforgiving Servant

Then Peter came to Jesus and asked, "Lord, how many times shall I forgive my brother when he sins against me? Up to seven times?"

Jesus answered, "I tell you, not seven times, but seventy-seven times.

"Therefore, the kingdom of heaven is like a king who wanted to settle accounts with his servants. As he began the settlement, a man who owed him ten thousand talents was brought to him. . . . The servant fell on his knees before him. 'Be patient with me,' he begged, 'and I will pay back everything.' The servant's master took pity on him, canceled the debt and let him go.

"But when that servant went out, he found one of his fellow servants who owed him a hundred denarii. He grabbed him and began to choke him. 'Pay back what you owe me!' he demanded.

"His fellow servant fell to his knees and begged him, 'Be patient with me, and I will pay you back.'

"But he refused. Instead, he went off and had the man thrown into prison until he could pay the debt. . . .

"The master called the servant in. 'You wicked servant,' he said, 'I canceled all that debt of yours because you begged me to. Shouldn't you have had mercy on your fellow servant just as I had on you?' In anger his master turned him over to the jailers to be tortured, until he should pay back all he owed.

"This is how my heavenly Father will treat each of you unless you forgive your brother from your heart."

—Matthew 18:21–35

Stretch your brain muscles

* Go back and read this story again—*slowly*. This time underline the words and phrases that jump out at you. Circle anything that doesn't make sense to you, and then take your questions to your pastor, youth pastor, or small group leader. Finally, write a one-line summary of what this parable tells you about forgiving others.

DAY 274 Don't Worry

Version 1.0

> Do not be anxious about anything, but in everything, by prayer and petition, with thanksgiving, present your requests to God. And the peace of God, which transcends all understanding, will guard your hearts and your minds in Christ Jesus.
>
> —Philippians 4:6–7

Version 2.0

> Don't fret or worry. Instead of worrying, pray. Let petitions and praises shape your worries into prayers, letting God know your concerns. Before you know it, a sense of God's wholeness, everything coming together for good, will come and settle you down. It's wonderful what happens when Christ displaces worry at the center of your life.
>
> —Philippians 4:6–7 Message

Version 3.0

* **Circle words or phrases of the translations above that really speak to you. Next, write your own version of Philippians 4:6–7.**

DAY 275 No Spirit of Fear

When I saw the movie *I Am Legend*, I left halfway through, terrified that the world could end any minute in mass chaos and carnage. (OK, I'm kind of a wimp when it comes to seeing blood and destruction.) I did eventually finish watching *I Am Legend*, but that experience helped me see that everyone has limits when it comes to fear. And that's OK.

That experience reminded me that God doesn't give us a spirit of fear, but one of power and self-control (2 Tim. 1:7). After all, fretting about the future (and trying to predict it) doesn't help—it just makes us more fearful. In fact, Christ tells us not to worry about what will come tomorrow and beyond. He says, "Each day has enough trouble of its own" (Matt. 6:34).

Yes, there is plenty to fear. However, if you have trusted Christ as your Savior, you have nothing to worry about. In Psalm 91:14–15, God says, "I will rescue those who love me. I will protect those who trust in my name. When they call on me . . . I will be with them in [times of] trouble" (NLT).

—Michelle

Stick it in your head

* Choose one of the Bible verses in Michelle's story to look up and memorize this week.

DAY 276 The Rope

My memory is a long rope
stretching backward from where I stand.
If I let go I will tumble into the darkness
of a future filled with fear.

So I cling tightly to the rope,
knowing it is thick and strengthened
by many smaller strings twisted together:
with stories of joy and celebration;
with stories of pain turned to hope;
with stories of lessons learned.

Stepping now into the future,
I will continue to cling to my memory
each step of the way,
trusting I won't fall
into the dark unknown,
because my past is anchored to
the eternal love of God.

—Marie

319

Think it through

* Marie is wrestling mainly with fear of what?

* What helps calm Marie's fear?

Pray it through

I will remember the deeds of the LORD; yes, I will remember your miracles of long ago. I will meditate on all your works and consider all your mighty deeds.

—Psalm 77:11–12

DAY 277 Worry Gets Us Nowhere

That is why I tell you not to worry about everyday life—whether you have enough food and drink, or enough clothes to wear. Isn't life more than food, and your body more than clothing? . . . Can all your worries add a single moment to your life?

—Matthew 6:25, 27 NLT

* What do you tend to worry about the most? What does this passage tell you about these worries?

DAY 278 What's It Saying?

There is no fear in love. But perfect love drives out fear, because fear has to do with punishment. The one who fears is not made perfect in love.

—1 John 4:18

* What it says about fear:

* What it says about God:

* What it means for me:

> Don't be bluffed into silence by the threats of bullies. There's nothing they can do to your soul, your core being. Save your fear for God, who holds your entire life—body and soul—in his hands.
>
> —Matthew 10:28 Message

* What it says about fear:

* What it says about God:

* What it means for me:

> The seed that fell among the thorns represents those who hear God's word, but all too quickly the message is crowded out by the worries of this life and the lure of wealth, so no fruit is produced.
>
> —Matthew 13:22 NLT

* What it says about fear:

* What it says about God:

* What it means for me:

DAY 279 Tough Question

Q: I have a hard time witnessing. I'm not ashamed of God. I am just afraid of making a fool of myself or being rejected. Does this make me a bad Christian? How can I witness without these fears?

—Anonymous

A: Very few people aren't afraid of rejection when sharing their faith. This is normal. My best advice is this: instead of worrying about what to say, just live out your faith in front of people. The apostle John gave great advice when he wrote, "My dear children, let's not just talk about love; let's practice real love" (1 John 3:18 Message). My friend Jon is a good example of what it means to live out this verse. His loving actions make people feel special and important. One person has even described Jon like this: "Whenever I am with him, I feel like the privileged guest at a party in my honor." What a great witness to God's love.

Witnessing is sometimes easier than we think. I remember in high school I really wanted to witness to my best friend. He and I had never talked about faith and I was very scared about witnessing to him. After praying for a while, I invited him on a retreat. There he found Christ. Wow. A simple invitation to a retreat was all it took to make an eternal difference in my friend's life. Why was I so worried about it?

My encouragement to you: keep your eyes on eternity and it will be easier to face your fear of sharing your faith in the present.

—Jim

Make it personal

* How could Jim's advice about this person's fears be applied to whatever you are worried or scared about right now? Circle phrases in Jim's answer that give you peace or encouragement.

DAY 280 Letting Go of Fear

I used to be terrified of bulldozers. Every time I saw one, I'd grab hold of my dad's leg and refuse to let go. I thought those big, yellow monsters were going to capture me in their buckets and take me far away from my family. Irrational? Maybe a little. But I was a child, and my fears seemed very real.

We all fear things. Whether it is the imminent presence of sickness and tragedy or the pain of lost dreams and failures. Some days my fears consume me, leaving me confused and doubtful. I spend countless hours worrying about stuff that may never happen. I know life's not supposed to be like this—God never intended for me to live this way.

Jesus says, "Do not let your hearts be troubled. Trust in God, trust also in me" (John 14:1). Sounds simple. But we know it's difficult to do.

Especially when it seems God has his own agenda—which can sometimes be much different from our own.

God has a plan for *all* of us (Jer. 29:11). So how can we question the will of God for our lives when he is the very one who gave us breath? God promises to make our fears disappear and to calm our shaking souls. And when my fears threaten to overwhelm me, he's there showing me I can trust this promise.

—Amber

Imagine it

* Think about the scene Amber describes: a young girl grasps tightly to her dad at the sight of a scary metal monster. Close your eyes. What feelings would she feel in that moment? What does her father provide? How is that similar to how God comforts?

A calming father

I am the LORD, your God, who takes hold of your right hand and says to you, Do not fear; I will help you.

—Isaiah 41:13

DAY 281 God Is . . .

My confidence

Have no fear of sudden disaster or of the ruin that overtakes the wicked, for the LORD will be your confidence and will keep your foot from being snared.

—Proverbs 3:25–26

My shepherd

The LORD is my shepherd. He gives me everything I need. . . . He gives me new strength. . . . Even though I walk through the darkest valley, I will not be afraid. You are with me. Your shepherd's rod and staff comfort me.

—Psalm 23:1, 3–4 NIrV

My shelter

> He will cover you with his wings. Under the feathers of his wings you will find safety. He is faithful. He will keep you safe like a shield or a tower. You won't have to be afraid of the terrors that come during the night.

> —Psalm 91:4–5 NIrV

DAY 282 | I Wanted to Fit In

A thick haze of cigarette smoke hung in the air of the fraternity house and the air reeked of alcohol and strong cologne. It was my first weekend in college and I'd come to a frat party with some other freshman girls. It didn't take long, though, for me to lose them in the crowd.

For the first time in my life, I had no one looking over my shoulder to see if I was doing the "right things." And while I didn't want to throw away my Christian values, I also didn't want to feel like an outsider. I was sure going to this party would help me fit in.

But without a beer in my hand, I definitely looked out of place. So I grabbed a can of beer, wedged my finger under the tab, and nervously pushed upward.

Before I forced myself to take my first swig, I heard someone say, "I've never seen anyone inspect their drink so much."

I turned to see a guy standing behind me.

I gave a nervous laugh and said, "I guess I'm a beginner."

"So you're a freshman."

"Is it obvious?"

"Only because you look like you're about to drink poison."

As I fidgeted awkwardly with my can, I saw that he wasn't holding one. "Where's yours?"

"Oh, it's not my thing."

"You don't drink?"

"Nah."

"But you're at a frat party. You're supposed to, right?"

"Not necessarily. I live here, actually. And hi, I'm Kevin."

"Nice to meet you, Kevin. I'm Elizabeth. . . . This is your fraternity? And you don't drink?" I noticed a cross necklace around his neck.

"Right. I still go out and have a good time, just without the alcohol."
He smiled and nodded toward my beer. "Are you sure you want that?"

I didn't say anything, but simply put down the can. I immediately felt relieved.

"Doesn't it get frustrating being the only sober person at a party?" I asked.

"Not anymore," Kevin responded. "But it wasn't always easy for me to turn down a drink."

"Did you used to drink?"

"I drank once at the beginning of my freshman year, just to see what it was like. But now I've seen what the other side is like, and it's not worth it. Just look at all these people." He motioned toward all the people who were stumbling around and shouting vulgar things. "I didn't want to be that."

"But it seems like everyone is into partying."

"Not everyone is into drinking. Have you ever heard of Campus Crusade for Christ?"

"No, what is it?"

"It's a Christian group on campus," he said. "It meets every Thursday night. That's where I met people who shared my faith but still wanted to have fun on campus."

The next Thursday night I went to the meeting for Campus Crusade for Christ and I realized that Kevin and I weren't the only Christians on campus. In fact, there were hundreds of other students there. Soon I had a close group of Christian friends.

I still face difficult choices. Each time I do, I turn to God and my Christian friends for guidance. As for parties, I now know I don't have to pick up a beer so I can fit in with the crowd. I want to be the kind of person that I would seek out at a party. Amidst the haze, I want to shine.

—Elizabeth

Think it through

* What can you learn from Elizabeth's story about making God-honoring choices?

DAY 283 Stretch Your Brain Muscles

Don't copy the behavior and customs of this world, but let God transform you into a new person by changing the way you think. Then you will learn to know God's will for you, which is good and pleasing and perfect.

—Romans 12:2 NLT

* Go back and read the passage again—*slowly*. OK, read it a third time and underline the words and phrases that jump out at you. Circle the ones that make no sense at all. Now try to answer this question: what does Romans 12:2 tell you about making godly choices? Not sure? Take your questions—and your circled words and phrases—to your youth pastor, pastor, or small group leader.

DAY 284 What My Choices Say about Me

I don't want to say no. After all, my friends are going. I don't want to feel left out. Sometimes they think I'm weird anyway. They tease me about being a "goody-two-shoes." They tell me, "Not all R-rated movies are bad." Maybe they're right.

But I'm feeling pulled. My parents would definitely say no. They're strict about stuff like movies. But are they always right? Can't they trust me to make the right decision?

And what about *me*? How do I feel about R-rated movies?

I'm not sure.

I've seen a few on DVD, and to be honest I've felt a little dirty afterward. Like I needed to have my brain dry-cleaned. So I made a promise to myself: no more R-rated movies. But now all my friends are going.

Some decisions are just plain easy: Will I push the button for Pepsi or Sprite? Mushrooms or green peppers on my pizza? Those are no-brainers.

Some decisions, though, are tougher. Like, will I take another year of Spanish?

Then there are decisions that go a bit deeper. That say something about who I am. And about what I believe and value.

Take the major paper I have to finish for English class. There's a box in our attic with all my big sister's term papers. One of those papers is an English assignment with a huge, red A+ at the top. I could take it, change it a bit. My teacher would never know. After all, I need a good grade on this paper. Without it I could flunk the class, not to mention disappoint my parents and my teacher.

I can't escape something that's true about me. I have these things called values. I know keeping them will make me a better person. I know keeping them will make me feel better about who I am.

After much thought, sweat, and prayer, I've made a couple of decisions: The R-rated movie is out. And I'm going to leave my sister's paper in that box in the attic.

Suddenly I feel kind of, well, free. No, my decisions don't set me free to do what I want. And right now they don't make me feel very happy. But they do set me free from all the bad stuff that can come from wrong decisions.

I know I'll eventually feel good about the decisions I've made. After all, there will be no guilt. No regrets. That's the kind of freedom I can live with.

—Michael

DAY 285 Difficult Decisions

* What difficult decision are you facing right now?

* Why is it a difficult decision?

* What could be some positive results of the right decision?

* What could be some negative consequences of the wrong decision?

* Who is someone you could go to for advice before you make your decision?

DAY 286 Before You Decide . . .

Whatever tough decisions you're facing, you can't go wrong following these tips:

Ask God about it. Jesus put it like this: "Ask and it will be given to you; seek and you will find; knock and the door will be opened to you" (Matt. 7:7). When it comes to making decisions, you can expect God's help. Be sure and ask for it.

Listen for an answer. By speaking through your conscience, God often lets you know what you should do. It's important to remember, though, that God's "voice" will never contradict his Word, the Bible. If it does, it's not God's voice.

Look for an answer. When faced with a tough problem, go to the Bible for help. Use an index or concordance to look up the issue or topic that concerns you. And don't overlook Proverbs, a book in the Bible that contains tons of practical advice.

Make a list of pros and cons. Ask yourself: What are the pluses of doing this? What are the minuses? Getting the positives and negatives on paper can give you a clear picture of what you should or shouldn't do.

Talk to someone. Proverbs 12:15 says, "Fools think their own way is right, but the wise listen to others" (NLT). When faced with a tough decision, get help from your parents, your youth pastor, or a trusted Christian friend.

DAY 287 My Friends Make Stupid Choices

Q: Many of my friends do things that are legal—but just stupid. Some are eighteen and smoke. One rides a motorcycle without a helmet (and our state has no laws against it). When something's legal, how do I discourage stupid things?

—Anonymous

328

Your turn

* How would you answer this question?

How IYF's expert answered:

A: You're right—just because something is legal doesn't mean it's a safe choice. To make it worse, studies show that part of the brain that helps with making those safe choices isn't fully developed until after we get into our twenties. This means there are a lot of sad stories of people who made one bad decision early in life and faced heavy consequences like addiction, paralysis, or even death.

What can you do? Remind your friends that decisions they make today will affect them for the rest of their lives. Most of all, strive to model a standard of wise decisions for your friends. Let your standard be to live for more than yourself. Colossians 3:17 is a good guideline: "And whatever you do, whether in word or deed, do it all in the name of the Lord Jesus." God wants us to live full lives and have fun, but to do all things in his name—and that means doing them with love and respect for ourselves, others, and God.

—Jim

DAY 288 What's So Great about Good Decisions?

When you're tempted to give up your values and beliefs, remember these five reasons for making good decisions:

1. *Good decisions make you a better person.* You can't help but feel good about yourself when you know you've made the right choice.

2. *Good decisions win the trust of others.* Do you want to be known as a person of your word? The best way to win trust is to prove yourself trustworthy through the decisions you make.

3. *Good decisions make for a good reputation.* While not everyone will agree with your decisions, you'll win some respect when you stick to your values and beliefs.

4. Good decisions show others the right way to go. You can talk about good and bad decisions. You can pass on good advice. But if you really want to influence someone, set a good example by making good decisions.

5. Good decisions create lasting habits. One cool thing about good decisions is that they build on one another. A series of good choices creates a very good habit. And once something becomes a habit, you hardly have to think about it. You simply do the right thing.

DAY 289 Good Advice from a Wise Guy

If you want to make wise choices, you can't go wrong checking out this very practical advice from Proverbs—sometimes called the book of wisdom:

Tempted by gossip?

> A gossip betrays a confidence, but a trustworthy man keeps a secret.
>
> —11:13

Wondering about that "harmless" little lie?

> Like a madman shooting firebrands or deadly arrows is a man who deceives his neighbor and says, "I was only joking!"
>
> —26:18–19

Are you working overtime just to get more stuff?

> Don't wear yourself out trying to get rich; restrain yourself! Riches disappear in the blink of an eye; wealth sprouts wings and flies off into the wild blue yonder.
>
> —23:4–5 Message

To party or not to party?

> It isn't smart to get drunk! Drinking makes a fool of you and leads to fights.
>
> —20:1 CEV

Daily advice for a whole month

* This is only a taste of all the great wisdom and good advice you'll find in Proverbs. Take a month to read through this book's thirty-one chapters.

DAY 290 Why Wouldn't God Listen?

My grandma was almost ninety years old when two strokes left her unconscious. Doctors said she probably wouldn't wake up. I knew Grandma was a Christian, but I wasn't ready for her to die. I needed to say goodbye.

I had faith that God would heal her, so I prayed constantly.

But Grandma didn't get better. She had another stroke. As she got sicker, my faith slowly slipped into doubt. I felt like God wasn't even listening. I didn't want anyone to know I was feeling pretty far away from God, but my mom didn't give me the choice to skip youth group that week.

As soon as I arrived, Sarah, my small group leader, gave me a hug and told me she was still praying for my grandma. I swallowed hard and did my best to hold back my tears.

Later that night, Sarah talked to our small group about prayer and how cool it was when you could see God working in your life.

"Do you feel connected to God when you pray?" Sarah asked us.

No one said anything for a long time. Then my friend Kelly spoke up: "Sometimes I pray and pray. But I feel like God isn't really listening."

"I think we all feel like that sometimes," Sarah said gently. "But remember, even if you don't feel God, that doesn't mean he's not there. He's listening to everything you say."

"Then why does it seem like he's not answering my prayers?" someone else asked.

Sarah paused for a minute. "He answers every single prayer," she said. "Even if you don't understand why you're going through something difficult, God really is in control and he loves you. That's why you can have faith and trust in him."

I spent the entire night just listening to Sarah and my friends. The more I listened, the more I felt like God was talking directly to me.

I went home and prayed, "Lord, even though I don't understand it, I know your plan is best. Protect my grandma and keep her from any pain."

A few days later my grandma died. She never woke up so I could say goodbye.

My faith was challenged that week. But I can also see how it grew until I learned to trust God, even when it was hard to understand why bad things happen. I eventually got the courage to tell Sarah that I had doubted God. After talking to her, I could see how God was in control the whole time my grandma was sick.

Because Grandma was unconscious, she was never in any pain. If she had woken up she may have been confused and really hurting. I still regret that I didn't get to say goodbye to her. But God did answer my prayers, even if it wasn't how I expected.

It's not always easy to completely trust God. And when it's hardest to do so, I know Sarah and my youth group friends are always there for me.

—Rita

Think about it

* Why was Rita afraid to talk about her doubts and pain?

* Why is it difficult to be vulnerable with each other?

* Why is it important to open up?

* What should be our response to friends who are grieving or struggling over some deep hurt or disappointment?

DAY 291 Love Hurts

Even though my mom died several years ago, I still feel sadness. Some people think I should have gotten over it by now. Jesus thinks we should never get over it.

332

In fact, he says people who don't get over it are blessed.

Bible break

Blessed are those who mourn, for they shall be comforted.

—Matthew 5:4 ESV

. . . the rest of the story

We can't do anything about the death of a loved one. There's no reversing it. We can't get back in control. We can't do anything to bring the loved one back to life. I can remember the good times we shared, but even that makes the loss all the more painful. In the end, I simply have to accept the death and accept my grief.

That's what Jesus is saying in Matthew 5:4—accept the grief. Accept the mourning. Don't fight it. Don't deny it. Don't wall yourself off from people. Don't kill the feeling with drugs or alcohol or other risky behavior. Just let the pain make its way through you. It is a blessed pain. It means you are a healthy individual. You have entered into relationships that mean something; you've risked caring about others. You've decided to love, and sometimes that leads to grief.

And for those who let themselves grieve, there comes a promise: "Blessed are those who mourn, for they shall be comforted." God designed us so that we will feel joy in the presence of loved ones and grief when we are separated from them. He also designed us to receive comfort.

That comfort comes in the hug of a friend, in the prayer of a pastor, in the encouraging words of Scripture, in the fellowship of friends who "weep with those who weep" (Rom. 12:15 ESV). Grief has a way of bringing people together to love each other even more deeply. So while love will eventually lead to grief, it turns out that grief leads to more love. It's as if Jesus is saying, "Blessed are those who mourn, for they shall be loved, and blessed are those who love and grieve, for they shall comfort and love others even more." Such is the way of love—it always gets the last word. Even over death and grief.

What's that look like?

* What does it mean to "weep with those who weep"?

DAY 292 Source of All Comfort

All praise to God, the Father of our Lord Jesus Christ. God is our merciful Father and the source of all comfort. He comforts us in all our troubles so that we can comfort others. When they are troubled, we will be able to give them the same comfort God has given us.

—2 Corinthians 1:3–4 NLT

Mark it

* Write 2 Corinthians 1:3–4 on a slip of paper and use it this week as a bookmark in a school text, a novel you're reading, or this book. Every time you use it, read it. Every time you read it, think of: (1) a different way God has comforted you, and (2) a different person you could be comforting.

DAY 293 I Hid My Pain

I chucked a stack of old CD cases across my room. *They can't do this!* I thought, grabbing a pillow and hurling it against the wall. *They're Christians. Christians don't get divorced.*

My parents had just told my brother and me that their marriage was over. All evening long, one word screamed over and over in my mind: *Why?* But I kept the question to myself. I didn't want to talk to anyone about my hurt. When asked how I was, I'd say, "I'm fine."

Deep down, though, I wasn't fine. Sometimes I thought maybe I should pray, but I really didn't think it would do any good. While I'd prayed to accept Christ when I was a small child, my faith wasn't something I'd really thought that much about. As I looked at how awful my life had become, God couldn't have seemed farther away.

Eventually I'd had enough. I decided to run away. I didn't know where I'd go; I just had to get out. I reached the front door with my duffle bag. I paused.

As badly as I wanted to leave, I couldn't make myself open the door. I headed back upstairs to my room. Flopping onto the bed, I couldn't think of anything else to do but pray.

"All right, God," I said aloud. "If I'm going to stay here, you have to help me."

I not only needed him to help me through this awful experience, but I knew I needed him all the time. Sobbing, I begged God to forgive me for not trusting him, for trying to get through this tough time without his help. While I was still very sad, I no longer felt like I wanted to throw stuff, and I certainly didn't feel like I had to run away.

I prayed more after that day. I didn't know what to say, so I just repeated again and again, "Help me, please help me! I can't do this."

At youth group one night, my buddy Mike grabbed my arm. "You OK, man?"

My first thought was to tell him I was fine. Instead, I took a deep breath and said, "Um, not really. Can we talk?"

Talking to Mike felt good. Since his parents had also divorced, Mike knew exactly what I'd been going through. After that conversation, I started opening up more with my close friends and youth pastor. It even got a little easier to talk with my family. The more I talked to others, the easier it was to pray. Soon I found myself talking to God all the time—about decisions and problems and even everyday stuff.

Those difficult days taught me that I couldn't make it on my own. It's such a relief to open up to people who really care about me. Most importantly, I discovered how much I need God and how important it is to really live for him.

—Alex

DAY 294 A Prayer for the Hurting

LORD, show me your favor. I'm in deep trouble. I'm so sad I can hardly see. My whole body grows weak with sadness.

—Psalm 31:9 NIrV

* Turn Psalm 31:9 into a prayer either for yourself or for someone you know who is hurting.

DAY 295 Ready to Walk Away

When my mom went into the hospital for minor surgery, a blood clot unexpectedly rushed to her lungs and surgeons gave her a 2 percent chance to live. My brother, my dad, and I struggled with the reality that she was going to die.

I made up my mind that if my mom didn't make it, God wasn't a God I could believe in. I thought, *If she dies, I'm not going to church anymore. I'm not gonna believe in God.*

Miraculously, she lived. I knew her survival was not man's doing. I know it was Jesus who worked to save my mother's life. I was overjoyed, but also devastated by the way I acted in the face of trial. My faith was immature and self-centered. I wasn't focused on what God wanted. I was too busy with my own desires and wishes.

I now realize that if something doesn't go the way I want it to, it is all for a reason. I won't always be happy with what happens, but I shouldn't get so caught up in my own heartache and pain that I'm selfish. By looking at what the Lord did all my life, how could I have prayed that prayer? How could I have sworn to walk away from him if things didn't go my way?

—Kierra

Don't forget your promise to me, your servant. I depend on it. When I am hurting, I find comfort in your promise that leads to life.

—Psalm 119:49–50 CEV

DAY 296 Tough Question

Q: My cousin committed suicide, and now his father is blaming God for it. What can I do or say?

—*Anonymous*

A: I can only imagine how painful this is for your uncle and the rest of your family. It is not unusual for God to get the blame during tragedy. That's a pretty normal response to the kind of grief your uncle is going through. It's almost as if we need someone to blame so the subconscious mind says, "Why not God?" Believe me, God is big enough to handle your uncle's pain, blame, and anger.

In fact, I believe God grieves along with your family. Death and loss is not something he wants either. I think the very best thing you can do for your uncle is pray for him and show the same unconditional love God shows all of us. Your uncle doesn't need a theological lesson as much as love and understanding. I firmly believe your uncle will see the love and compassion of God through the love and compassion you show him.

Be there for him. In times like these, he will regard your very presence as a sign that someone cares for him. Don't push God on your uncle, but every so often you might want to hand him a comforting card that says your prayers are with him.

While it's wonderful you're concerned about your uncle, you're probably also hurting. If you haven't already, I'd encourage you to let your pastor or youth pastor know what's going on.

Finally, don't expect your uncle to change too quickly. In fact, he'll never totally get over his terrible loss, but he may eventually seek comfort in God's love. And it's just good to know that a caring person like you will be there for him if he does.

Fill-in-the-blanks prayer

* Lord, as I think about showing love to the hurting, I think about _____. Help me know how to be there for _____ _____. I pray that you'll open doors for me to be supportive, loving, and reflective of your love to this person this week. Amen.

DAY 297 Strength When It Hurts

Eighth grade was horrible. I was beat up by a girl who thought I wanted her boyfriend, and everyone seemed to like picking on me. So-called friends dug up old, embarrassing photos of me and emailed them around to others. Then, with profanity and insults written in, the photos got taped up in the school halls and bathrooms.

The abuse didn't stop all year. It was rough. But still, I felt this odd comfort. I didn't know what it was, but it kept me strong.

The next year I transferred to a new school. I had a new start and good friends. My family also started going to a new church about this time. For the first time I began to understand Jesus's love in a real way.

Here's the funny thing: the feeling I had when I came to Christ was that same feeling that got me through the abuse. I realized the comfort I'd felt was Jesus. He was there for me and holding me every step of the way, even when I didn't know it. I thought it was awesome that even if you don't know about God, he's still there for you.

—Jessie

Can't erase Jesus

* Get a blank sheet of paper. With a pen write "Jesus" (or draw a picture of him if you'd like). With a pencil, completely shade out your picture or word. Sometimes life gets so dark it's hard to see Christ, but if you now erase the pencil shading, you'll see he was there all along.

DAY 298 "You're Better than This"

I was standing at my open locker when I felt something small hit the back of my neck. I ran my fingers through my hair and fished out a sunflower seed. Immediately I felt another graze my forehead. I then spotted my annoying classmate Steve, who was holding a giant bag of sunflower seeds.

"Cut it out!" I shouted.

Two seconds later I felt another seed flick my earlobe. My cheeks got red hot.

"Kevin, leave it alone," my friend Tyler said. "Let's get to class."

Stop and think

* What would you have done if you'd been Kevin? Tyler?

. . . the rest of the story

"What? And let this fat jerk get away with zinging stuff at me? No way!" I'd said it loud enough so Steve heard every word.

"Bring it!" Steve shouted.

I slammed my locker door shut and lunged at Steve, slugging him hard in the gut. Steve cried out in pain and started to fall, but not before grabbing hold of my shirt. I hit the floor first and then Steve fell on top of me, pinning me beneath his massive frame.

The next thing I knew, a few teachers were pulling Steve off me and hauling us down to the principal's office to issue detentions.

Even though I was in pain when I got home that afternoon, my mom wasn't at all sympathetic. After all, it was my second fight in less than a month.

"You are *so* grounded," she said.

"But Mom!" I pleaded. "This kid was being such a jerk!"

"You should've walked away."

Yeah, right! I thought. *Everyone knows that not sticking up for yourself is social suicide.*

Mom looked me in the eye, placed her hand on my shoulder, and softened a bit.

"You're better than this," she said. "Your dad and I know you're a good kid. So does God. But people determine who you are based on your behavior. Kevin, if you keep acting like this, you'll be known at school as the punk who settles things with his fists."

"That's not true," I insisted with a huff. I went upstairs to my room and lay on my bed, staring up at the ceiling and repeatedly tossing a Nerf football in the air.

339

What if Mom's right? I thought. I had recently transferred to this school and hadn't made many friends. Maybe everybody was afraid to get to know me because they thought I had a bad temper.

As I continued to toss the football in the air, I began to calm down. I thought a lot about what Mom had said. I also started feeling kind of guilty for letting my temper get the best of me. I leaned back on the bed, closed my eyes, and began to pray, "God, give me the strength to step away from situations where I feel the urge to fight. And give me the patience to keep my cool when kids at school give me a hard time."

—Kevin

Think it through

* What causes you to lose your temper?

* What do you have to gain from losing your temper?

* What do you have to lose?

DAY 299 When God Got Mad

The Bible tells us, "Be angry and do not sin" (Eph. 4:26 ESV). For a long time, however, my life verse was closer to "Be angry and sin."

There was the time I tore up a baseball card because my favorite player failed to produce in the clutch.

And the time I put my fist through a wall. Well, not quite. You see, there was this two-by-four stud behind the drywall right where my fist hit. Better to say my hand bounced off the wall, and I ended up in the emergency room so the doctor could mend my broken bones.

Temper has been one area where I've been spiritually challenged. Thanks to some caring people in my life and God's grace, I'm not nearly as challenged as I used to be.

But one thing I've learned along the way is that anger, by itself, wasn't the problem. Sinful anger was.

Grab a Bible and read John 2:13–16. Here we see Jesus mean and wild—acting like a pro wrestler doing some stunt in the ring. Except with

Jesus it wasn't a stunt; it was anger. He turned over tables. He applied the whip. He shouted.

So here we have Jesus, God's love incarnate, rearranging the furniture. Apparently it's right to be angry sometimes.

My problem: I got angry for all the wrong reasons. It was about me and what I wanted. It wasn't about defending the oppressed, fighting for human rights, or standing up against blatant immorality. It was all petty, selfish stuff.

Pause and think

* What makes you angry? Is it the kind of stuff that makes God angry?

. . . the rest of the story

That's the difference between Jesus and me: Jesus got angry only when something important was on the line. In this case, it was God's honor.

People had turned a place of worship into nothing more than a store. There was so much business going on, it destroyed the ability of people to worship in peace. And that made Jesus angry. People couldn't worship his heavenly Father, the very thing they were created to do. They were acting like money was more important than God!

The interesting thing is that even though such a thing might annoy most of us, we wouldn't get angry. Likewise, we may be troubled when we hear a racist remark, when a friend mistreats another, or when a TV preacher uses God's name as a way to make money, but such things don't make us *angry*. We usually get angry only when we don't get our way.

We need this story to help us see that while much of our anger is selfish, there is such a thing as godly anger. We don't want to get rid of our anger, because a person with no anger is a person who doesn't care about anything. But we do need God's help to train us to be angry about the right things.

When we're angry about the right things, we'll know we really care about the things God cares about.

—Mark

DAY 300 Letting Go of Anger

"What did you say?" I glared at the other waitress.

"You heard me," she shot back.

I *had* heard. She'd made a racist comment about my Mexican family.

"If you have a problem, we can talk in private," I said icily.

I could feel my temper rising. Then she pushed me on our way to the break room. I warned her to quit, and she pushed me again. My anger exploded, and I punched her in the face. Both of us lost our jobs.

My fiery temper earned me a reputation as someone who wouldn't take bullying from anyone. I refused to be anybody's victim. If it took angry outbursts and an occasional fight to make people respect me, fine. And if I had to be fired, that was OK too.

Then something happened to change all that. At youth group one Sunday night, two guys got into a shouting match, and one of them shoved the other to the floor. The next week they stood in front of the group and apologized to each other, to us, and to God. One of the guys read Proverbs 22:24: "Do not make friends with a hot-tempered man, do not associate with one easily angered."

That verse is talking about me.

And what was it saying? *Don't be friends with angry, hot-tempered me.* I thought about the fights . . . the people I'd yelled at . . . being fired from my job. I thought about a guy from school who'd recently made a rude comment to me. I'd backed him against a locker and warned him never to mess with me again.

The next day at school, I took my seat next to the boy I'd threatened. When our teacher passed back some homework, I handed him his paper.

"Thanks," he said.

"You're welcome."

My friend in the desk ahead of mine turned around and stared at me in shock. I felt stunned too. *Where did that come from?* Normally I would have antagonized the kid for at least a week. After class my friend asked me what the deal was, and I told her something had happened at church to change my attitude.

I've noticed a lot of changes since I decided to let go of my anger. I've even tried to say I'm sorry to people I've hurt. I also have been biting my tongue—something I *never* used to do. I find I'm able to stay cool in situations that used to send me into a rage. Instead of blowing up, I find myself saying a silent prayer.

In spite of all the positive changes, I still get angry and swear sometimes, and I feel frustrated and wonder if I'll ever get things right. I know if it were up to me, I wouldn't. Thankfully it's not. I know Christ is working on my heart to change me little by little from the inside out.

—Madolyn

Your turn

* Think about something that makes you angry. Now grab a coin and look at it. Let the coin represent your anger. Close your fist. Squeeze it tightly. Tell God how you're feeling right now. Then open your fist and turn your hand so that the coin drops out of it. As the coin falls from your hand, say this prayer: "Lord, I let go of my anger. I give it over to you. Keep working in my heart. Keep changing me from the inside out. Amen."

DAY 301 My Guilt Turned to Anger

Throughout the entire test period, my so-called friend Joel kept trying to cheat off me. I covered my paper so that he couldn't. He obviously wasn't happy about it.

When the class ended, I stood to leave and faced Joel's icy glare. If looks could kill, my parents would have been planning my funeral that afternoon. I stood there for a moment wondering what to say. *Why do I feel guilty for not letting him cheat?* I thought. Then the guilt suddenly turned into anger. *He has no right to make me feel guilty!* I felt like telling him off. But then a verse I'd memorized came to mind:

Do not be overcome by evil, but overcome evil with good.

—Romans 12:21

As I stood there in silence, I felt my need for revenge melt away. While I needed to let him know I felt cheating was wrong, I didn't want to destroy a friendship—if I could help it. My mind searched for the right words.

"Sorry, Joel, but you know me well enough to know how I feel about cheating," I said slowly and gently. "But maybe I could help you study before the next test."

I watched as Joel's expression softened just a little.

"OK, Allison." He cracked a slight smile. "It might not be easy, but I'll give it a try."

Then he turned and walked away. I stood there for a moment more, finally able to breathe again. I felt relieved that my friendship with Joel hadn't been destroyed. Even more, I was glad I'd stood up for my values in a way that would make God happy.

—Allison

* *Memorize Romans 12:21.* Then repeat this verse to yourself each time you're tempted to lash out in anger or seek revenge.

DAY 302 Keeping the Peace

When tempers flare, Jesus calls us to be peacemakers. Here's how:

Go to God immediately. Just saying a quick, silent "Lord, help me show your love" will do.

Count to ten. Or five or three or whatever. Just remember that the first thing that comes to mind might not be the best thing to say.

Watch your words. No matter what the other person is saying, resist the urge to fight back with mean, angry words.

Don't blame. Don't be accusatory by saying things like, "You did this!" Instead, gently say things like, "My feelings are hurt when . . ." or "I'm sorry, I didn't know you felt that way."

Apologize. If the confrontation is a result of something you said or did, say you're sorry—and mean it. Then ask the other person to forgive you.

Forgive. This may not be possible in the heat of the moment, but you
need to forgive the other person for whatever happened—and soon.

Go to God again. While you may have had time for only a quick prayer
during the confrontation, you'll have time for more in-depth prayer
later. Ask God to resolve the situation and to make you a better
peacemaker.

—Mark

God blesses those who work for peace, for they will be called the children
of God.

—Matthew 5:9 NLT

DAY 303 My Anger Hid My Insecurities

I was always yelling at somebody. I yelled because I didn't want other
people to know the real me. It kept people from getting too close, so
they wouldn't figure out my insecurities. It was like I built a wall around
myself.

Instead of going out with friends after school or doing something fun
on the weekends, I just stayed home. There was lots of yelling at home
too. And I wasn't the only one yelling.

That's until my grandparents came to visit from Seoul, South Korea.

While they were staying with our family, I was having stomach problems. Everything I ate seemed to make me sick.

One night before bedtime, my grandpa sat beside me, told me about
God, and prayed for me to be healed. That was probably the first time
someone had told me about God, although I had clearly seen God in
Grandpa's life. I noticed he'd spend hours in prayer and Bible study. And
even in his old age, he found a church to walk to in my neighborhood.

He told my family about this church and encouraged us to go. So my
mom and I tried it. The first time I went to youth group I was amazed at
how cool these people really were. I had fun being with them.

One night the youth pastor told us about Jesus and how he could be
our Savior. He said if we wanted Jesus to come into our hearts, all we had

to do was ask. I remember praying, "God, I know I have really messed up, but please come into my heart."

After that night, I felt so clean. I really knew my Savior loved me, regardless of how I'd acted.

I know God changed my heart because his love has affected the way I feel about myself and interact with other people. Sometimes I still struggle with yelling, but the walls I had built around me are slowly coming down. Instead of always putting up an angry front, I actually have a smile on my face when I walk the halls of my school.

—Thomas

Dig deep

* Think about your own angry or hurt feelings. Where do they come from? Do they come from insecurities? Do they come from a desire to keep others out? Do they come from pressures others are putting on you? Use the space below to journal about whatever you're feeling right now.

DAY 304 How to Conquer Anger

From my room I listened as my parents argued in the kitchen. At that time it was pretty much a nightly occurrence. Usually I blocked out the noise with music. This night I just listened as they fought over the most insignificant things.

With voices rising in the background and my stomach in knots, I pulled a Bible off my bookshelf and opened it randomly. I came upon these words in Ephesians:

"In your anger do not sin": Do not let the sun go down while you are still angry, and do not give the devil a foothold.

—Ephesians 4:26–27

I sat staring at those words. Wasn't that what was happening? Through anger, the devil was gaining a foothold in our home.

Anger, I have come to realize, can so distort your viewpoint that you may begin cooperating with the devil without even realizing it. Then a little later in Ephesians, it says:

Get rid of all bitterness, rage and anger, brawling and slander, along with every form of malice. Be kind and compassionate to one another, forgiving each other, just as in Christ God forgave you. Be imitators of God.

—Ephesians 4:31–5:1

What keeps the devil from gaining a foothold? What conquers anger? Forgiveness. As you see what God has done for you and then begin to imitate him, you can move toward self-control, even when you'd rather explode in anger or nurse grudges.

—James

DAY 305 Trust . . . No Matter What?

I cautiously checked the belay—the rope attached to my climbing harness. I gave it a tug, trying to make sure it was securely clipped.

"On belay?" the student next to me yelled.

"Belay on," I said back, not sounding nearly as loud or as confident as she did.

"Permission to climb?" I asked.

"Climb away."

These commands bounced around the gym walls as I started up our school's rock-climbing wall. The higher I got, the sweatier my hands felt.

347

If I slipped and started to fall, I was totally in the hands of the girl who held the other end of the belay. Would she keep me from falling like a rock if I needed her to?

One foot after another, I finally reached the top. I forced one shaky hand to loosen its grip on the rope and ring the bell on the ceiling. Then came the part I'd been dreading. I had to rappel—push away from the wall and let myself fall—and hopefully the girl holding my rope would do her job. *Hopefully.*

Placing one foot flat on the mustard-colored wall, I thought for just a moment about something I'd heard so many times in Sunday school. *Trust. Trust what you can't see. Have faith.*

It was amazing what went through my head as I gripped the rope and hesitated. Suddenly this experience wasn't just about getting down a wall in my gym. I thought about all those times I'd hesitated to trust God. *Trust God.*

So often I've found it hard to believe that he would see me through difficult times, that he wouldn't let me fall or turn into a failure.

Bible break

He will not let your foot slip—he who watches over you will not slumber.

—Psalm 121:3

. . . the rest of the story

Now it felt like God was saying, "Trust me, Allison, I know what I'm doing. I'm big enough, strong enough, and loving enough to take care of you."

Then suddenly my thoughts shifted back to the sweat-smelling gym and the girl below me holding tightly to my belay. I took a couple of breaths and shouted, "Rappelling!"

I pushed away from the wall and my partner held the rope firmly. Her steady grip on the belay made me feel confident and safe. Before long, I was standing next to her with my feet planted on the floor.

As I removed my harness, I gave my partner a quick "thank you for not letting me smash to the earth" smile. Then I whispered a thanks to

God for being there for me and for showing me, through what should have been just another gym class, that he will always be there for me. He will catch me when I stumble, make mistakes, and even fail him. He will be there . . . no matter what. I can trust him.

—Allison

DAY 306 Why Trust God?

* I have the hardest time trusting God when _____
_____.

* Three reasons I can trust God:
  1.
  2.
  3.

DAY 307 Your Trust Prayer

Write a short prayer that demonstrates your trust in God's love and faithfulness. Memorize the prayer and say it each time you face a difficult situation.

DAY 308 Cure for the Common Bully

One day while I was playing basketball on the school playground with some friends, a bully named Justin started saying that I couldn't make the shot, that I was a loser and a bed-wetter (standard bully talk). Something in me snapped. With ball in hand and eyes focused, I took my shot. Not at the basket, but at Justin's big bully face.

It was a bold move. And a dumb one. The bully suddenly came charging at me.

I did what any self-respecting fourth grader would do. I screamed. As Justin's body slammed into mine, I heard a familiar voice above my howls. It was my older brother. He and two of his eighth-grade buddies had heard my screams like a bat signal sent out over the kickball field. They grabbed Justin and carried him to the recess lady. From that day on, Justin left me alone.

Nothing beats an older brother. Nothing beats the feeling of knowing someone bigger than you has your back. The Bible tells the story of Gideon, a guy who discovered someone was there for him too—even in the face of an army of bullies.

The Midianites threatened to destroy Israel. They were bad enough and big enough to do it too. The Bible says they filled the valleys like a swarm of locusts (Judg. 7:12).

It seemed like God had forgotten the Israelites. But in Judges 6:16, God told Gideon not to worry because "I will be with you. And you will destroy the Midianites as if you were fighting against one man" (NLT). It was hard for Gideon to believe, but in faith he put together an army of around thirty-two thousand soldiers.

Then God told Gideon with an army that big, Israel might take the credit and forget God was the one who won the fight (Judg. 7:2). So Gideon began to downsize . . . all the way down to three hundred soldiers!

In the dark of night, God sent Gideon to spy on the enemy's plans. He overheard one of the Midianites describing a dream that apparently had only one interpretation: Israel would beat the bully! Gideon ran back to his camp, woke up his three hundred soldiers, and set out for the attack.

But instead of packing swords or shields or ninja stars or grenade launchers, Gideon had each soldier take only a trumpet in his right hand and a lit torch hidden under a clay jar in his left. Gideon and his three hundred soldiers surrounded the enemy camp. At midnight they blew their trumpets and smashed their jars to reveal the light. The Midianites were so freaked out they began fighting each other and nearly wiped themselves out. Gideon's men just stood there watching God do what only God *could* do.

Imagine walking into each day with that kind of confidence. What if your strength and confidence came from God and his unconditional love for you? What if instead of relying on your own strength, you actually asked God to go before you and with you into each day, each problem, and each fear? I bet you'd begin to see things like Gideon did. You'd begin to see God a whole lot bigger than you thought—and your personal bully a whole lot smaller than he first seemed.

—Jarrett

DAY 309 Spinning out of Control

As I stared at the Cessna 150 that I'd soon be flying all by myself—for only the third time—my flight instructor, Jim, said the words I didn't want to hear: "I want you to work on your stalls today, Sue."

Learning stalls is a critical part of any flight training plan. A stall happens when the plane's air speed drops too low to keep flying. Pilots routinely practice their stalls at five thousand feet or higher, where there is plenty of room to recover safely.

As Jim and I both knew, stalls were not my best maneuver. They left me feeling shaky, so I tended to recover much sooner than necessary.

As I boarded the plane, Jim said, "Don't be afraid to really stall the bird, Sue. You can do it."

A few minutes later I was airborne and on my own.

At five thousand feet, high above a small farming community, I took several deep breaths to relax. Then my right hand grasped the throttle to gradually reduce the engine's power.

As the air speed began to drop, the stall-warning buzzer went off, its whine filling the tiny cockpit. Normally I would recover at the earliest annoying sound of that buzzer. Not this time. I decided to let that buzzer screech as loudly as I could stand before pulling out of the stall.

I waited too long.

A slight, dropping lurch from the propeller was my only warning. Almost instantly, the left wing dipped, then tipped over, pitching the plane into a wing-over-wing spin.

Precious seconds grew incredibly long as I desperately tried to regain control over the plane. My frantic efforts only plunged it—and me—into an ever-tightening death spiral.

As I yanked and fought against the inevitable pull of gravity, I suddenly remembered something Jim told me: "If you ever get into a spin in a Cessna 150, just let go of the controls. It's built to fly on its own."

But my hands seemed glued to the controls.

I threw my arms up in the air, releasing my stranglehold on the yoke. I covered my face, bracing for impact.

Yawing and pitching wildly, the Cessna made grotesquely odd noises. Then, amazingly, the airplane faithfully returned to straight-and-level flight. I had fallen more than half a mile, but now all was well.

Back on the ground, I told Jim what happened. And I told him I never wanted to fly again.

"The plane looks fine to me, and you do too," he said, smiling. "You obviously remembered my advice. It worked, didn't it?"

I learned an important lesson that day—and it was about so much more than flying.

When I find myself in situations seemingly spinning out of control, God reminds me to let go of the controls of my life and trust him.

He'll always return me to a straight-and-level course.

—Susan

Think it through

* When was the last time you tried to "take the controls" from God? What happened? Why is trusting in God better than trusting in yourself?

DAY 310 There

When tears are shed
And anger rages
When fear takes hold
And hangs on tight
When skies are gray
And umbrellas needed

You are there

When goodbyes are said
And hearts are broken
When glass shatters
And cannot be fixed
When greed controls
And sin creeps near

You are there

Like a shield guarding me
A blanket comforting
A tower protecting

You are there
Surrounding me
—*Amy*

Journal your thoughts

* Reread the poem and then ask yourself: *How does this poem make me feel? What struggles am I facing right now that make it difficult to trust God?* Take a couple of minutes to journal what's going through your head and heart right now.

DAY 311 A Nice Place to Hide

Pray this

You are my hiding place! You protect me from trouble, and you put songs in my heart because you have saved me.
—Psalm 32:7 CEV

Answer this

* According to this verse, what does God do? What should be our response to what he does?

353

DAY 312 "Put It in Neutral!"

Pulling up to the gas pump, I shook my head and realized how totally distracted I was: I didn't even remember driving to the gas station.

This is making me crazy, I thought. I was trying to choose a college and I really didn't know what to do.

I had been praying about this decision. But days, then weeks, passed and God wasn't delivering the answer I was asking for. I was beyond frustrated.

I finished pumping the gas and pulled around the corner to receive the automatic car wash that came free with my fill-up.

"Put it in neutral, hands off the steering wheel."

The bored-looking man's instructions didn't register with my brain any more than the drive to the gas station had. I started driving forward toward the suds and spinning brushes.

"Hey. Hey! HEY!"

The attendant's voice had lost its monotone and was now cutting sternly into my private thoughts.

"I said put it in neutral and keep your hands off the steering wheel!"

It seemed to take all the restraint he could muster to keep from adding the words "you moron."

"Oh, I'm sorry," I said. "I was thinking about something else."

The man's weather-beaten face softened noticeably when he heard my apology, then he tempered his impatience with a little car-wash wisdom: "It's automatic, son. You just bring the car up to the line. I do the rest."

As my car was slowly being changed from filthy to clean, I started to wonder about God's apparent silence in the face of my prayers. Maybe the silence was his way of telling me I hadn't yet put my will in neutral and allowed him to steer my life. I'd been leaning on my own understanding. I wasn't really trusting God to guide me. I was merely asking him to give me what I wanted.

A couple of weeks later, God provided an answer to prayer that was better than anything I'd imagined. I realized how important it had been to put my will in neutral when seeking God's guidance. And the words of the car-wash man echoed in my mind:

"It's automatic, son. You just bring the car up to the line. I do the rest."

—Nate

DAY 313 The Night of the Flying Kitten

"Jill, turn off your light!" Amy's muffled scream came from across the bedroom. I couldn't see my younger sister buried beneath a mess of blankets, but I could certainly hear her. She yelled again—and again and again.

"Chill out! I'm almost done."

A few minutes and seven outbursts later, I turned out my light.

"FINALLY!"

I hated sharing a room with my little sister. *I'll never get my own space*, I fumed.

Can you relate to this?

* **What advice would you give Jill?**

At breakfast the next morning, I vented to Mom. "I can't deal with Amy anymore."

She gave me her standard response. "I know it's hard right now. But there's nothing we can do about it." I slammed the refrigerator door and rolled my eyes.

At bedtime the next night, Amy threatened me. "You better turn your light off earlier tonight," she said, with all the menace a fourth grader could muster.

"Ooooo, I'm scared." She gave me her dagger eyes and then turned her back to me. I clicked my lamp on and started another chapter of my book.

Soon the yelling started. "Turn it off!"

I chose not to reply this time. I was concentrating only on making her mad. Our bedtime routine had turned into a game. Winning was the only option.

Suddenly, a furry, soft, but heavy object bounced off my cheek. I looked down and saw a small, gray kitten—a stuffed animal from Amy's massive Beanie Baby collection. I threw down my book. "You are going to be sorrrrrrry," I warned.

I chucked the Beanie back at her and retreated to the space behind my bed. She fired giraffes, dolphins, and sheep in rapid succession. I retaliated, firing them back. She blocked the attack with fluffy pink pillows.

Somewhere among the flying barnyard livestock, sea creatures, and exotic zoo animals, we started giggling. The giggling soon erupted into all-out laughter interspersed with cheers of triumph, screams of defeat, and trash talk.

Finally, I scooped up as many teddy bears and bunnies as I could, charged her side of the room, and dumped them on her head. Then I tickled her and tried to control her flailing arms. We laughed so hard we cried. When our tickling and fighting had slowed from exhaustion, I rolled off the bed.

Later, before drifting off to sleep, I had a shocking thought: *I had fun with my little sister tonight.* The next shocking insight was that, basically, I was selfish. I prayed, "Father, I admit I'm selfish. Give me the strength to love my sister when I don't feel like it." On the days she still annoyed me, I would pray, "God, help me to be thankful for the blessing of a sister and to treat her the way I'd want to be treated."

—Jill

Try it

* Are you struggling to get along with one of your siblings? Choose one of Jill's two short prayers to say right now.

DAY 314 Honest Words from Real Siblings

Catie and Pat

A year and a half ago, I was too caught up with my own stuff to care about my relationship with my brother Pat. But a lot of things changed after I became a Christian. I realized where my priorities needed to be. Now we talk a lot. We're so open with each other that we talk about issues before they become a problem. When we have disagreements, they're usually over the annoying everyday things that come up when you live with somebody.

—Catie

I really think we get along because of our faith. Before we knew Christ, I think we loved each other. But until you know God, you can't truly love. So because of God, our relationship is stronger.

—Pat

Stacy and Christy

My sister Christy and I have this rivalry. We're both so competitive that it often results in a yelling match. But I think we're gradually realizing we're our own people. I really like Christy's openness. It's hard for me to be open sometimes, but Christy shows me that she wants to know about me, and that means a lot to me.

—Stacy

Stacy just makes friends so easy. I used to get so jealous of her. Now, instead of comparing myself to Stacy, I'm starting to look at the things I do have. When we have disagreements, we know we need to give each other some space and move on. We don't hold grudges or anything.

—Christy

Michael and Danny

I admit, I can be an annoying little brother. I like to pick fights with Danny because he has a short fuse. I think it's funny when Danny gets mad. Even if he's pushing me or beating me up, I'll just keep laughing. But all fighting aside, I definitely look up to Danny and consider him a friend.

—Michael

357

We usually fight about stuff that doesn't matter. Like today, Michael was sitting on my bed, and he knows I don't like it when people sit on my bed. So we started pushing each other a little bit. We goof off like that a lot. That's why our fights aren't so bad; we usually laugh about how dumb they are. I'm actually really proud of my little brother. He's got a lot of determination and a lot of heart.

—*Danny*

Your turn

* Write down what you admire or appreciate about your brother(s) or sister(s).

DAY 315 Pick One

There's a saying: "You can pick your friends, but you can't pick your family."

That may be true, but you *can* pick your attitude toward your family. Now, pick one of the activities below:

1. Tell your sibling why you appreciate him or her. (If you have more than one sibling, choose the one who's hardest to get along with.) Ask if there's any way you can serve him or her this week. Bonus challenge: end your conversation with a hug and tell your bro or sis, "I love you."
2. Handwrite a letter, poem, or short note to a brother or sister. Like in the first option, focus on what you appreciate about your sib.
3. Do activity 2, but use email or Facebook or texting.
4. If you don't have a sibling, do any of the above activities for a cousin, parent, aunt, uncle, or grandparent.

DAY 316 Why Won't She Listen to Me?

When my younger sister Brooke started dating Kevin, we knew very little about him. He seemed like the "strong, silent type," and it didn't seem like he'd open up to anyone. We all assumed he was just shy. Then one of my friends told me Kevin had a drug problem, drank a lot at parties, and had been physically abusive with his ex-girlfriend. I expressed my concern to Brooke, but she said Kevin wasn't like that. She acted like everything was perfect and told me not to tell our parents.

I didn't tell Mom and Dad everything, but I made enough comments to raise their suspicions. When they finally confronted Brooke, she refused to stop dating Kevin. She was also furious that I didn't keep my mouth shut.

More and more, Kevin jealously guarded my sister's every move. He was totally possessive. Soon Brooke was canceling planned outings with us and with her friends because Kevin didn't want her to go.

Brooke sometimes had tears in her eyes when she got off the phone with Kevin, but she always acted like it was no big deal. We watched as he pulled her away from those of us who loved her most.

When Brooke and I headed to college, the pattern continued. Early in the semester, Brooke started going home only to see Kevin—and not our parents. At college, she rarely came to see me—even though she and I were living in the same town.

Finally, Brooke broke down and told my parents that Kevin had been emotionally and verbally abusive. She hated her own body because Kevin constantly accused her of dressing like she was trying to show herself off (even though she had always dressed conservatively). At the same time, he'd said she was lucky to have him because no one else would want her for a girlfriend.

I don't really understand why Brooke is still with Kevin. I get angry with her sometimes because she refuses to see what Kevin is doing to her, and to all of us. But I can't be mad, because I know she needs my love and support more than anything else.

I know that God's in control and I can't manage this situation by myself. But I also realize that God doesn't necessarily work on my time schedule. He might not answer my prayers the way I want him to, and Brooke might not listen to me at all, but God is still in control.

Brooke and I will always be sisters, even when she doesn't seem to want me in her life. I will always reach out to her and wait for her to reach back.

—Angela

* Do you have concerns about any of your own siblings? Are you feeling like your relationship is strained? Take your concerns to God, asking him to: (1) heal hurts, (2) help your sibling with whatever he or she might be struggling with, (3) give you wisdom about what to do or say, and (4) protect your brother or sister during this difficult time.

DAY 317 My Brother and I Fight All the Time!

Q: My brother is a year younger than I, and we fight all the time. We both go to church and attend our youth group. But he's not interested in really living for Christ. He uses bad language and listens to a lot of raunchy music. We used to have a great brother/sister relationship, and I'd like to have that again. How can we get past our differences and learn to get along?

—Anonymous

Your turn

* How would you answer this question?

How IYF's expert answered:

A: Restoring your relationship is going to take patience, understanding, and a lot of commitment on your part. With that in mind, there are a few things you need to remember.

First, think about other relationships in your life. I'll bet each of them has had ups and downs. Even best friends argue, disagree, and think differently about important issues. But when you are committed to a friendship, you're willing to work through those differences and repair the friendship. The same is true in your relationship with your brother.

So don't let yourself get too worried that the way things are right now is the way they will be forever.

Also realize your brother may be going through a rebellious stage in his life. But no matter how he acts on the outside, he most likely still needs to feel loved and cared for. By sticking by him and continuing to show him you care, you'll send an invaluable message to your brother—one that says your love is permanent and unconditional.

To show that kind of love to your brother, you need to focus on what's right in your relationship. Think about some of the things you have in common. Do you both like sports? Is there a movie or TV show that always makes you two laugh? Anything that helps you stay connected with your brother can help get you through this tough time.

Even if you can't find any common interests, you can still connect with your brother by expressing interest in his life. Yes, he's listening to music you find offensive, but do your best not to judge your brother. If you really want to be close to him again, you won't get very far by criticizing him or pointing out all the ways he's messing up.

Finally, keep a close eye on your brother. His change in behavior may indicate more dangerous changes, like alcohol or drug use. If you become concerned about anything, talk to your parents, youth pastor, or another trusted adult.

Most importantly, pray for your brother. Ask God to be with him and to guide his decisions. And ask for God's wisdom as you work to repair your relationship.

After all of this, remember that your brother may not respond the way you want him to. But be patient. Hopefully he will move out of this phase. My guess is that he really does want to be close to you too, but he may not know how right now.

—Jim

DAY 318 Smiles-on-a-Stick

I smiled as I opened the package that my sister Carmella sent for my birthday.

"I'm sad that I can't be there to hang out with you on your special day," Carmella wrote, "but hopefully this will help!"

My sister had cut out a photo of her head and glued it to a Popsicle stick. "Even though the real Carmella can't be there, here's a Carmella-on-a-stick! Now let's go to the mall!" she wrote. I laughed out loud. Carmella-on-a-stick is probably the most creative gift anyone's ever given me.

Bible break

Dear children, let's not merely say that we love each other; let us show the truth by our actions.

—1 John 3:18 NLT

Since I'm always up for a good joke, Carmella-on-a-stick and I went to the mall for some quality sister time. We joined a couple of friends for celebratory meals. And we went to a movie, which we both liked.

Now, it probably took Carmella (the real one) five minutes to make Carmella-on-a-stick. But her little gift really touched me. It was a reminder that Carmella thinks of me often, even when we can't be together.

—LaTonya

DAY 319 Memorize This

Be completely humble and gentle; be patient, bearing with one another in love.

—Ephesians 4:2

And . . .

* Think about practical ways you can apply this verse to the way you relate to the members of your family.

DAY 320 No Dad to Call

My youth group was hundreds of miles from home on a mission trip. We were piled in the van on the way back to our motel when everybody else started talking about their dads. It was Father's Day, and everyone needed to call home. Everyone but me. Since my dad had died when I was four, I had no reason to celebrate Father's Day.

I felt so sad and so alone. Sure, I had my mom and my three brothers. *But who am I supposed to call today?* As the day went on, I thought about all the things I'd missed. I never had a dad to cheer for me at softball games. I had to find a substitute for father-daughter events. By the end of the day, I was convinced I'd been wronged in a horrible, unforgivable way.

In the days that followed, working with young kids helped me get through each day.

I especially enjoyed afternoons with six-year-old Devin. As I worked with this serious, tough little guy on his crafts, I loved trying to make him laugh.

"Not quite so much glue," I advised as Devin squeezed about half a bottle onto his construction paper. He scowled but put the bottle down. He then picked through several pieces of colored tissue paper.

"Are you gonna be here for a long time, Heather?" he asked suddenly.

"Not really," I told him.

"What do you have to leave for, anyway?"

"I don't live here. I have to go home."

"I don't ever want to go home," Devin declared fiercely.

"Why not?"

He picked up a piece of tissue and smooshed it down. "Because no one there loves me."

"Devin, that's not true."

"Is too."

I then remembered that most of these kids were from broken homes. Some were being raised by grandparents because their parents were in jail or had abandoned them. A lot of them saw drug use every day.

363

"I bet there are lots of people who love you," I finally said. "And God loves you an awful lot too."

He shrugged. He stuck a few more pieces of tissue paper down and then held up his creation. "Look—I made a stained-glass window." He grinned from ear to ear. I'd never seen him do that.

Suddenly I felt terribly ashamed. I had spent so much time pouting about what I didn't have that I'd completely forgotten about all the really good things in my life. Right then my family was looking pretty great.

Sure, sometimes it still makes me sad to think of all I've missed. But then I try to remember Devin and his difficult life. No matter how much I may think I'm missing, there's surely someone out there who would consider me very blessed.

—Heather

Fill-in-the-blanks prayer

* Dear God: It's easy for me to get upset about _____.
  But one thing I'm thankful for right now is _____. Amen.

DAY 321 Gratitude

I'm grateful
for the big and the
small ways
God brings joy
into my life:
Grandma's successful surgery,
the pizza lunch
I ate this afternoon,
the sermon I heard on Sunday,
the pair of jeans
my new job let me buy,
the friend I told about God,
our family vacation
to the beach,
but most of all

the security I have in knowing
God's gifts to his children
are good.

—Kate

Give thanks to the LORD, for he is good! His faithful love endures forever.

—Psalm 107:1 NLT

Try one

* Write your own gratitude poem.

* List ten things you're thankful for.

* Write a thankful prayer.

DAY 322 Amy's Quiz: What's Your Gratitude Attitude?

1. Your parents bought you a used laptop. Your best friend's parents got him a newer, faster one. You:
   A. Don't give it a second thought.
   B. Feel a little slighted, but don't let it get you down.
   C. Feel pretty jealous. It doesn't seem fair.
2. When you pray, you spend most of your time:
   A. Reminding God about the new things you need.
   B. Asking for help with the things that weigh on your mind.
   C. Thanking God for providing for your needs.
3. After you have your tonsils taken out, your best friend delivers your homework for an entire week. You:
   A. Drop him a quick email, just to say thanks.
   B. Take him out to dinner once you can swallow again.
   C. Totally forget to thank him—but you're not worried, because he knows you appreciate him.
4. Your dad lost his job just before Christmas. You:

A. Let them know that Christmas gifts are *really* important and that they still have credit cards they could use.

B. Tell your parents not to worry about giving you gifts this year. You have everything you need.

C. Feel sorry for yourself, but try not to complain. After all, your parents really need your support right now.

5. Your parents agree to help you buy a mountain bike if you chip in half. You're:

A. Really grateful. It's nice of them to help you.

B. Annoyed. Why should you have to pay for any of it?

C. A little down. Your half will probably wipe out most of your checking account.

Scoring

1. A (3), B (2), C (1)
2. A (1), B (2), C (3)
3. A (2), B (3), C (1)
4. A (1), B (3), C (2)
5. A (3), B (1), C (2)

13–15 points: Your heart is in the right spot! You don't need a reminder to see how well God and your family have provided for you. It's not often that you find yourself wanting more than you have. A grateful heart pleases God.

9–12 points: You're grateful for what you have . . . most of the time. Sometimes you do find yourself wishing for bigger and better things. Try not to get wrapped up in always wanting more—and don't forget that God will take care of all your needs.

5–8 points: It can be tough for you to be happy with what you have. Be sure to say thanks when someone does something nice for you. And remember, the gift of God's love is better than anything in the world.

DAY 323 The Problem with Grumbling

God led a great escape. A million oppressed people left the slavery of Egypt by following his clear guidance. Things began spectacularly. Then the grumbling started. The people became impatient. They complained about Moses; they complained about God. "Why have you brought us up out of Egypt to die in the desert? There is no bread! There is no water! And we detest this miserable food" (Num. 21:5).

How did God respond? "Then the LORD sent venomous snakes among them; they bit the people and many Israelites died" (21:6).

Judgment was swift and strict.

Such stories seem embarrassing to us. We want to apologize for God, or make excuses for him. We say, "Well, this is the Old Testament. Things are different. God didn't *mean* to hurt people with those snakes. If you forget to thank your mom for hamburgers, God won't kill you." But the unmistakable point, the unchanging point, is this: *ingratitude is more serious than we think.*

In God's mind, thanks matters. He speaks through the apostle Paul about thankless people: "They knew God. But they didn't honor him as God. They didn't thank him. Their thinking became worthless. Their foolish hearts became dark" (Rom. 1:21 NIrV).

No honor.

No thanks.

Worthless thinking.

Darkened hearts.

In God's mind, thanks matters.

—James

DAY 324 Reasons to Say Thanks

* Look up these verses, and then draw a line to the reason that fits the verse.

1 Chronicles 16:34   Because God wants you to

1 Corinthians 15:57   Because God always does what's right

Psalm 118:21   Because prayers are answered

1 Thessalonians 5:18   Because God's love never fails

Psalm 7:17   Because Jesus makes us winners

DAY 325 One Miserable Day . . .

Raindrops trickled down my nose as I ran from my friend Bethany's car up to my front porch. It was a Friday afternoon, and I'd just gotten out of school for our weeklong Thanksgiving break.

I should have been excited about having some extra time away from school. But the awful weather, a nasty head cold, and a huge amount of homework left me feeling miserable.

As I walked into the kitchen, I looked over at the table and saw a big bouquet of flowers wrapped in tissue paper. Not stopping to look at the card attached to the flowers, I figured somebody had dropped them off for Mom.

I dragged myself up the stairs and into my room to rest until supper. I hadn't been in my room more than ten minutes before Mom came upstairs and asked, "Rachel, why didn't you open up those flowers? After all, they're for you."

Before Mom finished, I'd rushed downstairs to see who in the world had sent me flowers. I opened the card and discovered they were from my friend Sara, who lived in another state. Included with the flowers was a stuffed panda bear. I didn't remember telling Sara I loved pandas. I'd even collected them when I was younger. *How could she have possibly known?*

I carefully arranged the flowers in a vase and brought them up to my room. I placed the panda on my bed. As I lay beside the thoughtful gift, I couldn't help thinking about how grateful I was for a friend like Sara.

Grateful? Just a few minutes earlier I'd been anything but grateful. Even though it was Thanksgiving break, I'd pretty much decided to spend the whole time in a foul mood, feeling miserable and sorry for myself. I wasn't planning on being thankful for anything. Not even turkey and dressing.

Yet my friend's beautiful gift reminded me that I had many things to be thankful for. Friendship, for one. And wonderful memories, like that old panda collection I'd almost forgotten about. And then there was the simple joy of small surprises in my life—especially when I least expected them.

Philippians 1:4 says, "I thank my God every time I remember you." That's what I need to do every day: I need to thank God for friends who care about me, and for just showing me in little ways how much he loves me and cares about me.

—Rachel

Who?
* Think of a friend or family member you really need to thank.

Why?
* What is it about this person that makes you so grateful?

How?
* Show your gratitude by sending a card . . . making a phone call . . . writing on a Facebook wall . . . sending a text message. Just think of some small way you can say "Thank you!"

When?
* Why not right now?

DAY 326 Exchange Worry for Thanks

Don't worry about anything; instead, pray about everything. Tell God what you need, and thank him for all he has done.

—Philippians 4:6 NLT

Do this

* Grab a handful of coins (pennies would work well). Place a coin on the word *Thanks* and then whisper one thing that worries you or causes you stress. Grab another coin and place it on the word *Thanks*, again whispering something that causes you worry or stress. Do this until the word *Thanks* is completely covered up. Now think of something you're thankful for. Turn your thought into a one-sentence prayer. As you whisper your prayer, move a coin from *Thanks* to *Worry*. Do this until *Worry* is all covered up.

DAY 327 A Surprising Discovery

I sat in my guidance counselor's office, squirming under the glow of the fluorescent lights. I checked my watch, knowing I would be late for soccer practice. *Why do I have to meet with my guidance counselor anyway?*

"I've looked at your transcript, David, and there's a problem," my counselor said. "You haven't enrolled in an art class, and it's a requirement to graduate." I slumped back into the chair and stared blankly at her. *Does she know how much I hate art?*

She laid out my options: ceramics or photography. I figured photography was the least painful, so I enrolled.

When I walked into class the first day, I was definitely out of place. While some of my classmates had portfolios of photos or their parents' hand-me-down cameras, all I had was my soccer duffle and a pen.

I rolled my eyes as my teacher described our first homework assignment—shooting a series of still lifes. *How am I going to pull this off?* I wondered. Then I glanced at the soccer ball poking out of my duffle and figured it would probably make a decent subject.

To my surprise, something strange happened during that first assignment. As I was setting up my soccer ball in the bathroom (an admittedly strange location for a photo shoot), the sun made a cool shadow through the window and created a series of lines, illuminating the Nike swoosh. I tried out different lighting and settings, crawling on the cold linoleum like I was a *National Geographic* photographer spying on a lioness with her cubs. The hours flew by.

A couple of classes later, my teacher called me to the front of the classroom. *Great . . . now she's going to use me as an example of what not to do.* To my surprise, she used my shots as an example of how to do the assignment. As she excitedly showed the entire class each of my pictures, everyone got real quiet and leaned forward to get a good look. I felt a rush of adrenaline. In the past, I'd only felt that good when I dove to save a goal on the soccer field.

Riding that high, I began spending as much time as possible in my school's photo lab. I couldn't get enough of it. And instead of taking my soccer ball with me everywhere, it was my camera.

—David

Think it through

* Have you ever had an experience similar to David's?

* Were you ever surprised to discover a gift or ability you never knew you had?

* How could you use—or how are you using—this gift or ability to serve your church, school, or community?

* Could this gift or ability turn into a future career?

DAY 328 Characters Every Church Needs

Romans 12:4–8 and 1 Corinthians 12:4–31 compare the church to a body. In order to function, a body needs a lot of different parts. And each part needs special abilities. What kinds of abilities? Well, I thought of five movie characters who'd fit nicely in any church.

Professor X

In the *X-Men* films, Magneto believes that mutants must take care of themselves in a world that hates them. Professor X believes humans and mutants can and must live together.

Magneto's plan really doesn't sound that evil. But Professor X is able to see the lie behind Magneto's thinking. Just because a path seems easy and attractive doesn't mean it's right. Knowing the difference is discernment. We need people like Professor X in the church because of their ability to know right and wrong.

Mrs. Beaver

The first time Mrs. Beaver meets the young heroes of *The Lion, the Witch and the Wardrobe*, she says, "Come inside, we'll get you some food." She stirs the pot on the fire. She feeds the kids. She keeps them all warm.

She is the behind-the-scenes helper. In the church, these people do tasks—however small—to free others to use their own gifts for ministry. So who's Mrs. Beaver in your church? It's the person in the kitchen washing dishes after a big fund-raiser. Or the guys setting up chairs. Or the people working in the nursery.

Summer Hathaway

When fake substitute teacher Dewey Finn forms a band out of his class in *School of Rock*, he makes the responsible Summer Hathaway the band manager. With a clipboard and many checklists, Summer makes sure everyone is where they need to be, schedules gigs, and keeps track of the band's gear.

This is the gift of administration. In your church, administrators keep things running so the leaders can concentrate on doing what God has called them to do.

Will Turner

When the governor's daughter, Elizabeth, is kidnapped in *Pirates of the Caribbean: The Curse of the Black Pearl*, the commodore wants to play it safe. But a lowly peasant blacksmith, Will Turner, steps up with a new plan. Before the movie ends, Will becomes a trusted leader. Why? Because he has the leadership qualities of confidence, decision making, and courage. He models trustworthiness and shows what it means to work hard. He isn't always the first to speak on issues, but he guides others—sometimes quietly—to address them. This is a big part of what leadership in the church is about: standing before people to direct and motivate them to accomplish goals.

Hagrid

Romans 12:8 says that if a person's gift is "showing mercy, let him do it cheerfully." Nobody displays that better than Hagrid from the Harry Potter movies. There are few people with a bigger heart than Hagrid. He gives everyone the benefit of the doubt, he has compassion for animals no one else would go near, and he does it all with a big goofy grin. At your church, Hagrid is the one who offers genuine sympathy, speaking words of love and compassion. He'd be everyone's shoulder to cry on. And that's one big shoulder.

—Scott

How do you fit in?

* What are your gifts? There are many more than the five listed here. See Romans 12:4–8 and 1 Corinthians 12:4–31 for more. Talk to your friends, parents, and youth leader about what gifts they see in you.

DAY 329 Was I Ready to Lead?

During my freshman year, our youth group had a great group of senior leaders. But after they graduated, no students stepped up to show leadership. That was painfully obvious on the first day of a team-building camp during my sophomore year.

We all sat in a circle with arms interlocked. The camp leader, Melanie, told us to figure out how to stand up together. Everyone had a different idea how to do it. The exercise turned into a big mess of people talking over each other and falling down.

"I'm not sure your group is ready for more difficult challenges," Melanie told us. "You don't work together at all."

Her words stuck with me as we walked through the woods to the next team-building station. I had done a rope web activity like this before and had confidence I could lead us. I took charge but let everyone share their ideas of what could work. Together we solved the challenge quickly. When Melanie gathered us all together, she said, "I can't believe you guys did this! I'm surprised at how well you came together!"

Later that day, Melanie took us on a challenge course forty feet in the air. I'm afraid of heights, but I gained real confidence from my friends telling me how much I helped in the day's earlier challenges. I felt I could do anything. I even took on the hardest course, the hourglass, which consists of three ropes that cross each other in the middle. I was the first group member to get across it. It felt great.

What felt even better was that I got to help others get across it too. When our head counselor, Jen, went on it, I instructed her every step of the way. She was scared but made it through. During that night's worship service, Jen told me she couldn't have done it without me. I thought, *Wow, I helped lead the leader?* I thanked God for how much he'd used

374

my youth group to encourage me, build my confidence, and help me realize I was a leader.

—Mike

Your turn

* Whether or not you see yourself as a leader, how do you think God wants to stretch your gifts, abilities, and interests?

DAY 330 A Skill I Thought I'd Never Use

When I was a senior in high school, I worked for an electrician. I was sure I'd never use those skills again. Not a Christian at the time, I also didn't think I'd end up on a Christian college mission trip helping build a home for a needy family. But when God comes into your life, you never know what's going to happen.

In my junior year of college, I joined nine other students on a summer mission trip to Tijuana, Mexico. We built a house for a family of four who had been living in a cramped shack with no electricity. Remembering my old skills, I spent a lot of time wiring up the house so that for the first time they would have a great new home, fully lit.

When it came time to turn on the electricity, I held my breath. *Would there be sparks? Would the whole thing catch fire because I'd done something wrong?*

All my fears were swept away as the warm glow of light filled the house. My team cheered, and smiles lit the faces of the family members who'd soon move into a new home. It was an incredible moment, one I will never forget.

The experience really changed the way I view my faith. As a non-Christian high school student, I'd learned a skill I thought I'd never use again. It was just a temporary job to help me earn some spending money. Yet God knew exactly what he was doing when he led me to the electrician's job so many years ago. Without my skills, I don't know how we would have completed that house.

375

The mission trip showed me just how much God has led me throughout my life—even before I had any idea that he was interested in me! Now when I learn something new, even if it seems unimportant at the time, I realize that one day God may use it to his glory.

—Carlos

List

* List three things you're pretty good at:
  1.
  2.
  3.

Do

* How could you use one of these interests to serve your church, school, or community?

Dream

* How could you turn one of these interests into a future career?

DAY 331 What Is God's Plan for Me?

Q: For a long time, I've had a desire in my heart to someday become a minister. But I don't know if God really wants me to do this. Please tell me how I can get direction from God about my future.

—Anonymous

A: I don't think there are simple formulas for finding what God wants us to do with our lives. It's true that we must be willing to follow God wherever he leads (Luke 9:57–62), but God has given you certain gifts, abilities, and desires to put you where he needs you. I think we find what we're supposed to do at the intersection of what we enjoy and what we're good at. Doesn't it make sense that God would want to use those gifts, abilities, and desires to serve him?

376

Of course, "to serve him" is key. Whatever we do, wherever we go, God wants our service to be for him. I don't think a Christian has to be in a career clearly labeled "Christian ministry." God needs teachers, company executives, computer techs, and janitors who will serve him in their places of work and influence. What's important is dedicating our work and career to God, wherever that place of work may be (Col. 3:23).

Here's a suggestion. If you think God wants you to be a minister, do what you can to be involved in ministry right now. In a sense, you're taking your heart's desire for a "test drive." Lead a small Bible study group. See if you can do a brief internship with your pastor or youth pastor. Interview them about what their jobs are like. These activities will give you a more realistic picture of what it means to be in full-time Christian work.

I'd also encourage you to talk to people who know you best or who have spent a lot of time with you. What have they seen you really shine at?

You also need to share your desire with God. Ask him to direct your decisions, and to help you find places where you can explore your various gifts and abilities. And thank him often for the gifts and desires he's given you.

Finally, I'd like to share a short Scripture that's very applicable here:

Delight yourself in the LORD and he will give you the desires of your heart.

—Psalm 37:4

This little verse is a big reminder to put God first. When you do, you can expect him to give you your true heart's desire. Now, he may change your desire. He has a way of doing that. But those new desires are still your desires.

—Jim

Follow Jim's advice

* 1. Write down two or three college majors or types of careers that might match up with your abilities.

* 2. Which of these majors or careers do you feel you'd really enjoy and be passionate about?

* 3. Take your interests for a test drive. Enjoy writing? Keep a journal or develop a blog—and write daily. Ask for helpful guidance and critiques from your English teacher. Think you'd like to be a coach? Help out with a Little League team.

* 4. Seek guidance and advice from those who know you well.

* 5. Talk to God. Tell him what you're interested in. Ask for his guidance. And strive to put and keep him first. Dedicate your plans to him and trust that he truly will "give you the desires of your heart."

DAY 332 Amy's Quiz: Me, My Stuff, and I

Take this quiz to find out if you're thinking a little too much about clothes, cars, and cash.

1. Your best friend is holding your cell phone when he slips and falls. He's OK, but the phone's broken! He tells you he doesn't have the money to replace it. You:
   A. Refuse to talk to him until he replaces it.
   B. Tell him you're glad he's OK, then ask if he can pay you a little bit every couple of weeks until you have enough money to replace your phone.
   C. Are more concerned with how he's doing. You know he'll replace the phone whenever he can.
2. Your parents just traded in their old car for a used minivan. You:
   A. Are glad you won't be squished between your two brothers anymore.
   B. Are totally embarrassed. There's no way you're riding in a lame minivan.
   C. Ask your dad if you can use the money you were saving for a DVD player to buy one for the van.
3. When you pray, you:
   A. Always pray for more stuff.
   B. Are thankful for all you have.
   C. Praise God, but sometimes ask for things too.

378

4. Your sister's getting a total room makeover. You:
   A. Volunteer to photograph "before" and "after" pictures of her room.
   B. Help her paint. That'll help you think of ideas for your own room. You can't wait till it's your turn.
   C. Are jealous of all her new things.
5. You strike up a conversation with the new kid at youth group. You:
   A. Like his great sense of humor and can't help but notice his cool clothes.
   B. Think he's super nice and you could be good friends with him.
   C. Check out his two-hundred-dollar shoes and wish they were yours.

Scoring

1. A (1), B (2), C (3)
2. A (2), B (1), C (3)
3. A (1), B (3), C (2)
4. A (3), B (2), C (1)
5. A (2), B (3), C (1)

13–15 points: Less is better. Sure, there are things you want, but you rarely let those wants control you. Good for you. To help you continue keeping your priorities in check, read Matthew 6:33.

9–12 points: Balancing act. You're constantly trying to balance the stuff you need with the stuff you want. If you find yourself falling into the trap of wanting more, read and study Matthew 6:19–21.

5–8 points: Stuff matters. Things are really important to you. And even though it seems like more stuff will make you happier, it's not really true. Check out Philippians 4:4–8 to find out more about true happiness.

DAY 333 God and My Stuff

Sometimes I feel like ads and commercials do more than just make me interested in trying a new product. In some ways, they make me feel a little less content with what I have. A little dissatisfied with the clothes I have in my closet. A little like something new would make me happier.

Bible break

Those who love money will never have enough. How meaningless to think that wealth brings true happiness!

—Ecclesiastes 5:10 NLT

If we are too focused on having things, we can get to the point where we're never satisfied. We'll always want a new backpack, tickets to another concert, or whatever people at school are wearing. Maybe we'll even take on more hours at our jobs than we can handle—letting our schoolwork and church activities slide.

I know that if I'm not content with the stuff I already own, having more stuff isn't going to help. I'm not saying that we shouldn't ever go shopping for fun, or that it's wrong to have more than one coat. But we should remember that God has given us everything we have, whether it's extra babysitting money, a check from a job, or birthday cash from Grandma. How we spend our money is important to him. Jesus taught that we can know the condition of our hearts by thinking about what we treasure. He warned that we can't serve God totally and be obsessed with having more stuff at the same time (Matt. 6:2, 24).

So what's the answer? I'm learning to pray about my money and purchases. After all, God promises to provide for my needs (Phil. 4:19). I'm also trying to be more grateful for what I have and to seek first God's kingdom (Matt. 6:33). Lastly, I'm learning to think carefully when I see an ad or when I see something on a commercial I'd like.

—LaTonya

380

Your turn

* Think about something you've been wanting to buy. With that potential purchase in mind, respond to these questions:

   Have I given money to God's work?

   Have I saved some money?

   Is this something I need, or something I want?

   Why do I want this?

   Is that a good reason to spend money on it?

Fact

* God cares very much about the way I use what he's given me. In fact, seventeen of Jesus's thirty-eight parables were about money! The Bible mentions possessions more than two thousand times. Money and possessions definitely matter to God.

DAY 334 Where's It Go?

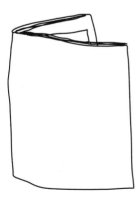 

In the wallet or purse, make a list of where your money regularly goes. Try to estimate how much you spend on those things each month, and write that amount beside each item. Think about gas for your car; new

381

clothes; coffee or smoothies with friends; video games; birthday gifts; money you give to your church.

Reread your list. Are you spending money carelessly on things you don't need? Are you giving generously? Could you benefit from a budget? And if you don't have a lot of money to spend, do you still have a grateful attitude?

Now, in large, bold letters write "It's all God's" over the purse or wallet. Think about what that should mean for your spending habits.

DAY 335 | I Need a Car!

I sat on the curb of my school parking lot waiting for Mom to pick me up. As I watched my classmates jump in their cars and peel out of the lot, tires screeching, I started counting up all my friends with cars. It seemed everyone had something to drive but me.

On the drive home, I once again bugged Mom about getting my own car.

"I don't care if it's a clunker," I said. "Just something to get around town."

"We've been over this," Mom replied. "Your dad and I have prayed and tried to find a way, but with both your brother and sister in college right now, we just can't afford it."

That night I called my brother Matthew at college to talk about how unfair my life was.

"It's true," he agreed. "It's not fair. When I turned sixteen, I got the old van. And Lauren drove the Ford Focus around during high school. I'm sure Mom and Dad feel bad about not having an extra car for you."

"Yeah, I know," I said. "It's just hard having it rubbed in my face that I'm the only one without wheels."

"Try shifting your perspective," Matthew suggested. "Your friends may have easy transportation, but look at all you've got."

"Like what?" I asked.

"Well, God has blessed you with a family who may be lacking in funds but who makes up for it in love and support. You know we've all got your back, Ry. If there was something that you really needed, medically or whatever, we would get it for you. God would help us find a way."

I knew Matthew was only trying to help, but there was a part of me that wanted to scream, "Well, I don't need a kidney! I need a car!" But I kept quiet so I wouldn't sound like a selfish jerk.

"I know you're right," I said without much enthusiasm in my voice. "But I still really want my own car. How am I supposed to just stop wanting that?"

"I don't have an easy answer for you," Matthew said. "There's no pill you can swallow to stop craving material things. My best advice is to take a hard look at your life right now. It's pretty amazing, really. Recognize it. Appreciate it. Thank God for it."

Instead of arguing, I got kind of quiet for a moment. I thought about the stack of auto magazines I'd been drooling over for the past six months. I thought about how shallow my thinking gets sometimes. There were way more important things to me than whether I had my own car—things like my family and my friends. (I was glad I had so many friends to be jealous of!) More than anything, I cared about my relationship with Jesus. I wanted to continue to grow in Christ—to love him, worship him, glorify him—and I didn't need a car to do that.

—Ryan

* List four things you're thankful for:
   1.
   2.
   3.
   4.

* Now thank God for the items on your list.

DAY 336 What about Tithing?

Q: I want to follow God's teachings. Can you explain what the Bible says about tithing? What if I only receive an allowance?

—Anonymous

383

Your turn

* How would you answer this question?

How IYF's expert answered:

A: The concept of tithing (giving 10 percent of your income to God) is taught in the Old Testament. God's people were told to give the first 10 percent of their field and flocks to God. "A tithe of everything from the land . . . belongs to the LORD" (Lev. 27:30). And "'Bring the whole tithe into the storehouse. . . . Test me in this,' says the LORD Almighty, 'and see if I will not throw open the floodgates of heaven and pour out so much blessing that you will not have enough room for it'" (Mal. 3:10).

In the New Testament, the emphasis is on recognizing that everything we have comes from God and belongs to him. We are simply stewards, managers of the stuff that God has given us to use for his purposes. We're to give cheerfully to God and to meet the needs of others (2 Cor. 9:7).

Is tithing as a teen a good idea? Yes! It's a good starting place to develop the discipline of generosity. We learn to give every week, whether we feel like it or not. It's a way of remembering on a weekly basis all that God has given us. And it also trains us to live on less than we earn—an absolutely vital lifelong skill.

—Marshall

DAY 337 Prized Possessions

I met Yolanda about a month ago on a mission trip in Venezuela. One day our group went to the barrios (very poor neighborhoods) to help start a church building. Ten-year-old Yolanda helped me in whatever way she could. After a long day of work, I searched my backpack to find something to give her. I found lots of things I could give her, but I was only willing to part with a colorful pen and a whistle. Her eyes lit up as I handed these trinkets to her. They were just taking up space in my backpack, but to her they were treasures. She gave me a hug and a kiss on the cheek, then proceeded to unlatch the black beaded necklace around her neck and put it on mine. Right then I was humbled. She was giving me one of her precious treasures, but I only gave her my "leftovers."

—Krishana

DAY 338 Toss This . . . and That

1. Find two big boxes or bags. Label one box "Give Away." Label the other "Throw Away."
2. Now spend some time going through your closet, dresser, bookshelf, CD rack, and desk.
   - If you find things in good condition that you haven't used for a while, that you don't need, or that are just taking up space, put them in the Give Away box. Bonus challenge: Add one thing to the box that's brand new or that you like a lot.
   - If you find things in poor condition, put them in the Throw Away box. If possible, try to recycle those things.
3. After you've tossed the Throw Away box and taken the Give Away box to a homeless shelter, Goodwill shop, or Salvation Army store, take a minute to enjoy the feeling. You've not only de-cluttered and simplified your life; you've also given things to people who need them more than you.

DAY 339 Materialism Madness

Sometimes when I'm upset or frustrated, I have this intense desire to go buy something. I don't care what it is. Clothes, shoes, half of Target's beauty aids aisle, whatever. I think superficial, cosmetic items that change my appearance will also change my mood.

This week my desire was to highlight my hair. When all the steps were completed, my brown hair was streaked with orange. Since Halloween is over, my "quick fix" was a total failure. Now I was not only upset, but I felt worse about myself than I did before I bought the highlighting kit.

Our society tells us the more stuff we have, the better we look, the more places we travel, the happier we'll be. Yet Jesus tells us a whole different story. In Matthew 16:26 he asks, "What good will it be for a man if he gains the whole world, yet forfeits his soul? Or what can a man give in exchange for his soul?"

No amount of money can buy my salvation. A cool wardrobe won't give me a VIP pass to heaven. And most certainly, my hair color isn't going to make God love me any more or any less than he does at this very moment.

Jesus told his disciples, "If anyone would come after me, he must deny himself and take up his cross and follow me" (Matt. 16:24).

Some days I might deny myself that new sweater, but other days I might buy it in an attempt to "cure" my bad mood. Following God sometimes means giving up the quick fixes and getting to the root of the problem—no matter how difficult it is.

When I think about the things I fill my life with in an attempt to make a gloomy day bright, I'm disgusted. But I'm also thankful that I worship a God who can see past my materialism and knows the hurts of my heart; who heals me every time I ask; who loves me, cries with me, died for me.

Now I have a plan to bypass the temporary solutions. When I'm feeling down or getting the urge to run to the nearest store to buy something, I'll drop to my knees. I'll ask God to fill me with peace. A peace that's been bought and paid for by the blood of a Savior. I don't have to make payments. I just have to ask for it.

Rest assured, my hair isn't streaked with orange anymore. But if you're looking for a quick pick-me-up, you won't find it at the store. Just look up.

God is the permanent answer to our temporary problems.

—Autumn

Think about it

* What are you using or buying that's a temporary solution to a longing only God can fill?

DAY 340 No Rich People in Heaven?

Millions and millions of people all across the planet don't have what I have: ten pairs of shoes, a couple dozen shirts and pants, a TV, an iPod, a car.

The fact is, I'm rich. Your family is probably just as rich, or close to it. And according to Jesus, this can be a big problem. He put it this way in Matthew 19:24: "It is easier for a camel to go through the eye of a needle than for a rich man to enter the Kingdom of God!"

Wow. He seems to be saying it's impossible for a rich person to get into heaven. That's why the disciples were shocked when they heard this. They exclaimed, "Then who in the world can be saved?"

Jesus, of course, knows what he's talking about. Rich people don't have many needs. It's easy for them to get out of the habit of asking God for help.

Rich people have a lot of toys. When you have too many toys, like electronic gadgets or lots of extra clothes, it's easy to get distracted from your focus on God. And when you have a choice between taking a weekend ski trip or staying home to go to church, well, most of us know what we'd do. When this sort of thing happens time and time again, the spiritual life of the rich can get starved.

Rich people are used to having their act together. Being rich is often about being in style, acting like you're in control, looking cool. But cool people have a hard time humbly asking for forgiveness for their sins. It just spoils the image.

This is the main reason wise people never want to become rich. It puts the soul in a delicate situation, to say the least. But here's the problem: most of us in North America are rich whether we like it or not. We're doing pretty well when we compare ourselves to the rest of the world.

* Have you ever considered yourself rich? Why or why not?

So what are we supposed to do?

Well, lots of things. We have to realize that we are in a delicate soul situation. We have to give money away—the usual guideline is 10 percent (Mal. 3:8). We have to use our wealth and influence to help the needy—

387

check out the websites for World Vision (worldvision.org) or World Relief (worldrelief.org) for some ideas.

And we have to pray . . . and pray . . . and pray for God to save us from our basic tendency to be selfish.

And here's the kicker: he will! As Jesus put it to his shocked disciples, "There are some things that people cannot do, but God can do anything" (Matt. 19:26 CEV).

If we rich were left on our own, it would be impossible to enter the kingdom. As impossible as it is for a camel to go through the eye of a needle. But if we rich, knowing how desperate things are, throw ourselves humbly on the mercy of God, admitting we are spiritually poor, he'll make us rich in salvation. And he'll begin to give us an attitude adjustment about our wealth, and to use us and our possessions for his kingdom.

—Mark

Check it out

* Visit the websites Mark mentioned: worldvision.org and worldrelief.org.

DAY 341 Verses to Think About

Not that I was ever in need, for I have learned how to be content with whatever I have. I know how to live on almost nothing or with everything. I have learned the secret of living in every situation, whether it is with a full stomach or empty, with plenty or little. For I can do everything through Christ, who gives me strength.

—Philippians 4:11–13 NLT

If you see some brother or sister in need and have the means to do something about it but turn a cold shoulder and do nothing, what happens to God's love? It disappears. And you made it disappear.

—1 John 3:17 Message

Your fill-in-the-blanks prayer

* God, I really like having _____ and _____. And I'd really like to buy _____ and _____. But I also know that stuff won't make me happy. Help me to remember that you've blessed me with everything I have. Help me to be content with those things, to give to those who have less than me, and to desire you over anything I possess. Amen.

DAY 342 Defeated!

For the past five years, wrestling had been my life. For some of the guys, working out at our daily practices was enough, but not me. I'd often work out more *right* after practice. I lifted weights, I ran, I swam, I sat in the sauna to drop an eighth of a pound—all for wrestling.

My wrestling became the center of many of my prayers. *Lord, if I win today, please use it to bring you glory*, I would pray as I warmed up for a match. *And if I lose, God, please comfort me.*

By my senior year, my hard work had really paid off. I was captain of the team and had the best win-loss record. And I was close to my big dream: the state tournament. I just had to win one more match. *God, this is the goal I've been working toward for so long*, I prayed. *Please, help me to do my best and to win.*

But when I looked at the wall where the upcoming matches were posted, I couldn't believe who I'd be wrestling next: Chuck Banners.

We'd wrestled each other several times, and he'd beaten me every time. I was sure my wrestling career was all but over.

When the referee blew the whistle, I felt a surge of adrenaline. I lunged across the mat and scooped Chuck up by the legs. I twisted hard with my torso and arms, slamming Chuck down in one of the best double-leg takedowns I'd ever done. Chuck stayed down.

I turned toward the audience and flexed my arms. *I've done it. I'm a state qualifier now.*

But Chuck got up before the ref finished the count. And for the next four minutes, he tossed me around like a rag doll. His score soon passed mine.

Then it was over. My season. My dreams. My hopes.

I shook Chuck's hand and ran out of the gym. I didn't want anyone to see me cry. *God, why did you let this happen? All that work, all that prayer, for what?*

Think about it

* When have you prayed a similar prayer? Is there any activity or goal you're placing too much value on right now?

. . . the rest of the story

God taught me a huge lesson through that painful defeat at the tournament. He taught me that life isn't really about winning. It brings glory to God whenever I focus on serving him through whatever I do. God has shown me that he loves me not because of what I achieve; he just loves me.

—Matthew

DAY 343 Character Failure

* List five movie, book, or TV characters who failed.
   1.
   2.
   3.
   4.
   5.

* *Pick one character* from the list, and answer the following questions:

   How did he or she handle that failure? Did he or she ask for help or go it alone?

   Did he or she persevere or give up?

Did he or she set a good example or bad?

Did you leave the movie, book, or TV show encouraged, depressed, or ambivalent? Why do you think you felt that way?

DAY 344 | I Tried So Hard

As I watched my friend Carla get in her mom's minivan after the speech and debate meet, I imagined her glowing with excitement as she talked about her victory.

My own parents finally drove up, and I hurled my bag into the backseat.

"How was the competition?" my dad asked, grinning.

"I thought I did all right." And I wasn't lying. I thought I gave my best performances of the year. I had practiced constantly during the weeks before the competition. Even before that, I went to every meet our school entered, and recently I'd been ranking high. But apparently it wasn't enough.

"So . . . did you make it to State?" my dad asked.

"No." Awkward silence. "But Carla did." I started to cry uncontrollably. "I'm proud of her, but I really thought I was going to make it, and I've been to so many more meets and practices than her, and . . . it's just so unfair. I tried so hard."

My mom handed me a tissue. "I'm sure God will bring something good to you," she said slowly. "Maybe you'll do better next year."

But no matter what my parents said, the same thoughts just kept running through my head. *I really thought I was going to make it. . . . I tried so hard.*

A few days after the meet, Mr. Louis, a theology teacher at my Christian school, dropped by my locker.

"Do you want to be a leader for the sophomore spiritual retreat?"

I definitely wasn't expecting that. I never really saw myself as a leader. I was quiet, neurotic, and, most of all, indecisive. Apparently, though, there was something the staff at my Christian school saw in me that rose above those shortcomings.

I walked into the first planning meeting, and I was relieved to see that many of the other leaders were my close friends. From there everything just got easier and easier. I spent most of my lunch periods helping organize activities, offering insight, and, most nerve-racking of all, writing the talk I'd have to give about service. I was passionate about the topic, and I was praying that my passion would carry through to everyone else.

As I worked on it, I couldn't help but laugh when I found 1 Peter 4:11: "If you have the gift of speaking, preach God's message. If you have the gift of helping others, do it with the strength that God supplies. Everything should be done in a way that will bring honor to God" (CEV). Finally it all made sense. God wanted me to hone my speaking abilities, but for reasons bigger than any ribbon or medal. Maybe I didn't make it to State, but God could use my hard work and abilities to serve him at the retreat.

I gave my talk a few weeks later. After I sat down and saw the expressions on the students' faces, I knew things had gone just the way they were meant to.

—Pauline

Repeat after me

* Failure is not the end of the world. Failure is not the end of the world. (Repeat ten more times.)

DAY 345 The Word on Failure

We strive not to fail

But I have pleaded in prayer for you, Simon, that your faith should not fail. So when you have repented and turned to me again, strengthen your brothers.

—Luke 22:32 NLT

Examine yourselves to see whether you are in the faith; test yourselves. Do you not realize that Christ Jesus is in you—unless, of course, you fail the test?

—2 Corinthians 13:5

The Lord never fails

So be strong and courageous! Do not be afraid and do not panic before them. For the LORD your God will personally go ahead of you. He will neither fail you nor abandon you.

—Deuteronomy 31:6 NLT

Now I am about to go the way of all the earth. You know with all your heart and soul that not one of all the good promises the LORD your God gave you has failed. Every promise has been fulfilled; not one has failed.

—Joshua 23:14

Praise be to the LORD, who has given rest to his people Israel just as he promised. Not one word has failed of all the good promises he gave through his servant Moses.

—1 Kings 8:56

So if you are suffering in a manner that pleases God, keep on doing what is right, and trust your lives to the God who created you, for he will never fail you.

—1 Peter 4:19 NLT

* **What do you think God wants you to learn from the passages you just read?**

DAY 346 Doomed to Fail

"OK, Courtney. Take it from the top," said Mr. Kunz, the band director.

I placed my fingers on the keyboard and played a few notes before hitting a wrong one.

"Nope," Mr. Kunz said, shaking his head. "Remember, the actors are relying on the five of you for their cues to start and stop singing," said Mr. Kunz, motioning to our five-man band that made up the orchestra pit. "That's why you have to be spot-on perfect."

Ugggghhhh! I thought. *Why did I let my parents talk me into doing this stupid school musical?*

393

I was perfectly happy with spending my time studying, hanging out with friends, and playing in the church's youth group band. But Mom and Dad said that colleges liked to see students involved in extracurricular activities.

Mom thought that with my musical background, I'd fit in perfectly with the school band. But I soon learned how different it was to play at school than at church.

As the weeks passed, my anxiety intensified. My bandmates, on the other hand, seemed at ease in the pit. I found myself praying that their self-confidence would somehow rub off on me. I also prayed for a miracle.

Please, God, I pleaded. *Help me not to mess up in practice today. Guide my fingers where they are supposed to go so that I don't make a fool out of myself!*

One day during lunch, I told my friend Katie how miserable I was.

"Maybe you're psyching yourself out," she said. "Maybe you can't concentrate because you're so worried about messing up."

It's true. I've always been the queen of psych-out. If I was nervous about a test, I'd convince myself I'd flunk. Not long ago, I'd told a friend my dream of becoming a nurse. When she told me how hard nursing school was, I immediately thought, *Oh, forget it then. I probably can't do it.* Talking to Katie got me thinking about how maybe I needed to adjust my perspective—as well as my prayers.

That night when I kneeled beside my bed, I prayed, *I want to thank you, Lord, for giving me the gift to play. I'm sorry I've been taking that gift for granted.*

As I talked to God, it became clear what I needed to do. Rather than simply praying to get better, I needed to rehearse more *outside* of school practice. So I started practicing at home in the evenings. And the more I rehearsed, the fewer mistakes I made and the greater my self-confidence became.

By opening night, I was actually *excited* to be in the pit. I couldn't wait to put on a great show. And we did. The whole cast delivered an unforgettable performance. And I'm glad God had given me the gifts *and the confidence* to be a part of it all.

—Courtney

Think it through

* Think about a time you convinced yourself that you would fail. What happened?

* How might a change of attitude help you succeed more often?

Memorize it

For I can do everything through Christ, who gives me strength.

—Philippians 4:13 NLT

DAY 347 The Problem with Perfection

Striving for excellence isn't always a bad thing. Doing our best is part of the Christian life. Way back in the Old Testament, God's people were told to "present as the LORD's portion the best and holiest part of everything given to you" (Num. 18:29). Even though God was talking about tithes and offerings, we know that our lives are offerings to God and that we need to give God our best.

But perfectionism is doing our best for all the wrong reasons. Perfectionism is about us, not about God. When it comes to God's love, we perfectionists tend to get the order of things all mixed up. We think, *If I'm good enough, if I do all the right things, God will love me.* But God reached out while we were still sinners (Rom. 5:8). God made the first move. The incredible gift of salvation is ours because God loves us, not because we earned it. (Check out Romans 4:4–5.)

Perfectionism is a losing game. Fortunately it's one we really don't have to play. After all, God reached out to us when we were as far away from him as we could possibly be. Being a Christian isn't about being perfect and never failing; it's about being forgiven. So we can relax and be confident that God knows we're not perfect and loves us just the same.

—Carla

* *Write down* five ways in which you're not perfect.
    1.
    2.
    3.
    4.
    5.

* Now, in bold, huge letters, write one word over that list: *FORGIVEN.*

DAY 348 Flat on My Face

I daydreamed about Trevor and decorated the inside covers of my notebooks with hearts and our initials. My first name and his last name sounded perfect together.

But I couldn't work up the guts to actually talk to him—not even when we ended up in the same Spanish class. I wasn't the type to chase after guys, but I found myself brainstorming ways to get him to notice me.

One day I got my chance. Some of my volleyball teammates and I were hanging around outside the school, waiting for our practice to start. Then it happened. The football team jogged across the parking lot at the end of their practice. A water fight broke out, and one of the guys sprinted toward my friend Kayla and me and dumped a jug of icy water on Kayla's head.

Just then I caught a glimpse of Trevor walking from the football field. My big moment! I grabbed my water bottle and sprinted after the guy who had soaked Kayla. He zigzagged across the parking lot, turning around and laughing as I tried to get close enough to do damage. I flung squirts from my water bottle and laughed loudly, hoping Trevor would hear and take notice.

That's when my toe caught the edge of the sidewalk, and I went sprawling. Gravel rushed up at my face, and with one hand holding a water bottle I didn't have a chance to brace myself. My chin took the force of the fall.

When I lifted my head, the first face I saw was Trevor's. I'd practically fallen on top of his feet, and he was staring down at me like a slimy alien had dropped out of the sky.

I put my head down and started praying. *Please, God, send an earthquake to swallow me.*

My friends helped me limp inside the school and pick the dirt and gravel out of my knees, elbows, and chin. Then, to make my nightmare even worse, our super-strict volleyball coach punished Kayla and me for being late to practice.

At home that night, I gingerly dabbed first-aid cream on my cuts. *I deserve gravel in my skin*, I thought. I'd wanted Trevor to notice me—and he did.

While I can't exactly say I'm glad I fell flat on my face in front of Trevor, I am glad about the lesson it taught me. Now I know no guy is worth changing who I am and how I act. My experience with Trevor taught me not to bother chasing after boys. It's much too painful.

—Karen

* **Write down a lesson you've learned from a failure or embarrassing moment.**

DAY 349 The Beauty Behind Failure

I take pride in the fact that I think I'm a nice person. Most days I'm pretty good at being kind to others. I go out of my way to help people. I give my time and money (the little I have) to others. In fact, there's been a lot of times I've thought, *Wow, God must be proud of me!* And that's when it happens. This little voice that speaks from both my head and heart begins to remind me of my shortcomings: "Hey, remember when you were venting about a friend this past week? You probably said some things you shouldn't have. And when you yelled at the guy riding his bike in the middle of the road? That wasn't very nice. Not to mention that you should have been more patient with your sister. And what about . . ."

I'm not perfect. And no matter how hard I try, I never will be.

397

This world has deceived us into thinking that if we just work harder, we'll eventually be "good enough." Good enough to win that scholarship, likeable enough to be the most popular kid in school, smart enough to get a promotion. But God doesn't work that way. No matter how hard we try, we will never be perfect. So are we simply destined to fail?

First John 1:5–7 says, "God is light; in him there is no darkness at all. If we claim to have fellowship with him yet walk in the darkness, we lie and do not live by the truth. But if we walk in the light, as he is in the light, we have fellowship with one another, and the blood of Jesus, his Son, purifies us from all sin."

There is freedom in knowing that I don't have to be perfect to be loved by God. Once I accepted Jesus into my heart, there was and still is nothing I can do or say that will make him love me any more or any less than he did the moment I believed. His perfect love encourages me to try to stop sinning. And when I fail to do this, his grace picks me up, dusts me off, and tells me to press on.

Perfection is an unrealistic goal in a world riddled with sin. But in heaven, God will give us one last gift, one final act of grace for our sinful souls. He will make us pure. He will make us perfect. He will make us just like him! And that is why our story of failure is ultimately a tale of triumph.

So when you're upset about your imperfections now, look forward to the freedom!

—Autumn

Fill-in-the-blanks prayer

* Lord, I know I'm bound to fail because I'm not perfect and I live in a sinful world. Just this last week, I've failed by doing _____ and _____. I confess this and ask for forgiveness. I praise you that you cleanse and forgive me every time! Please help me to gain victory in these struggles and sins: _____ and _____ and _____. Thank you that, by your power, I have the strength to fail less and less in these areas. And thank you that one day I'll be with you in heaven, and then I'll never fail again! Amen.

DAY 350 God with Us

The nativity scene taught me something very important about Christmas. It's there we get a glimpse into the core of Jesus's life and mission here on earth. The nativity scene reveals that Jesus came to be with us. *To be with us.* Everyone we see in a nativity scene reminds us of how important it was for Jesus to not only give his life for us but to live his life with us.

Jesus could have been born in some palace where he was instantly waited on by several high-priced nannies. He could have been born with only Mary and Joseph hanging around. He could have done it a hundred different ways, but Jesus showed early in his life how important it is for him to be with us. In fact, one of the many beautiful names given to Jesus is Immanuel, which means "God with us" (Matt. 1:23).

From his birth until his death, Jesus chose to live his life with people. Instead of making a name for himself, by himself, he was constantly surrounded by others.

—Jarrett

Think about it

* "Jesus chose to live his life with people." What does this say about God's character?

* If being with people was such a big deal to Jesus, what do you think it might mean for how you live?

DAY 351 Traces

Sometimes a person comes to Earth
just for a little while,
staying long enough
to live and love and die,
then he is gone,
leaving traces.

"Today in the town of David
    a Savior has been born to you."
"You will not always have me."
"I must return to my Father."
"In a little while you will
see me no more."
"Then he was taken up
    before their very eyes,
    and a cloud hid him from them."

The Word was made flesh
and lived among them for a little while.
They saw his glory,
then he went away
    and they became his glory—
leaving traces of him across the world.

        —*Ruth*

Reflect on this

* Reread the final four lines of this poem. In what ways do Jesus's followers reflect his glory? How are we still seeing traces of Christ's life? (Hint: Take a look at Matthew 5:14 and John 14:12.)

DAY 352 | I Found Jesus! (Todd's fake interview with a for-real Bible character)

Q: How did you find Jesus?

A: Well, I was at the temple worshiping God. I turned around and there he was!

Q: Oh, so you literally found him?

A: I don't think he was lost. He was with his parents and this guy Simeon, who also worshiped at the temple a lot.

Q: Did Jesus talk to you?

A: Well, he was just a baby. He cooed a little bit. And spit up.

Q: How'd you know he wasn't just a regular baby?

A: Well, I spent day and night in God's house worshiping, reading the Word, and praying . . . .

Q: Wait. You never left?

A: No, my life was about praying, fasting, and reading Scripture. I gave my daily life to God. Because I was so in touch with God, I knew from the Scriptures that the Messiah was coming. I'd been waiting and preparing for that moment, just like a faithful follower of God named Simeon. In fact, Simeon had been told by the Holy Spirit that he'd see the Messiah before he died. When he saw Jesus that day, he held him and worshiped him. He even told the boy's mother about what this baby would do for Israel and all who believed.

Q: What do you think God taught you through this?

A: That he is faithful and good. And the least we can do is live our lives for him. I'd made God my first priority and believed his promises. And he came through! He kept his promise to send the Messiah. So why wouldn't we devote our lives to him?

* *For the real story* behind Todd's fake interview, read Luke 2:21–35.

DAY 353 This Is No Fairy Tale

The Tooth Fairy grabs a tooth out from under a pillow and then leaves a buck in its place. A big, bearded, jolly guy parks his flying deer on roofs and leaves gifts under Christmas trees. A rabbit hops around the neighborhood and gives out candy-filled baskets. Admit it: you once believed all that.

It's OK, we all did. Then somebody tips us off—"It's not true! Nobody believes that kid stuff anymore!" We stopped believing in fairy tales. We no longer believed the unbelievable. We wouldn't be fooled again.

Jesus was born of a virgin?

How are we to make sense of this outrageous idea found in our faith? We know how babies get here, and it has nothing to do with fairy tales or storks.

The truth is, Mary knew this too. When told by an angel (yes, an angel) that she was going to have a baby, she reacted like any smart, young virgin would react. First, she kind of freaked out. Luke, a historian and not a writer of fairy tales, records that Mary was "thoroughly shaken" (Luke 1:29 Message). Then Luke records what Mary said: "But how? I've never slept with a man" (v. 34 Message).

Mary was right on target, wasn't she? She knew how women got pregnant.

The angel told her that she would conceive a baby by the power of the Holy Spirit. Mary may not have believed in fairy tales, but she did believe in the power of the God she followed. Here's how she replied to the angel's message: "I am the Lord's servant. May everything you have said about me come true" (v. 38 NLT).

The virgin birth is important. God wanted to get humanity's attention. He wanted to shout loud and clear, "Here I am on Planet Earth! And to prove it, I will be born miraculously from a young and godly woman."

—Jerry and Grady

DAY 354 Memorize This

Think the same way that Christ Jesus thought: Christ was truly God. But he did not try to remain equal with God. Instead he gave up everything and became a slave, when he became like one of us.

—Philippians 2:5–7 CEV

DAY 355 Imperfect

I sit staring at our
Christmas tree,
watching as a brittle
brown needle falls
onto a present I will soon unwrap
to discover something unwanted,
or too small (or too large) to wear.

Just above the gift unwanted
I see a dull, burnt-out bulb;
then, a little higher up,
dangles a cheap ceramic Santa,
with a chipped nose.

Christmas suddenly feels imperfect, broken—
just like the world
a baby dropped into (so long ago),
to be born in a barn reeking of animal manure,
to be placed in a feed box filled with scratchy straw.
A perfect child, all smudged with birth-blood,
sent to an imperfect, broken planet,
to bring peace, salvation,
and hope that (one day)
all that's broken
will be mended.
Forever.

—*Marie*

Reflect on this

* Think about your own life. What is broken or damaged? What feels beyond repair? What hopeful message does this poem offer for you and your imperfect life?

DAY 356 What's It All About?

Every December I look forward to seeing *A Charlie Brown Christmas*. I dig that funky little dance Snoopy does. But my favorite part is when Charlie asks, "Isn't there anyone out there who can tell me what Christmas is all about?"

Luckily Linus is there to give the answer. A big spotlight hits him as he recites:

And there were shepherds living out in the fields nearby, keeping watch over their flocks at night. An angel of the Lord appeared to them, and the glory

403

of the Lord shone around them, and they were terrified. But the angel said to them, "Do not be afraid. I bring you good news of great joy that will be for all the people. Today in the town of David a Savior has been born to you; he is Christ the Lord. This will be a sign to you: You will find a baby wrapped in cloths and lying in a manger."

Suddenly a great company of the heavenly host appeared with the angel, praising God and saying, "Glory to God in the highest, and on earth peace to men on whom his favor rests."

—Luke 2:8–14

"And that," Linus finishes, "is what Christmas is all about, Charlie Brown."

Linus is right. The importance of Christmas goes beyond just the birth of a baby in a manger. What makes Christmas meaningful is *who* that baby was—the Son of God—and what he grew up to do.

—Todd

Not just a baby

The Word became a human being. He made his home with us. We have seen his glory. It is the glory of the one and only Son. He came from the Father. And he was full of grace and truth.

—John 1:14 NIrV

DAY 357 Loud and Clear

Therefore the Lord himself will give you a sign: The virgin will be with child and will give birth to a son, and will call him Immanuel.

—Isaiah 7:14

* *Read* each of the following statements and let them sink in:

Isaiah 7:14 was written hundreds of years before Jesus was born.

The birth of Jesus is a miraculous event that happened only once in history.

The virgin birth allowed God to be with us in the flesh.

DAY 358 He's Been There . . .

Here's a cool thing about Jesus: He wasn't just God on high shouting down orders. He experienced what we experience. When he told us to live a certain way, it was coming from a guy who'd been there. He lived on earth, felt our temptations, experienced happiness and sadness, and saw what this world he created looked like from our perspective. He understands. And he modeled what it looks like to live a truly godly life.

—Todd

. . . and done that

Since we have a great high priest, Jesus the Son of God, who has gone into heaven, let us hold on to the faith we have. For our high priest is able to understand our weaknesses. He was tempted in every way that we are, but he did not sin.

—Hebrews 4:14–15 NCV

DAY 359 Amy's Quiz: Finisher or Quitter?

Take this quiz to see how good you are at finishing what you start.

1. Your youth group is reading through the Bible in a year. Two months into the readings you:
   A. Are so far behind you give up.
   B. Are right on track.
   C. Need to catch up on a few days you skipped.
2. Your older sister needs a babysitter every Tuesday night for the next three months. You volunteer to do it, but after a month of watching your rowdy little nephew, you:
   A. Stick with it—no matter how much the kid drives you crazy. A promise is a promise.

405

B. Throw in the towel. There's no way you're spending every Tuesday night chasing around a little kid.

C. Tell them you can't watch your nephew every week, but you give them a list of a few dates you're willing to babysit.

3. Your friends are playing Ultimate Frisbee in the park and they call and ask you to join them, but you're right in the middle of studying for your algebra test. You:

A. Study for an hour, play for an hour, then come home and hit the books again.

B. Race to the park. You'll cram for the test in study hall tomorrow.

C. Tell them to definitely count you in for the next game, but you have to finish studying now.

4. You were really excited about joining the soccer team, but halfway through the season you haven't spent one second on the field during an actual game. So you:

A. Practice even harder and try your best to prove yourself to the coach.

B. Ask your coach if you can be the team manager. At least you'll be helping the team.

C. Quit. Why waste your time?

5. You promised your little brother you'd help paint his room. Where are you when the first coat is dry and it's time for the second one?

A. Long gone. You helped out with most of the first coat; he can finish it up.

B. Dipping your brush in paint.

C. Taking a break for a burger with friends. But you'll be back in time to help with the finishing touches.

Scoring

1. A (1), B (3), C (2)
2. A (3), B (1), C (2)
3. A (2), B (1), C (3)
4. A (3), B (2), C (1)
5. A (1), B (3), C (2)

13–15 points: As it says in Matthew 25:21, "Well done, good and faithful servant!" You are always good on your promises and a faithful finisher. Dedication and perseverance are great qualities and definitely go hand in hand with studying, work, and especially your spiritual life.

9–12 points: You're usually pretty good about seeing things through to the end. Although you try to finish everything you start, you do sometimes cut corners to get it done. When you agree to do something, remember these words from 2 Timothy 4:7 (NLT): "I have fought the good fight, I have finished the race, and I have remained faithful."

5–8 points: You're easily sidetracked and you often look for the easy way out. This may not seem like a big deal—but it is, especially when it comes to your spiritual life. Proverbs 12:24 offers this advice and a warning: "The diligent find freedom in their work; the lazy are oppressed by work" (Message). As you seek to break free from old habits, start small, set realistic goals, and work on a task until it's completed.

DAY 360 | Decided to Quit

As I peeled the sweaty, grass-stained clothes from my aching body, I thought about the last three exhausting weeks at football camp. I went home every night bruised, battered, sore, and stiff. I'd had it. I decided to quit.

When I told my coach, he simply grunted, "Why?"

"I'm not having any fun," I said lamely.

"Son," he said, looking me directly in the eye, "these practices prepare you for the games. That's when the fun begins."

Yeah, right, I thought. *Like I'll ever make it into a game.*

Coach Walker placed his hand on my shoulder and said, "I'll make ya a deal. Stick it out this year, and if you don't wanna come out again next fall, I won't hassle ya about it."

It sure didn't seem like a "deal" to me, but since no one ever won an argument with Coach Walker, I agreed.

When I got home from school, I hurled my book bag across the room.

"What's with you?" my brother Scott asked.

"Why can't I be decent in one stinkin' sport?!" I complained. "Is that too much to ask?"

I told Scott about the deal Coach had struck with me, and Scott smiled.

"I'm glad you're not giving up this time," he said, tossing me a Nerf football.

"When have I given up?" I snapped, purposefully nailing him in the thigh with the Nerf.

"Uhhh, baseball, basketball, piano," Scott said. "Want me to go on?"

"I just haven't found my thing yet."

"Listen, anything worth having takes effort," Scott said. "Hey, I don't blame you for hating the drills and stuff, but is there anything about football you like?"

I thought for moment.

"Well, I've kinda gotten into weightlifting. I've been lifting with this guy Matt from the team, and even after just a couple of weeks we're getting stronger."

"So try focusing on the progress you're seeing," Scott suggested. "You won't reach your goals instantly, but every little bit gets you closer."

That night after dinner I went to my room to think about my conversation with Scott. As tough as it had been, I realized my time on the team had already benefited me in at least three ways: I'd gotten into better shape, I'd discovered that I liked lifting weights, and I'd become really good friends with Matt.

There were still plenty of times that season when my body ached to quit, but I just pushed myself to keep going. Finally, toward the end of the season I made it into a couple of games. One in particular was really great. Coach Walker put me in at running back and I caught a thirteen-yard pass for a first down.

I'll never forget that amazing moment. If I'd quit when I felt like it, it never would have happened.

—Todd

Reflect on this

All athletes are disciplined in their training. They do it to win a prize that will fade away, but we do it for an eternal prize. So I run with purpose in every step. I am not just shadowboxing. I discipline my body like an athlete, training it to do what it should. Otherwise, I fear that after preaching to others I myself might be disqualified.

—1 Corinthians 9:25–27 NLT

DAY 361 Jesus says, "Wait"

Jesus told stories of the spiritual life, comparing it to a tree that needed time to grow and produce fruit (Luke 13:6–8); to a building that must be carefully planned and conscientiously constructed (Luke 14:28–30); to the process of birth (John 3:3–8); to a coin that, through diligent searching, must be found (Luke 15:8–10); to a seed that must be planted, cultivated, and harvested (Mark 4:26–29). None of these pictures suggests something instantaneous or immediate. It is a process, requiring time, patience, persistence. Waiting.

Jesus gave his friends a reminder of himself and his self-sacrificing love: communion. Then he announced that he would not share this bread and cup with them again until the future kingdom (Luke 22:14–17). Waiting.

Jesus spoke of judgment at the end of the age, and he urged watchfulness. Patient, active waiting. And he condemned those who would grow tired of the wait and impatient at his absence (Matt. 24:36–25:13).

Some will lose patience with the wait. They will ask, as Peter explained it, "Where is this 'coming' he promised?" And the question is answered: "With the Lord a day is like a thousand years, and a thousand years are like a day. The Lord is not slow in keeping his promise, as some understand slowness. He is patient with you, not wanting anyone to perish, but everyone to come to repentance" (2 Peter 3:4, 8–9).

Christ is patient.

He can wait.

For us.

And we are challenged to wait for him.

We may wonder about God's will—his plans for our education, career, marriage. Our future lies clouded in mystery. We must wait. And wait. It is hard to be patient. Yet the most significant things God wants to do for us (the hope for our eternal salvation, for example) come with the demand that we wait. So when it comes to less significant things (a good college, a job, a spouse), why do we so quickly become impatient and tired of waiting for answers?

—James

Think it through

* What are you waiting for right now?

* How do you remain patient during the wait?

* What does it mean to "wait actively"?

DAY 362 What Are We Waiting For?

We are told to wait for mercy, for pardon, for comfort, for salvation, for guidance and teaching, for fulfillment of God's promises. We are told it is good to wait, and that God calls us to wait *with the soul* (Ps. 130:5–6), with earnest desire, with patience, with resignation, with hope, with confidence. We are told that if we wait, we will renew our strength, we will inherit the earth, we will rejoice, we will receive all that's promised.

If only we will wait.

And wait.

There are things achieved through waiting that would never come through immediacy, or getting what we think we want without the wait.

Waiting builds our character, grows our patience, helps us sort out what really matters. We are willing to wait only for what we continue to believe is of deep value.

What good comes through immediacy? We get what we think we want, when we think we want it. But it spoils us. It softens us. It erodes our gratitude. It leads us to expect good things, as if they are owed to us, when we should be receiving in thankfulness. Almost in surprise. Like we're receiving a gift.

God owes us nothing. Life owes us nothing. We are not cheated if good is withheld. We are blessed when good is given—even if we must wait.

And wait.

—James

Here's something worth waiting for

But we are citizens of heaven, where the Lord Jesus Christ lives. And we are eagerly waiting for him to return as our Savior. He will take our weak mortal bodies and change them into glorious bodies like his own, using the same power with which he will bring everything under his control.

—Philippians 3:20–21 NLT

DAY 363 Perseverance through Pain

In the sports movie *We Are Marshall*, nearly the entire Marshall University football team dies in a plane crash. There isn't a soul in the school's hometown unaffected by this tragedy—everyone lost someone. They can't understand their loss or see how to continue. After the tragedy, football seems so trivial.

Still, football becomes a way for the town to keep going, to persevere, and to come together. Football gives them hope. It gives them something normal again. It's not about winning. It's about getting back on the field and playing. And very slowly, the town's trials eventually lead to greater strength.

Being a Christian doesn't exempt anyone from hard times. It's never easy to understand why bad things happen. But like in *We Are Marshall*, we have to continue living in faith that our hard times will be redeemed.

—Tom

411

Consider it pure joy, my brothers, whenever you face trials of many kinds, because you know that the testing of your faith develops perseverance. Perseverance must finish its work so that you may be mature and complete, not lacking anything. . . . Blessed is the man who perseveres under trial, because when he has stood the test, he will receive the crown of life that God has promised to those who love him.

—James 1:2–4, 12

Your turn

* Write down the name of a favorite movie or book character who experienced growth and positive change through perseverance:

  _____

* How does this character change as a result of persevering through difficult times?

* What can you learn about living your faith through this character's experience?

DAY 364 Faith and Tough Times

Therefore, since we have been made right in God's sight by faith, we have peace with God because of what Jesus Christ our Lord has done for us. Because of our faith, Christ has brought us into this place of undeserved privilege where we now stand, and we confidently and joyfully look forward to sharing God's glory. We can rejoice, too, when we run into problems and trials, for we know that they help us develop endurance. And endurance develops strength of character, and character strengthens our confident hope of salvation. And this hope will not lead to disappointment. For we know how dearly God loves us, because he has given us the Holy Spirit to fill our hearts with his love.

Romans 5:1–5 NLT

Try this

* Rewrite Romans 5:1–5 in your own words, or express it as a prayer, a poem, or lyrics to a song.

DAY 365 Give Me Patience . . . Now!

If the only way to develop patience is to go through difficulty, we'd probably just as soon skip it. Every day brings some exasperation—some need, small or great, that forces us to exercise patience. Patience is just part of the equipment we need if we are going to cope with life.

Think through the past few weeks. Who or what has tested your patience? A teacher who didn't understand you? A friend who annoyed you? A brother or sister in an obnoxious mood? A parent's expectations that seemed unreasonable? A disappointing grade? A broken-down car? Other drivers? Sickness?

OK, now which of those situations did you have any control over? Probably not many. Yes, it's good to try to control those things you can

413

control, just to simplify your life. But usually the things that test our patience are simply out of our control. We just have to live with them.

So now what?

Paul tells us to be "strengthened with all power according to [God's] glorious might so that you may have great endurance and patience" (Col. 1:11). Yes, God can actually give us the power to be patient.

Or think of it another way. What if the only thing you ever had to wait for was God? If the only thing that demanded your patience was someone who loved you, who ruled the universe, and who always had your best interest at heart, wouldn't patience come more easily?

We struggle with patience because we don't like the circumstances we face. Patience is difficult because things feel out of control. The timing seems wrong; the wait drags on and on.

And yet, because God is in control, we can be patient. Because God loves us, we can relax. Because God's wisdom is flawless, we can wait.

The only thing that ever demands our patience is the wise God who loves us. When we want circumstances to change, we wait for God to change those circumstances—or to help us change them. Or to help us accept whatever circumstances we're in.

When hardships test our patience, it is the powerful, loving, wise God who will, in time, lift our burdens—and give us the patience to wait for better things.

—James

Three-step prayer

* 1. Forgive me, Lord, for those times I've been impatient.

* 2. Give me that desire to show patience toward you, toward myself, toward others.

* 3. Help me to wait patiently for better things to come.

God will strengthen you with his own great power so that you will not give up when troubles come, but you will be patient.

—Colossians 1:11 NCV

ACKNOWLEDG-MENTS

To all of the teens whose stories are told in this book. Your experiences, honesty, and desire to follow Christ help demonstrate that God is powerfully at work in the lives of teens everywhere.

To all the behind-the-scenes professional writers who offered their insights, interviewed teens, and simply worked hard to help readers understand what it means to be on fire for Christ.

To Todd Hertz, Jill Meier, and Marilyn Roe—the hard-working team that helped compile, edit, and proof each and every word.

To Doug Fleener for a cover design that captures the energy and spirit of what this book is all about.

To our many friends at Revell. Thanks for your belief in this book and for giving us the freedom to make it happen. It's been a fun and faith-stretching experience!

Chris Lutes
Editorial Director
Ignite Your Faith

START STUDYING THE BIBLE FOR ALL IT'S WORTH!

Maybe you've heard this before: "Jesus is the Rock." But what does it really mean? And what does it mean to you personally? Find out in these devotionals on the words of Jesus from bestselling author Melody Carlson.